The Complete Book of
Machine Quilting

Other Books Available from Chilton

Robbie Fanning, Series Editor

Second Edition

The Complete Book of
Machine Quilting

Robbie and Tony Fanning

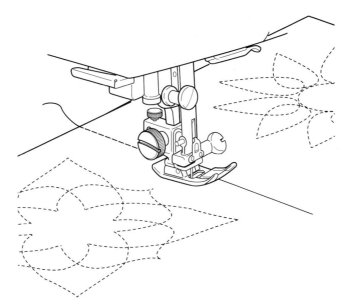

CONTEMPORARY
QUILTING

Chilton Book Company
Radnor, Pennsylvania

Published in Radnor, Pennsylvania 19089,
by Chilton Book Company

Designed by Martha Vercoutere

Line drawings by Pamela S. Poole

Black-and-white photos by Robbie Fanning

Edited by Rosalie Cooke, Gil Bowers, and Gaye
Kriegel

Production by Nora Kruger, Kendra Armer, and
Robbie and Tony Fanning

Manufactured in the United States of America

A CIP record for this book is available
from the Library of Congress

ISBN 0-8019-8388-6

1 2 3 4 5 6 7 8 9 0   3 2 1 9 8 7 6 5 4

Contents

Foreword

It's true: I first met Robbie Fanning on a bus in Chicago over 20 years ago. We were attending an embroidery seminar and were on our way to an art museum for dinner. The bus was packed, I was late, and I slipped into the closest empty seat—next to Robbie. The bus ride wasn't long, but by the time we reached our destination, I found out we were on the same wave-length. You know how it is—sometimes you meet someone, something clicks, and you feel as if you've known them all your life.

Over a period of years Robbie and Tony have asked me to design projects for them (can I do that?), Robbie asked me to write articles for her *Open Chain* and *Creative Machine Newsletters* (can I do that?), then write my own series of books (are you sure I can do THAT?). Robbie convinced me I could, assured me she'd be there to help me get organized, answer questions, and get me out of trouble when I needed it. But best of all, as my editor, Robbie let me exercise my creativity.

When I began reading Robbie and Tony's book, I was reminded of our history and thought of you who'll ask, "Can I do that?" Read on. Robbie and Tony will convince you that you can. Whether you are interested in quilting projects, keep your book close by for reference, or enjoy it for both, Robbie and Tony get you organized, answer your questions, encourage your creativity, and guide you through a first—or fifteenth—machine-made project.

I feel I'm loaning you my two most valuable resources and enthusiastic cheerleaders. Of course you can machine quilt—and here's the book that will make you a believer—as Robbie and Tony steer you to success.

Jackie Dodson
LaGrange Park, Illinois

Note to Readers Who Use Metrics

In the first edition of this book, we converted all imperial measurements to metrics. Instead of measuring by half and whole centimeters, we made a strict conversion. 1-1/2" became 3.8cm.

Books coming into the United States also made strict conversions in the imperial direction. A wallhanging would measure 22-13/32" x 30-7/17".

We're working with fabric, where that kind of precision is not only impossible, it's ridiculous.

In all these years since publication we have received letters from readers around the world. Never once has someone thanked us for including metrics. Nor has anyone commented on some blatantly incorrect examples given in the first edition. We debated whether to include metrics with each measurement in the second edition. Robbie asked penpals in Europe and elsewhere whether our metric conversions made sense. People replied that the widths of fabrics, battings, and beds are different outside the United States, that they never pay any attention to imperial measurements, and that they use the markings, for example, on their needle plates—1cm, 1.5cm, 2cm. People are going to do it the way they've always worked, no matter how we complicate measurements.

So we've decided not to include metrics within the book. Here is a reasonable approximation of equivalencies.

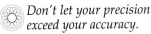 *Don't let your precision exceed your accuracy.*

Yards to Meters		Meters to Yards		Inches to Centimeters		Inches to Centimeters		Inches to Centimeters		Inches to Meters	
1 yd	0.9 m	1 m	1-1/8 yd	1/4 in	.6 cm	1-1/2 in	4 cm	15 in	38 cm	40 in	1m
2 yd	1.9 m	2 m	2-1/8 yd	3/8 in	1 cm	2 in	5 cm	20 in	50 cm	45 in	1.1 m
3 yd	2.8 m	3 m	3-1/4 yd	1/2 in	1.3 cm	3 in	8 cm	25 in	65 cm	54 in	1.4 m
4 yd	3.7 m	4 m	4-3/8 yd	5/8 in	1.5 cm	4 in	10 cm	30 in	76 cm	60 in	1.5 m
5 yd	4.6 m	5 m	5-1/2 yd	3/4 in	2 cm	5 in	13 cm	35 in	89 cm	108 in	2.7 m
6 yd	5.5 m	6 m	6-1/2 yd	1 in	2.5 cm	10 in	25 cm	36 in	92 cm	120 in	3 m

Many Thanks

Tony's Dedication

To Robbie and Kali, between whom I am just so much batting.

Robbie's Dedication

I'm one of those people who believe that the answer to every question is somewhere in print, so this book is dedicated to writers everywhere, published or not, for crafting words to educate, enlighten, and inspire.

We would like to acknowledge four people who are not thought of as machine quilters, but whose actions have facilitated the amazing advances in machine quilting:

• Bonnie Leman, for founding *Quilter's Newsletter Magazine*, where quilters find each other

• Karey Bresenhan, for infusing vitality into the quilt market with the high-quality show she runs in Houston and other places

• Donna Wilder, for starting the Fairfield Fashion Show, where so many machine-quilting artists have thrived

• Jean Ray Laury, for pollinating the quilting world with inspiration and ideas

Thanks also to our Chief Research Engineer, Mary M. Losey of West Lafayette, IN. Robbie could not have written this book without the financial support of her sister—not support of the Fannings, but of the entire quilting industry. Mary buys all the newest, most clever gadgets; reads every wonderful new book; subscribes to all publications; takes classes and visits shops and quilt shows all over the country. All of this she shares unselfishly with us and others.

And then, of course, there's her fabric collection….

Despite a demanding job, many community commitments, and a "far-left brain," Mary steadily produces quilts. She's an inspiration.

TV is a powerful way to communicate. We are lucky to have so many programs available and doubly lucky that many TV hostesses feature machine quilting. We've shown some of them in this book: Shirley Adams, Georgia Bonesteel, Sue Hausmann, Donna Wilder, Kaye Wood, and Nancy Zieman. Thank you for covering our favorite subject.

To thank all the manufacturers who supplied us with information, slides, and materials; all the artists who trustingly sent slides; all the authors who shared techniques and ideas; all the people at Chilton who waited patiently for this book to be finished, would expand this book another 50 pages. Thank you, everyone. (Special thanks, though, to Jan Saunders, Jackie Dodson, Gail Brown, Clotilde, Deb Wagner, and Kathy Conover; and to our West Coast team—Martha Vercoutere, Pam Poole, Rosalie Cooke, Gil Bowers, Kendra Armer, Nora Kruger, and Gaye Kriegel.)

Preface to the Second Edition

It has been 15 years since we began writing the first edition of this book. Much has changed in machines, materials, and techniques. But the biggest change has been in interest level: machine quilting has exploded.

In 1979 some people machine quilted; now everyone's doing it, because it's fast, fun, and easy.

When our first book came out, it was one of only a few. Today there are many "machine quilting" books. Yet upon close examination, few are truly about machine quilting—most are about piecing, appliquéing, or designing quilt tops.

In the first edition, we put emphasis in *The Complete Book of Machine Quilting* on the word "complete." In this edition, we're shifting the emphasis to "machine quilting." Our guideline was: is it relevant to machine *quilting*? We've tried to report on all facets of quilting by machine as applied not just to quilts, but also to clothing, crafts, and interiors (home *and* business).

As women have returned to full-time work, both inside and outside the home, the single most frequent comment we've heard over the years is "I don't have time for large projects," so we've kept the learning projects small. We often quilt the design of the fabric, calling these projects "F.A.S.T." That means Fabric-Aided to Save Time, in sympathy for those of us who have lots of ambition but little time.

We've included information on all sewing machine brands and some specialty machines, like the serger, OmniStitch, and room-sized quilting machines. But best of all, Chilton has planned glorious color throughout the book. Now we can inspire you with spectacular examples of machine quilting.

We've had 15 years of help from:

- kind readers who've written with ideas, suggestions, even stitched samples
- talented authors Robbie has worked with in Chilton's four book series (Creative Machine Arts, Contemporary Quilting, StarWear, and Crafts Kaleidoscope)
- artists who generously shared slides and ideas
- machine company educators, who tested techniques and accessories and sent items for photography
- industry contacts who suggested new products and supplied materials
- the wonderful team who crafted this book in California and our Chilton colleagues in Pennsylvania

It is a thrill to have the opportunity to incorporate all this richness. Perhaps in 15 years, we'll have another chance to update, so we invite your suggestions, questions, and improvements. Write to us c/o Open Chain Publishing, Inc., PO Box 2634-MQ, Menlo Park, CA 94026-2634.

Robbie and Tony Fanning
Menlo Park, California

A Note About This Working Partnership

We both shared all of the work of writing the book, from conception to overall form to photography, writing, and fussing over deadlines. As artist, Tony did most of the drawings in the first edition and the bulk of the designing. He was the first to question exactly how a stitch is formed on the machine (I'd never bothered to understand) and the first to notice that the feed dogs on the machine go up and down, not back and forth. He loves the color, texture, and general sensuousness of quilting—but he doesn't machine quilt. I, Robbie, love machine quilting, to the point of dreaming about it. I did all the machine work you see. I also did the first draft of writing and it seemed silly, in explaining how to do a technique, to say "we did this and then we did that." Therefore, the "I's" in the book are the female in the partnership.

Never have I felt more humble than in gathering the information for this book. Almost every idea in it came from talking to students, authors, and other quilters. Some of these led me to yet other sources—old books, personal libraries and collections, and even experienced hand quilters.

But this funnel of knowledge makes machine quilting special. It is part of the "caring and sharing" that all needleworkers cherish. Therefore, whenever possible, I attribute where I first heard or saw a technique, either from the (alleged) originator or from the friend who first told me.

And there truly is nothing new under the sun. Every needleworker eventually begins to develop new-to-me techniques and wants to share them. I'm no different. But I soon found that what I thought were great flashes of genius and personal discovery have been done somewhere before by someone else.

Another note: In this book, we concentrate on quilting with the sewing machine. There are many other decorative machine techniques besides the ones mentioned here, but lack of space kept us from including them all. For those who want to pursue these, consult our earlier book, *The Complete Book of Machine Embroidery*.

And now a confession: I'm new to machine quilting. I've only been at it for 25 years. Ernest B. Haight, whose work is shown later, machine quilted for more than 50 years. In his prime, he made and gave away 10 – 12 machine-quilted quilts a year.

But Mr. Joseph Granger of Worcester, MA, takes the machine-quilting prize. His wife had won a quilt contest the year before with a handmade quilt and he felt she took too much time, so he sat down at the treadle and machine quilted this 46" x 38" cotton crib quilt in 1879.

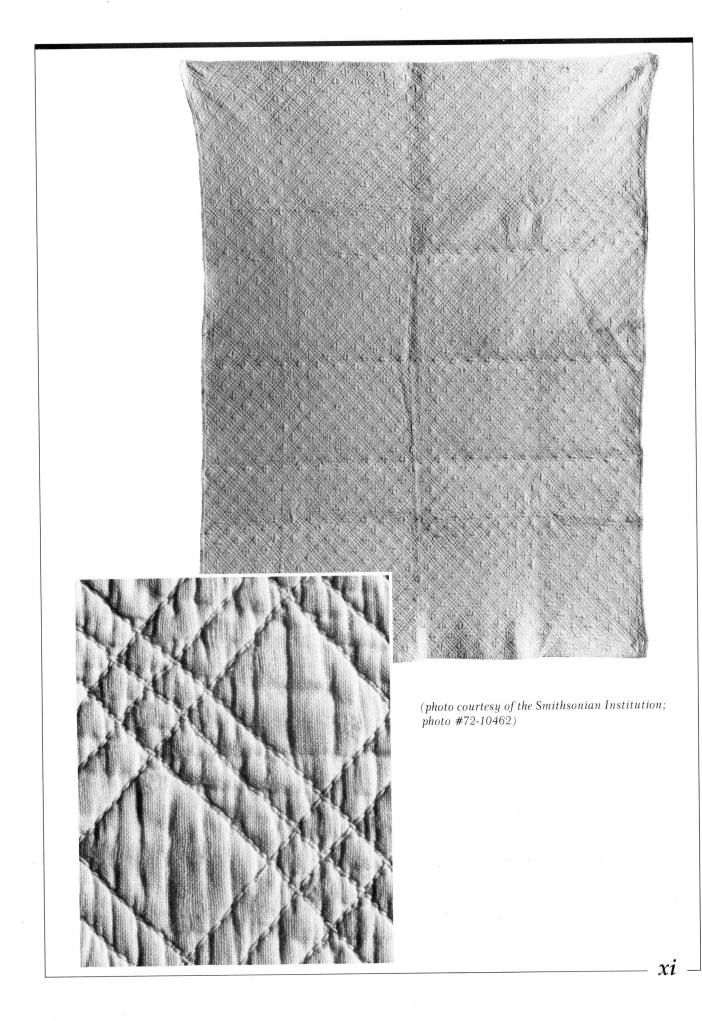

(photo courtesy of the Smithsonian Institution; photo #72-10462)

Introduction

Why I Machine Quilt

I'd like to tell you why I machine quilt. It has more to do with the value I put on things than with anything as abstract as aesthetics, creativity, or even practicality.

I'll express it in terms of quilts, but the concept applies to all quilted items. I love quilts. They are soft, comfortable, and warm; and they carry suggestions of home, family, protection, and practicality. I would also rather make something like that for my family than buy it.

Let me put it in perspective, starting with the drastic. If there were a fire in my house, I would save my husband and child before I saved a quilt. I would save the cat before a quilt. I would, if I had time, also save my computer, sewing machines, sergers, and camera before a quilt. Finally, I'd save the quilts.

In less drastic perspective, if our daughter wandered into the bedroom with a peanut-butter-and-honey sandwich, snuggled up to me on top of the quilt, and said, "Mom, it seems to me like every time I tell the truth, someone laughs at me," I'd seize the moment and talk to her, rather than scream about getting honey on the quilt.

And to put it in the most delicate perspective, any time my husband wants to grab me and throw me on the bed for a friendly wrestling match (or vice versa), I'm not going to say, "Wait! The quilt!"

Since any quilts in my house are so obviously doomed, you can see that there's no room for irreplaceable heirlooms on our beds. And if I am going to make a quilt, I'm reluctant to spend years making one by hand.

Why would it take me years to make a quilt? Because I work full-time, like the majority of women today, and I have an active life after work. My time for doing anything outside of work—reading, walking, movie-going, entertaining, being a bum—is limited to a few hours a week. If I'm both lucky and persistent, I actually get to use some of those few hours for quilting.

I've tried making hand-worked quilts (just as I've tried to handknit over the years). It never seems to work out for me. I do love handwork and I usually design a quilt in quilt-as-you-go modules, so I can take it with me when visiting friends or traveling (something admittedly not easy with machine quilting). But somehow, after working sporadically for three or four years, these grand ideas never get finished. I end up giving them to Goodwill with a great sense of relief.

In the meantime, is our bed bare? No! In the same time I've made several quilts by machine. Because with a machine-quilted quilt, I can have something durable, machine-washable, friendly, *fast*, and not at all so precious that I don't feel free enough to crush or desert it.

Add that to my love of the sewing machine as *the* tool to mold thread and fabric into something warm and touchable—and that's why I machine quilt.

What Is Machine Quilting?

There are so many forms of machine quilting that it is almost meaningless to say "I machine quilt." It's like saying "I'm involved in aerobic sports" and expecting the other person to understand which sport: running? soccer? bicycling? swimming? The phrase "aerobic sports" does not give us enough information. Neither does "machine quilting."

To some people it means a bed cover with all-over squiggly thread lines done by an industrial programmed machine and resembling a mattress pad. To others, machine quilting means a diamond-shaped grid over a whole quilt top, done with the presser foot and a straight stitch. Some people mean free-machine quilting when they say "I machine quilt"; others really mean "I machine piece patchwork for hand quilting." Machine quilting is all of these and more. It doesn't mean only quilts, either.

Also quiltable are outer clothing, vests, tea and coffee cozies, potholders, chair seats, valances, bags, wall pictures, banners, pillows, stuffed toys—anything that needs either additional warmth or additional emphasis.

But before trying to explain all the possibilities of machine quilting, let's ask ourselves a more basic question.

What Is a Quilt?

Technically, a quilt is merely a sandwich of three distinct layers:

• a *top*,
• some *filler* (usually called "batting" regardless of the material used), and
• a *backing* (sometimes called a "lining").

The top is secured to the backing through the filler with thread to keep the three layers from shifting around.

Nowhere is it written that the connecting thread has to be worked by hand.

And yet there are those who want to make a big issue of this.

A dying but not quite dead attitude still exists toward machine quilting: in the subtle pecking order of the quilt world, machine quilting still suffers wicked jabs. It is not uncommon to hear people who should know better say such things as: "This is the best piece of machine quilting I've ever seen. It was sort of sewn down the seam so it still puffed out like a real quilt but you could only see the stitches on the back."

Why does this antediluvian attitude continue?

Ignorance of the variety of machine quilting techniques, the misunderstanding of the nature of a quilt (it's also a "real quilt" if it's done by machine), and the assumption that machine quilting means generally low standards of

Quilt sandwich (squilt)

Top

Batting

Backing or lining

Quilting line

Quilt

Saying "quilt sandwich" trips my tongue. I call it a "squilt." Three layers in the process of being quilted make a squilt; once the quilting is completed, you have a quilted object.

workmanship—these explain some of it. Those who express this attitude aren't yet aware that among experienced quilters it's already a dead issue.

Good workmanship—the perfect blending of materials, design, and technique—is a result of personal standards of excellence and of experience. In some machine-made quilts, bad workmanship is embarrassingly obvious: colors of the top design are cheap and garish, the quilting lines are sloppy and relate neither to the top design nor to the capabilities of the machine, or the quilt is puckered on the back and hangs unevenly. But this is the fault of the quilter, not of the machine. I've also seen hand-quilted quilts with all the same characteristics (but I don't blame hand quilting).

How do you develop good workmanship? The key is experience. If you are new to machine quilting, start with easy small projects. For your first large project, practice on a simple design, such as quilting a crib sheet or the duvet in Chapter 5, where the quilting doesn't show. It won't be long before you are satisfied with the quality of your workmanship.

Nicky's Quilt: *Jean Ray Laury wrote a delightful children's book called* No Dragons on My Quilt. *In the back are directions for a hand-appliquéd quilt. I machine appliquéd the quilt for Nicky Armor and gave it to him with the book, both of which quickly became a favorite. Photo by Lee Lindeman.*

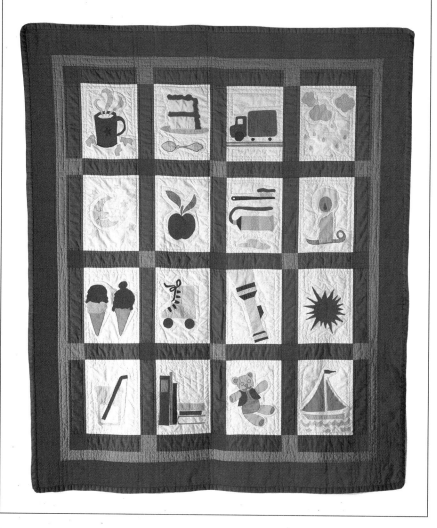

How To Use This Book

We reorganized this second edition in two major ways:

1. After you learn basic information about sewing machines, we encourage you to plunge in on a learning project immediately. Then the rest of the book will make more sense to you.

You don't have to know much to machine quilt. Get started!

2. Rather than bog you down with information early on, the details are in the back (see the Mini-Encyclopedia). We'll show you choices of binding, for example, in Chapter 7, but the details of doing it are at the back, where you can easily find them year after year.

The book gives an overview of your choices in technique, design, and application (quilts, clothing, interiors, crafts), and includes several learning projects. Once you've made these choices, read about the tools available to you, as well as the nitty-gritty of marking, basting, quilting, and finishing.

In every case, we encourage you to experiment and come up with *your* best way to work.

To get the most from this book, use it up. Underline what strikes you. Write notes in the margins as ideas hit. Make small samples (test cloths) of new-to-you techniques and pin to the appropriate page, or set up a notebook. Pencil in the machine settings, threads, and fabrics you used for a project. Put ribbons or tabs on the charts you use most often. Staple an envelope (the bigger, the better) to the back page of this book, into which you put magazine clippings, sketches on scraps of paper, addresses, resources, and other odd-sized pieces of paper about quilting that tend to lose themselves otherwise. The Bibliography lists some of the best references we've found; use it when a technique strikes your fancy and you want to know more about it. The Resource list is there for your use, too, when you can't get supplies locally.

In short, enjoy this book—and use it up!

Harriet Hargrave, Arvada, CO, 58" x 78". Machine-quilted with Harriet's Heritage Wool Batting from Hobbs, on a Bernina 1630. Harriet's book, Heirloom Machine Quilting, *caused an explosion of interest in machine quilting. She was the first to use extra-fine monofilament nylon with traditional quilting designs, as well as bicycle clips, clamps for table basting, continuous-curve stencils, cotton thread for quiltings (instead of cotton-wrapped polyester), and natural fibers for battings. An updated version of Harriet's book will be available in Spring 1995. Photo courtesy of the artist.*

Get Started Immediately

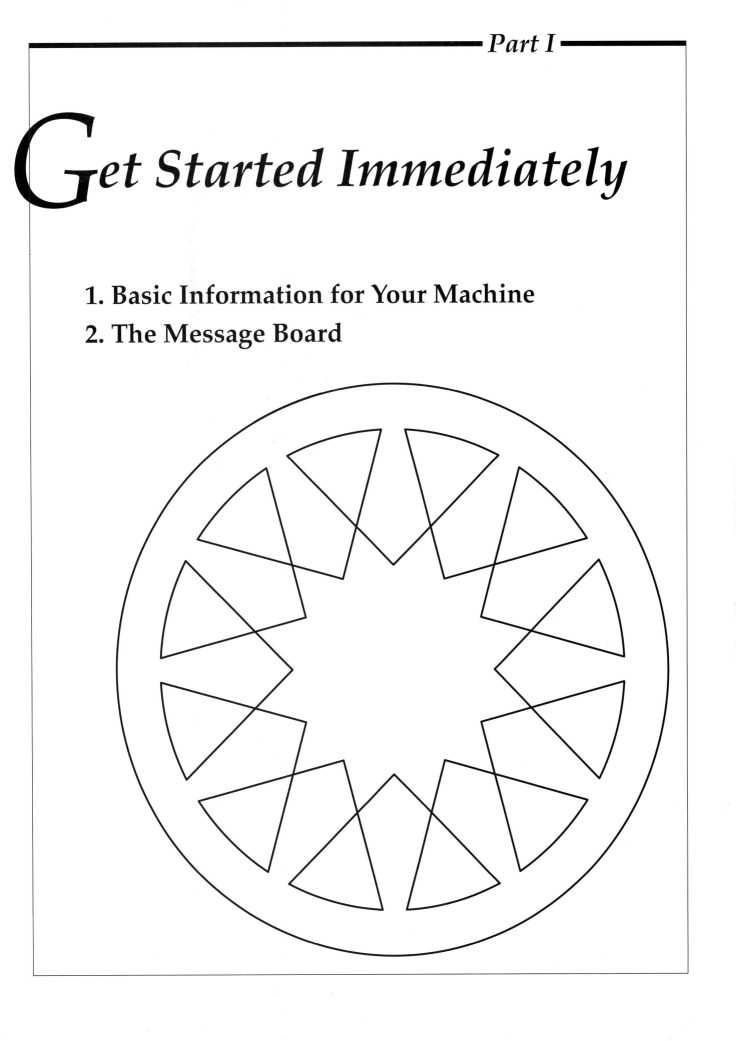

Chapter 1

Basic Information for Your Machine

There are quilts and there is quilting; this is a book about the latter—specifically, machine quilting. Once you understand how a stitch is formed on your machine, you can quilt anything. This chapter introduces the basics.

Left: *Caryl Bryer Fallert, Oswego, IL, Cosmic Pelican, 58" x 68", 1992. Striped and hand-woven ikat fabric in inner borders, string-pieced outer border, Cotton Classic batting, free-machine quilting without marking a design. Collection of Ray and Susan Scott, Pintlala, AL. When Caryl won the Viewers' Choice Award at the AQS Show in 1985 with a machine-pieced, machine-quilted piece, the world of machine quilting opened up. Photo courtesy of the artist.*

Machines

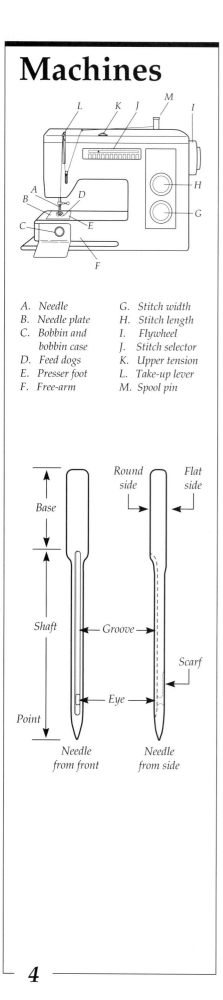

A. Needle
B. Needle plate
C. Bobbin and bobbin case
D. Feed dogs
E. Presser foot
F. Free-arm
G. Stitch width
H. Stitch length
I. Flywheel
J. Stitch selector
K. Upper tension
L. Take-up lever
M. Spool pin

Round side   Flat side

Base

Shaft

Groove

Scarf

Eye

Point

Needle from front   Needle from side

How a Sewing Machine Works

Must you own a zigzag sewing machine to machine quilt? No…but it certainly is more fun to work on a good machine. (If you need help buying a machine, see page 256.)

More important than owning the latest marvel of sewing technology is keeping your own trusty machine in good condition. If you keep your machine in smooth working order—periodically cleaning out the lint from the bobbin case, oiling it before every major project (if your machine takes oil), using new needles, not sewing over pins, and hugging it regularly—you can machine quilt.

The beauty of the modern sewing machine is that it can be adjusted to suit your sewing conditions. The standard settings for your machine are for seaming together two layers of medium-weight fabric. In machine quilting, you are asking your machine to perform in an out-of-the-ordinary way. Therefore, you must set your machine appropriately for these out-of-the-ordinary conditions. It's not difficult, but you must understand your sewing machine to machine quilt well.

Don't skip this information! You need to know how a stitch is formed on the machine (looking at the squilt from the side):

1. Above the eye of the needle is a groove called a "scarf." Some needles have deeper and larger scarfs than others; use the needle sizes recommended on page 238 and always use the needles specified for your brand. When the needle pushes through the squilt, the scarf eases friction, allowing thread to pass through the fabric.

2. After the needle passes through the fabric and begins to draw back up, a tiny loop is formed. If all adjustments are right for the materials you're working on, the loop stays below the bottom layer of fabric.

3. The bobbin shuttle hook grabs that loop and wraps it around the bobbin case and the bobbin thread. It's something like a jump rope. At first, the loop of top thread is on one side of the bobbin thread; then it's on the other. When the needle returns to the top surface, a stitch is locked on each side of the fabrics.

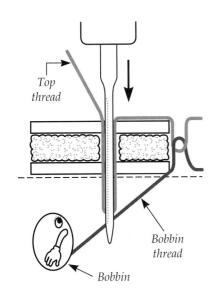

Top thread

Bobbin thread

Bobbin

The top thread meets the bobbin.

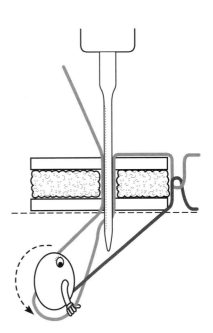

A tiny loop is formed by the top thread.

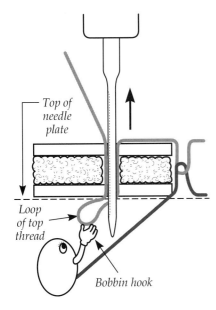

Top of needle plate

Loop of top thread

Bobbin hook

The bobbin grabs the loop and locks the stitch below the fabric.

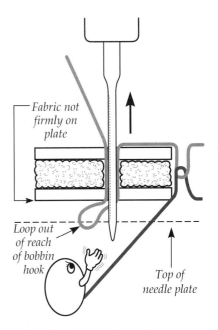

Fabric not firmly on plate

Loop out of reach of bobbin hook

Top of needle plate

If the fabric is not flat against the needle plate, the loop lifts out of reach of the bobbin and a stitch is skipped.

Common Problems

I f you understand that there is a set way in which your sewing machine works, you will be able to understand why it sometimes fails to work properly. And you will understand that there are simple remedies for the most common gremlins you'll encounter as you start to machine quilt. Let's look at each one now.

From upper left, clockwise:
Creep, Pucker,
Skip, and Fray.

Skip

You can see that if the fabric *lifts* as the needle passes back up through, the top thread loop also lifts up, the bobbin shuttle hook misses the loop, and a stitch is skipped. **You must keep the fabric absolutely flat against the needle plate as the needle passes through the fabric.** This may be done in a variety of ways. Use:

1. a presser foot
2. your fingers to press down on either side of the needle
3. a darning foot, darning spring, or spring needle
4. an embroidery hoop to keep the fabric taut.

You must also choose the correct point to the needle:

1. A *sharp needle* pierces the fabric fibers to make the hole for the thread. It is used on woven and most pressed (e.g., felt) fabrics. Sharp points are called H-J and now come in small sizes like 10/70 and 12/80.
2. A *universal needle* goes between the fabric fibers. It is used on both wovens and knits. Universal needles come in all sizes.

3. A *wedge-pointed* needle can pierce extremely dense fabrics like leather and imitation suede so that the material does not close up around the hole and bind the thread, thus causing skipped stitches. The wedge-pointed needles are usually 16/100 – 18/110.

If fabric is not pre-shrunk before sewing, the resin finish on it may deflect the needle on some machines enough that a stitch will be skipped. I prefer to preshrink my fabric (but see the discussion on page 174 for why you may prefer not to preshrink yours).

Pucker

It is very important to use the correct size and point of needle and correct thread for machine quilting—it will define your workmanship. Choose your fabrics first; then the fiber and weight of the thread; then the size and point of the needle. A general rule, broken often, is to use a thread that is as closely matched in size as possible to one thread of the fabric. Let me illustrate by exaggeration:

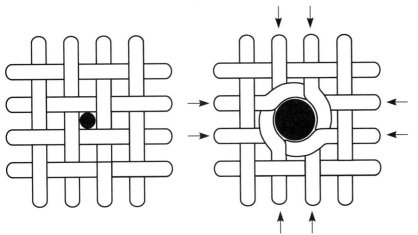

Because we can buy foreign threads in the United States and because different numbering systems are used around the world, it would be meaningless to give thread numbers here. Instead, divide your threads into extra-fine, ordinary, and heavy-duty (see the Resources at the end of the book for mail-order sources of threads).

Extra-fine are 100% cotton, rayon, polyester, and acrylic machine-embroidery threads, monofilament nylon, and size A silk thread.

Ordinary are those you use for normal sewing: cotton-covered polyester, regular 100% cotton and polyester, and metallics.

Heavy-duty are buttonhole twist, size D silk twist, carpet and buttonhole thread, and crochet and pearl cotton.

For an in-depth discussion of needles, see the Mini-Encyclopedia on page 239.

See page 169 and the Mini-Encyclopedia on page 250 for a further discussion of threads for machine quilting.

Left: *A thread the same size as or smaller than the threads of your fabric slips easily through the material.*

Right: *A thread too big for your material pushes the fibers apart and puckers your fabric. This shows up often in quilting lightweight cotton with too-heavy thread.*

A second meaning of the word "pucker" is tucks of fabric, usually seen on the back of a quilt at cross-seams or at the edge. These are caused by improper basting of the backing fabric and by fabric creep. Continue reading this chapter for how to prevent these puckers.

Fray

The function of the needle is to poke a hole in the fabric big enough for the thread to pass through the fabric easily. If the needle is too small for the three layers of the squilt, the hole will be too small, and the edges of the fabric around the hole will saw at the thread until it breaks. This is called fraying, and it can make your machine quilting distinctly less enjoyable. Every time the thread breaks, you have to stop and rethread the needle, pull up the bobbin thread, and reposition your squilt.

The remedy is to put in the next larger size of needle, and not necessarily to change threads.

In choosing a needle size, don't forget that if you are quilting a pieced top, you are periodically sewing through as many as five layers of material (if seams are pressed to one side, this can mean three layers + batting + backing). At the bound edges of the quilt, it could be as many as ten layers. Prepare for this *total* thickness when you quilt, instead of thinking merely of the thickness of the top fabric. Use a larger size needle. Otherwise you may be sewing merrily along when suddenly the light cotton fabric you see on top begins to behave like heavy denim and your machine objects to the load by breaking your thread or even your needle.

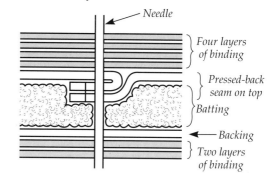

Machine quilting at its extreme. The needle must make way for the thread through eleven layers.

For all of these situations except sewing on knits, I like to use an H-J point. It punches through all the layers cleanly, without wobbling.

Creep

Choose fabric first, then the thread, then the needle size and point—this is the first rule for avoiding machine-quilting problems. You can also avoid further problems by choosing an appropriate presser foot.

The choice of presser foot depends on the machine-quilting technique selected. This will be covered more thoroughly in the following chapters.

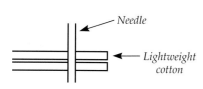

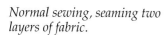

Normal sewing, seaming two layers of fabric.

See the Fabric/Thread/ Needle Chart on page 238 for more in-depth information.

The function of a presser foot is to help feed all three layers uniformly and to prevent skipped stitches. However, on three layers, the presser foot tends to move one layer farther than the other, and the overall effect of this is that one layer seems to creep past another. This causes misalignment of the squilt layers and/or tucks (puckers) on the backing, unless you (pick one):

1. Pin- or thread-baste properly (see Chapter 7).
2. Use a walking or even-feed foot.
3. Use a straight-stitch needle plate (small, round hole).
4. Decenter the needle to the left (and optionally, use a left-sided presser foot).
5. Choose a quilting design appropriate to the machine-quilting technique chosen, such as matching the diagonal diamond-grid (see Chapter 4) to the technique of quilting a whole top with the presser foot on.
6. Gain lots of experience and learn how to use your fingers as tools.

For most quilting with the presser foot on, the bobbin thread and top thread are balanced in tension. As a result, when a stitch is formed, both threads are interlocked in the quilt. This tension setting is called universal tension. If you are not sure whether your machine tension settings are correct, put one color of thread in the bobbin and use a different color of the same weight and brand as the top thread. Stitch a line of machine quilting on a small practice squilt (called a test cloth). Now examine both sides of the test cloth. Do tiny loops of the top thread show on the back? Then top tension is too loose and/or bobbin tension is too tight.

To correct this, turn the top tension dial to the right or higher, remembering Lucille Graham's phrase, "Right is tight." (Turn your head sideways to the left if your machine's tension dial is inset.)

On the other hand, if loops of bobbin thread show on the top layer of the squilt, then top tension is too great. In this case, loosening top thread tension or increasing bobbin thread tension will bring the threads back into the balance of universal tension.

While you are testing tensions on your test cloth, it is important that you experiment. Examine the results of purposely adjusting top and bobbin thread tensions out of balance. The effect can be decorative, especially if you use contrasting colors of top and bobbin thread. (Some people work a mock handquilting stitch this way. See page 28.)

The above discussion of tension holds for top and bobbin threads of the same weight. A slightly different situation holds when the threads are of different weights.

The heavier or stronger thread will always pull slightly to its side. Sometimes in machine quilting we use extra-fine

Machine Tension

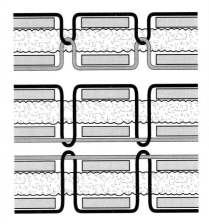

Top: *Universal tension.*

Middle: *Tight bobbin or loose top tension pulls top thread to underside.*

Bottom: *Tight top or loose bobbin tension pulls bobbin thread to topside.*

Testing stitch tension, length and width should be Standard Operating Procedure for you.

Form the habit of holding the top and bobbin threads as you start to sew. It will save you much grief. I press a forefinger to the needle plate, trapping the threads.

machine-embroidery thread on top and regular sewing thread on the bobbin. In this case, having tiny loops show on the back is unavoidable. Therefore for these conditions, be sure to choose a backing fabric of a color compatible to the top thread (the ageless trick to hide these loops is to use a small print on the backing).

Machine Set-up

If you have lost your manual, see the Resource list for places to re-order.

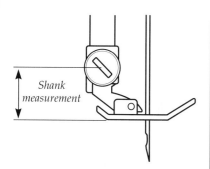

Shank measurement

Measure the distance from the center of the screw that holds on your presser foot to the bottom of the foot when it is in the down position. If the measurement is about 1/2", you have a low-shank machine; if it is about 1", you have a high-shank machine. Accessories from other similar-shank machines will sometimes fit your machine.

The best information about your machine is in its instruction manual. It will tell you how to keep your machine in good working order, how to manipulate tension settings, even how to do the simplest machine quilting.

If you've lost your sewing machine's instruction booklet, now is the right time to send away for another copy. Company addresses are given at the end of this book. When you send away, be sure to give the exact model number of your machine. You can usually find the model number on a metal plate attached to the machine, generally under it or near where the power cord plugs in. If possible, also give the year of purchase.

It is important to know whether your machine is a low-shank, high-shank, or slant-needle machine, because you can often use accessories such as a walking foot from other similar-shank brands on your machine. When the presser foot is down, measure the distance from the center of the screw that holds the foot on to the presser bar to the bottom of the foot. A low-shank machine measures approximately 1/2"; a high-shank machine, approximately 1". A slant-needle machine is obvious. Some brands, such as Bernina and Singer, have their own system. Some brands in the chart on page 255 vary according to the model you have, so you must measure to be sure.

Keeping in mind that each brand has several lines of machines, all slightly different, the chart in the Mini-Encyclopedia on page 255 shows what each company generally recommends for machine quilting (usually on their top-of-the-line models).

Since every machine is slightly different, it is important that you keep in touch with a good sewing-machine store that sells your brand to learn how to use the newest accessories for the newest techniques.

Here are what I consider the four essential presser feet for machine quilting. (But if I had to limit myself to these, I'd cry. For a more in-depth discussion of machine accessories, see page 168.)

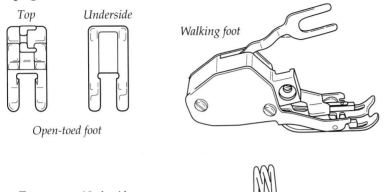

Top   *Underside*

Open-toed foot

Walking foot

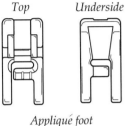

Top   *Underside*

Appliqué foot

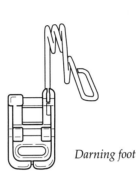

Darning foot

1. *Open-toed quilting or appliqué foot:* allows you to see exactly what the needle is stitching.

2. *Appliqué (or satin stitch) foot:* (plastic or metal) has a wedge on the underside that allows the extra thickness of satin stitch to pass easily under the foot.

3. *Walking foot (even-feed foot):* a box-like construction that helps all three layers of the squilt move evenly under the presser foot—a luxury worth owning if you plan to do a lot of machine quilting with the presser foot on (only one of many methods). The claw on the foot must grasp the needle screw.

If a walking foot did not come with your machine, ask your dealer for help in finding one that fits your machine. Also, check the Resource list for mail-order sources.

4. *Darning foot (or darning spring or spring needle):* optional for free-machine quilting…but indispensable for not sewing over fingers, especially if you tend to talk while sewing—it holds the fabric down on either side of the needle as it enters the fabric, so the top loop is caught by the shuttle hook (and simultaneously knocks the breath out of Skip).

Presser Feet

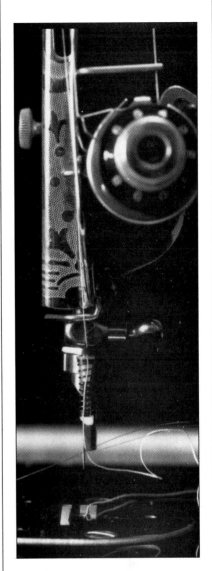

This is a Schmetz spring needle on my 1948 Featherweight. Clotilde's wire serger threader helps tired eyes thread the needle.

To help you see while stitching, some companies manufacture extra-wide openings in the foot, some make their darning feet clear, and some have openings in the front. You can modify any foot by cutting an opening in it. If it's made of plastic, use old scissors. If it's metal, use a file or ask for help.

Big Foot is a generic see-through darning foot that fits most machines. See Resource list.

Presser Feet and Seam Allowances

Because good machine quilting workmanship demands precise measurement of seam allowances, and a presser foot is one of the most convenient ways of measuring, it is extremely important to know exactly how wide each presser foot is. Measure from the needle hole to the right side of the presser foot (as you look at it). Put 1/8" graph paper, a fabric tape measure, or a ruler on the needle plate, perpendicular to the foot. Lower the needle to any inch or centimeter mark on the tape measure. Lower the presser foot. What is the measurement from the needle to the right side of the presser foot? If you own this book, write the measurement next to each foot you own in the list above, and write in any not mentioned. Now when you are figuring seam allowances, you will know, for example, when you can and cannot use the edge of the foot as a 1/4" seam allowance guide. (On some machines, you can decenter the needle to the right or left to make an exact seam allowance. If you use decentering with a favorite presser foot, mark with pencil on the dial where, for example, a seam allowance of 1/4" falls or write the settings on a Post-it Note.)

The seam allowance guides on your needle plate are not long enough for precision seaming. Extend them forward and back with a strip of masking tape. (I remove the tape and replace it each time I sew, as I don't like to gum up my needle plate.)

Some people use moleskin, a spongy material used by athletes to prevent blisters, as a seam guide. This gives a ridge to guide the fabric against and doesn't interfere with pins. A similar product is Sew Perfect by Creative Hearts, an

Measure the exact distance from the needle to the right side of each presser foot and write the measurement next to the appropriate foot in this book (if you own it). If you can decenter the needle on your machine, you can change the measurement to exactly 1/4" or whatever you need.

God bless Goo Gone! This yellow liquid, available in hardware stores, removes sticky residue. I keep a personal bottle in my sewing room and use it all the time.

Seam allowance guides: *Sew Perfect, white artist's tape, Bernina guide, Pfaff blindhem foot.*

adhesive strip about 1/8" thick (see Resource list). Stiff plastic adhesive strips are also available, but I find them less successful because pins catch on them.

I have had no luck with the magnetic seam guides available in fabric stores. Pins hit them and they move. However some quilters love them. Beckie Olson, author of *Quilts by the Slice*, gave me a screw-in guide for the Bernina which is handy. Don't be afraid to have a dealer or machinist put a hole in the needle plate so you can attach a guide. You don't really own a machine until you make a custom hole in it.

If your brand of machine has a movable blindhem foot, you can use it to make a perfect 1/4" seam.

Machine Location

A personal note about sewing-machine location: I occasionally hear the comment that machine work forces the quilter to be in isolation from her family. My response to this is, "Only by choice." When our daughter was born, I lost my tiny sewing room because we converted it to a nursery. For the next six years I complained loudly about having to move my machine around from table to table, a quilting gypsy, and about the pain of having to clean up fabric messes in order to eat or to greet guests. Finally we added a bedroom and I reclaimed my tiny sewing room...only to feel cramped and isolated. Soon I moved right back into the living room with the piano, the books, and the family—exactly like in the old days when the loom was an important fixture of every living room. I could talk as I sewed, and I liked incoming people to see what I was making. Now 15 years later, I have a wonderful long sewing room/office off the living room, right in the middle of everything.

Here are some suggestions for setting up a work area for machine quilting.

For regular sewing—clothing, wallhangings, small items for the home or office, craft pieces, gifts—a small table is fine. I bought two Sirco tables with cutouts to fit two specific brands of sewing machines. The left side lifts up around the free-arm, making a smooth surface.

For small projects, a little corner is fine but for large projects like king-size quilts, you need room for the quilt bulk to be supported behind and to the left of the machine. Otherwise, the weight of the quilt hanging down behind the machine drags it through and distorts the squilt (and in come Skip, Pucker, Creep, and Fray). Set up shop facing a large area.

A behind-the-machine support for overhanging quilts can be jury-rigged in several ways: a cardtable behind a larger table, a large piece of scrap cardboard (from appliance store or any large box opened flat) balanced on chairs in back of the machine, a pingpong table, a dining room table, or

Occasionally, when joining layers, each with many seam allowances, those underneath get tipped back instead of pressed open when they catch on the lip of the flatbed extension. Doreen Speckmann, author of *Pattern Play*, taught me to put a piece of masking tape over the crevass.

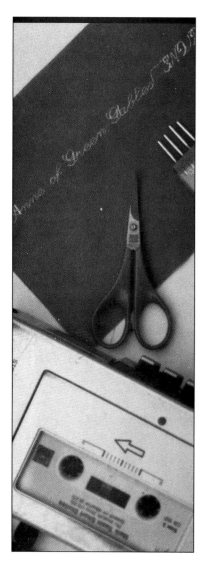

An essential part of any room I sew, cook, or clean in is my portable tape recorder and whatever recorded book I'm listening to. This brings me so much pleasure that I've taken to writing the name of the book along with my name and date on labels for whatever I've made. I especially like to rent books from the company Books on Tape, because the books are unabridged. (See Resource list.)

letting the squilt spill onto a bed. In dire circumstances, I have even sat cross-legged on the floor operating the foot pedal with my knee—a method not recommended, but at least the quilt didn't drag over the edge of a table.

To the left of the machine, set up the ironing board at the same height or rig another surface. Then you can feed the quilt through the machine without also fighting the weight of it.

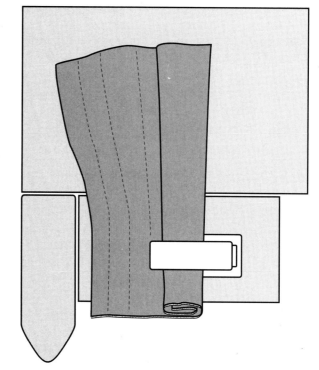

To keep the quilt from dragging off your work surface and causing problems in stitch evenness, rig a larger work area behind your machine and use a collapsible ironing board to your left. See also page 93

Try to sit in front of the needle, not to the right of it. You want your whole body centered, not leaning left, or you will soon ache.

A secretarial chair that lifts up and down and rolls easily helps your work habits. It allows you to adjust to various working heights without letting your head roll forward, which is part of what gives you a shoulder ache after hours at the machine. (Being able to rest your left elbow on a surface also helps.)

Most important, be sure your work area is well-lit. It can make the difference between eagerly wanting to work and deciding you're too tired. After observing Julie Nodine, the professional quilter (see page 258), and her well-lit work-room, I went to Home Depot and bought four $20 halogen lights. Wherever I sew in our home, I cart my machines, my tables, and my lights.

When you machine-quilt, ideas for all kinds of other quilted projects, realizations about subtleties of workmanship, and helpful hints for next time come fast. If you write ideas down as they strike you, you clear the way for more ideas to appear. Develop a system for capturing these valuable thoughts.

Years ago I began using a spiral-bound notebook with 1/4" graph paper. With the machine, I sew in squares of the fabric I used and date each work session. These notebooks have become a cherished part of my personal history. (See Resource list.)

If you don't have a Sewing Notebook, keep scrap paper near your work area. It's hard to believe that anyone wouldn't have scrap paper, but it can happen. If that's your problem, ask any office (bank, library, insurance) or recycling center to give you scrap computer print-outs, which are thrown away by the ton.

Don't eat or drink near your work-in-process or your notebooks. As I was writing this, I spilled milk all over my notes.

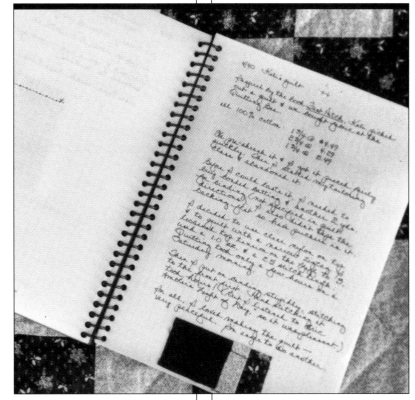

Keep track of your work in a Sewing Notebook. On the left, you can see the backside of a page with samples machine-sewn to the page.

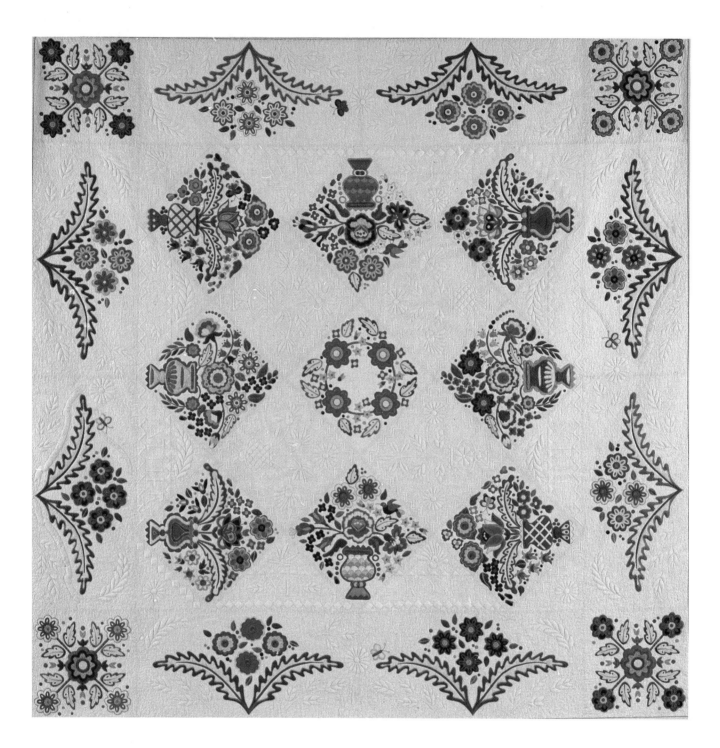

Deb Wagner, Cosmos, MN, Floral Urns, *90" square. This quilt won the $10,000 Bernina Award for Machine Workmanship at the 1993 AQS Show. Flowers are fused with doughnuts of fusible web to reduce stiffness, then zigzagged (not satin-stitched), using a width of 1, length of 1. Automatic stitches used in petals and centers of flowers. Free-machine quilted using Cotton Classic batting and DMC thread, then some areas trapuntoed, including a message as an inner border. Deb is the author of* Teach Yourself Machine Piecing and Quilting *(Chilton, 1992).*
Photo courtesy of Bernina of America.

Chapter 2

Get Started Immediately: The Message Board

You don't need a fancy machine that walks the dog and pays your taxes in order to machine quilt. Nor do you have to read an entire book in order to machine quilt. Let's get started—now!

Mail-order queen and world traveler Clotilde models a machine-quilted jacket designed by Annie Tulley. Photo courtesy of Clotilde.

The Message Board

Stay in touch by giving someone a message board, then sending periodic messages through the months and years. You can keep it simple or make it more complicated. Either way, you'll have a memorable machine-quilted gift within an hour.

Message Board: *Robert Kaufman Co. fabric, Glory Bee I batting, Sulky thread, Gingher appliqué scissors, Scotch Removable Mounting Squares, Velcro Sticky Back Tape, WT Rogers Magnetic Tape (can cut with shears). Quilted on a New Home Memory Craft 8000. Photo by Lee Lindeman.*

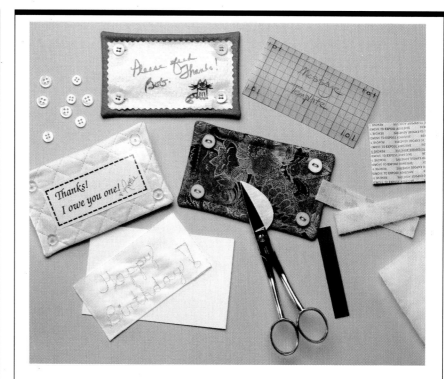

Message Board Size: *4-3/4" x 2-3/4"*
Technique: *Straight-stitch quilting*

Materials

- two pieces of fabric larger than 3" x 5" each
- 3" x 5" index card or ruler
- marking pen or pencil
- low-loft batting (I used Morning Glory's Glory Bee I)
- any thread in compatible color
- 12/80 needle
- four small buttons with two or four buttonholes
- point turner, chopstick, or retractable ballpoint pen
- Sewing Notebook
- *optional:* sticky-backed Velcro tape or self-adhesive magnetic strip (available at office supply stores), gluestick

Directions

1. Trace around the index card on the underside of one piece of fabric. Cut a slit about 2" long in the middle of the fabric, parallel to the long side.

2. Layer the fabrics rightsides together and place the batting underneath.

3. Using a regular straight stitch, stitch all the way around the squilt on the marked line, overlapping beginning and end stitches.

4. Trim the batting close to the stitching.

5. Batting side down, press the top seam allowance back on itself gently, in a half-hearted attempt to use dressmaking skills to get a better pressed-open seamline on the outside.

6. Trim excess seam allowances to 1/4". Clip diagonally across corners.

7. Turn Message Board rightsides out through the slit. Use a point turner, chopstick, or closed retractable ballpoint pen to push out corners (do not use sharp scissors). From topside, pin slit closed on either side.

8. Stitch a presser foot's width away from the edge, all the way around. Congratulations! You've just made a tiny quilt and machine quilted it.

9. Now sew a button in each corner. Turn the stitch length to 0. If you can drop or cover the feed dogs and decenter the needle, do so. Position the button just inside a corner of machine quilting (you can hold it in place with gluestick). Holding the top thread securely, carefully lower the needle into one hole of the button. Stitch in place several times to lock threads. Then set the stitch width lever to make a zigzag. You will have to try several settings, moving the needle by hand with the handwheel (not foot pedal), to find the exact stitch width for sewing each button. Satin stitch several times. Then set the stitch width lever back to 0 and lock threads again.

Some machines have special button-sewing feet.

10. Repeat Step 9 with the remaining three buttons.

11. Position either sticky-backed Velcro tape or a self-adhesive magnetic strip over slit on back or handsew slit closed.

12. Make notes in your Sewing Notebook about batting used, thread, needle, tension settings, decorative stitches, what you wish you'd done better.

13. Return tension settings to normal, if necessary. Throw away needle. Clean out lint and oil machine if necessary. Then hug it.

Your Message Board is done. You have many options for making messages to button onto the mini-quilt. Some ways follow. I'm sure you'll invent more.

Slit

Stitch on marked line

If you are nervous about sewing on buttons by machine, take your foot completely off the foot pedal. Do all the work by turning the handwheel. You can't do much damage that way, so relax.

Messages

Message Size:
4-1/4" x 2-1/4"

See page 22 for photo-copiable messages.

Materials

- paper or quilter's template material
- fabric or acetate or clear vinyl
- thread, pens, computer graphics, etc.

1. Trace the Message size on the paper or quilter's template material and cut it out. Center it over your Message Board and mark the position of the buttons. Since each Message Board is slightly different, mark the name of the owner on the template material. Then you'll know where to position the openings on future messages.

2. Options for messages:

- For a write-on surface, press HeatnBond Iron-On Flexible Vinyl onto topside of fabric, following manufacturer's instructions. It's easier to make a larger area, then cut it to size. Trace Message template on the backside with a pencil. Cut out with scissors or rotary cutter (I used Back Street Designs' wavy scissors). Write your message with a water-soluble pen like a Staedtler Lumocolor non-permanent pen (available at office supply stores). It will wipe off with a damp cloth.
- For a see-through surface, cut acetate or vinyl to Message size. Write your message on paper, by hand, typewriter, computer, or photocopy one of ours, and slip it behind the acetate. (This acetate is from overhead transparency kits.)
- For stitched messages, back fabric with freezer paper, Totally Stable stabilizer, or iron-on interfacing—anything to give the fabric body and to prevent it from fraying. (Or you could use nonfrayable fabrics like felt, Fabu-Leather, or Ultrasuede.) Stitch your message using your favorite machine-embroidery method.

3. Cut horizontal slits in the Message for the buttonholes. Slip it over the buttons.

Variation

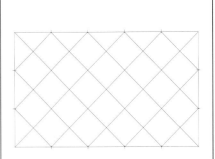

1. Draw around the index card on the topside with water-soluble marker. Mark every inch along all sides. Connect the dots as shown. Back the fabric with batting. Using metallic or shiny thread, straight stitch along the lines, starting in any corner and pivoting when you hit the side. You will be able to quilt in two passes.

2. Trim the batting close to the stitching.

3. Draw around the index card on the underside of another piece of fabric. Cut a slit in the middle about 2" long parallel to a long side. Use pins in the four corners to align the back with the quilted front, rightsides together. The quilting has probably shrunk in the top somewhat. Center the back over it.

4. Batting side up, stitch all the way around slightly inside the first stitching. Trim seam allowances and clip corners.

5. Turn rightside out and pin slit closed from topside.

6. Sew on four buttons. Cover or close slit.

7. Cut acetate to fit, so quilting will show when Message Board is empty. Cut horizontal slits in the acetate for buttons to slip through.

Send this message along with the Message Board (see next page for more messages):

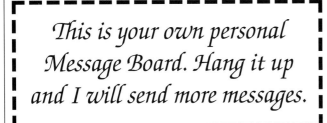

This is your own personal Message Board. Hang it up and I will send more messages.

No excuses:
Just do it!

Louder
and funnier

K.I.S.S.

Done is better
than perfect.

Congratulations!
You deserve it!

Good enough for
government work

Universal permission
to press seams open

Measure twice;
cut once.
Cut once; swear thrice.

Happy
Birthday!

You can never own
enough sewing machines.

Thanks!
I owe you one!

Hug your
sewing machine.

Lois Smith, Rockville, MD,
A Return to the Garden,
44" square. Recreates in fabric the impression of Monet's gardens and palette. A photo of Monet is screened onto fabric in the lower right quadrant. Lois is author of Fun & Fancy Machine Quilting *(AQS). Photo by Lee Lindeman.*

Shirley Nilsson, Sequim, WA,
March Winds, April Showers.
Shirley is author of Stitching Free
(C&T Publishing).
Photo courtesy of the artist.

Monica Calvert, Rocklin, CA,
Springs Promise, 91" square,
1991. Machine-pieced and -
quilted, gold metallic
thread in center.
Photo courtesy of the artist.

Melody Johnson, Cary, IL,
Technique Rebellion II, 52-1/2" square,
1991. Free-machine zigzag with two
threads through needle, built-in circle on
New Home 7000 used to machine-tack.
Quilt stolen in 1994.
Photo courtesy of the artist.

*C*hoices

Left: *Libby Lehman, Houston, TX,*
Tidewaters, *64" x 80", 1994.*
Rayons, metallics, Tinsel, Sliver.
Photo courtesy of the artist.

Below: *Sharon Hultgren, ColorBars Magic,*
using EZ International's ColorBar fabric.
Each of 12 fabrics has a stripe of pure color,
with three stripes each of lighter
and darker values.
Photo courtesy of EZ International.

Chapter 3

Techniques

This chapter is an overview of the types of machine quilting. They fall into three categories: with the presser foot on, with the presser foot off, and combination.

Once you understand your choices in techniques, practice on the simple project at the end of the chapter. Then look at the ideas for machine-quilted design in Chapter 4.

I define "machine quilting" as a thread stitched by machine through three layers. Therefore, out! goes Italian cording and traditional trapunto and the like.

Quilting With The Presser Foot On

Above: *Straight-stitch quilting after washing the sample. Diagonal lines are worked with Mettler 100% cotton, vertical lines with Coats Transparent Nylon, Metrosene Plus in bobbin, Warm & Natural batting, 12/80 H-J needle. You can also use two regular or fine threads in the needle.*

 I learned this technique through the Pfaff educators. They sometimes use a stitch similar to the triple straight or saddle stitch to emphasize the bobbin thread.

 Squilt = Quilt sandwich before quilting

Straight-Stitch Methods

Straight Stitch

Adding lines of straight-stitch quilting, whether regularly or irregularly spaced, immediately makes even plain muslin interesting. You don't have to use extra-fine or regular thread, either. For designs like sashiko (see page 68), use heavier thread like cordonnet, buttonhole twist, topstitching, or silk through a topstitching needle, with a slightly longer stitch length. If the bobbin thread color matches the top fabric, the top contrasting thread becomes more pronounced.

A mock handquilting stitch can be simulated by using monofilament nylon in the top and contrasting thread in the bobbin. Tighten top tension until the bobbin thread shows on the surface. The effect from a distance is like hand quilting. This technique can really pucker fabric, which you may or may not want. To prevent puckering, stabilize the quilting either by using heavier fabric as backing or by placing tear-away or typing-weight paper underneath the squilt, to be torn away later. The placemat project on page144 uses this technique with Timtex, a stiff batting.

Traditionally, straight-stitch quilting is worked in grids. See Chapter 4 for designs, including Ernest B. Haight's Whole-Cloth Method and Barbara Johannah's Continuous-Curve Method.

Above: *Mock handquilting worked both with a triple straight stitch (vertical lines) and saddle stitch. Tighten top tension, use monofilament on top, and use a contrast color in the bobbin. I used Warm & Natural batting and a pieced square from a Marsha McCloskey class. Worked with stitch #11 on a Pfaff 7550.*

Stitch-in-the-Ditch

If you have a pieced top, the most straightforward machine-quilting technique with the presser foot on is stitch-in-the-ditch. The term is borrowed from sewing on knits and was invented by Ann Person. After the squilt has been basted, stitch along selected major seam lines, using a regular straight stitch length or a narrow, short zigzag. If you have a walking foot, use it. Alternately, use an edgestitch foot.

Even though you're in the ditch, if you've pressed seams to one side, you'll see a slightly higher side. If you're using a straight stitch, guide the needle along the lower side.

Sometimes it's difficult to remember whether you've quilted a seam or not; when you're not sure, turn it over and examine the back.

Since the quilting does not always show on the top with this method, either you must use an interesting design on the top, or you must add additional quilting. The simplest addition is to machine quilt 1/2" in from all major seams, using the quilting guide or masking tape as a gauge. Continue to add quilting lines until your personal standards of craftmanship are met; mine is the Closed Fist Test (see page 214).

Scribble Quilting

Popularized by Bird Ross using an old Singer, scribble quilting stitches back and forth in spikes, using the continuous-reverse feature of the machine. The effect is free, not a controlled line.

Sally Lampi of Hayward, CA, designer of the well-loved Sally's Jacket, uses scribble quilting with children. After they make quilted yardage, she helps them cut it up to make baseball caps.

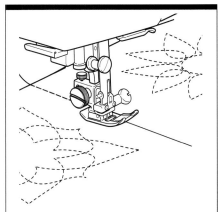

Stitch-in-the-ditch, a term invented by Ann Person of Stretch & Sew.

Left: *Scribble quilting, popularized by Bird Ross of Madison, WI, who made this jacket. Photo courtesy of the artist.*

If you have a machine that sews only one reverse stitch at a time, this technique is no fun.

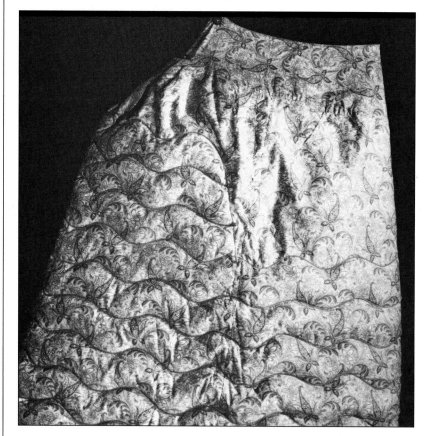

Right: *Pink sateen skirt with brown and white paisley design has channels filled with down. Quilting with a straight stitch through a cotton braid makes it appear to be chainstitched, (1886 – 1890, photo courtesy of the Royal Ontario Museum, Toronto, Canada)*

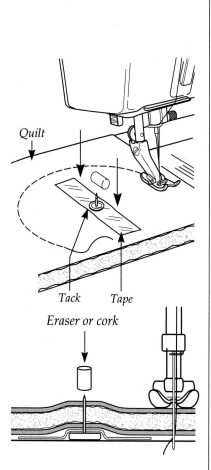

Quilt circles by taping a thumbtack, point up, on the bed of your machine. Stick the squilt over it and stitch, rotating the fabric under the needle.

You can hold down fabric appliqués and quilt at the same time by sewing straight stitches across the squilt and around shapes. The lines of straight stitch are usually a presser foot away from each other. The appliqués can be fused in place or as clever Jackie Dodson does (see page 61), held by a layer of tulle, which becomes almost invisible in the final work.

Circle Quilting

Circles are easily quilted on the machine. Tape a thumbtack head-side down to the left or right of your presser foot. Put the squilt over the tack point and cover it with an eraser or cork. The distance from the point of the tack to the needle is the radius of the circle. You can quilt circles or overlapping circles on a squilt (not too big or turning the bulk will be a nuisance) or circle-quilt finished shapes such as ears, wheels, and flower centers. Don't be shy about cutting up circle shapes after you've quilted them and then applying them with a satin stitch to other things—pockets, garments, quilts, pillows, wallhangings. The Elna 9000 has holes in the flat-bed extension. By putting a pin accessory through your work and into a hole, you can make perfect circles. That's how the circles for the Great Batting/Wheel Cover Test on page 174 and for the *Color, Wheels I* at the end of this chapter were stitched. Other machines also have circle accessories.

Outlining Printed Designs

Machine quilters seem to take absolutes as a challenge. As soon as it's generally repeated that you must do such-and-such, someone stomps defiantly to the machine and does it differently.

On the whole, it's easier and more successful to quilt whole tops on the machine with diagonal lines. But that doesn't stop machine quilters from stitching across the quilt or down it or in curved lines, if the pattern calls for it.

In particular, you may have a special print that you want to quilt. Here's how to ensure success:

1. Baste the squilt well (see page 206). Use the straight-stitch needle plate if you have one, or the left-needle position if you can decenter the needle.

2. Make sure it's worth the time to quilt your print. If it's surrounded by a busy design, you may not be able to see the puffiness and you'll be disappointed. Try to buy an extra 1/4 yd. of fabric to experiment on first. If outlining your print doesn't work with the presser foot on, try free-machine quilting (see page 47).

3. Choose the backing fabric carefully. A solid fabric is nice and can be brought around to frame the front, but it shows the goofs unless you match the top and bobbin threads to its color. A small print for backing fabric can work well as long as it complements the top.

4. Stay away from quilting small sharp angles and complicated turns—you're only asking for a visit from Pucker. In many cases, you can stitch around the general shape without delineating every in and out. However, if you stubbornly want to quilt each little nuance of your print, it helps to put one section or motif of the print in a hoop, put the presser foot on, and quilt. Don't try to force curves; stop with the needle in the fabric, lift the presser bar lever, move the quilt into position, lower the presser bar lever, and stitch merrily on.

5. If you are not using a hoop, choose your batting carefully, based on your experience. A thick batting looks beautiful quilted—but is harder to work without puckers. Use the open-toed presser foot so you can see where to quilt. For long straight lines down or across the quilt, work from the center out to one side, with the extra bulk under the head of the machine rolled up and pinned. Don't let the bulk of the quilt hang over behind your sewing area or it will pull away from the needle. Then turn the quilt 180° and work from the center out to the remaining side. If you are picky, pin on both sides of each quilting line before sewing. Admittedly, this takes more time, but you won't need to worry about the fabric pulling in unnatural angles.

Choose motifs to outline that are simple shapes with few complicated turns.

Looking at the bunny quilt reminds me that quilts take on a life of their own beyond your control. The backing has faded to a different orange, the batting is lumpy, the bunnies look tired—yet this is Jonathan's (Kali's husband) favorite summer quilt to sleep under.

Since the larger the area to be worked, the harder it is to handle and the more chance of error, consider breaking down a large fabric into smaller modules, adding units as shown in Chapter 5. If you don't have enough of this fabric print to use in both the center and the borders, copy the motifs onto tracing paper and use them actual size or blown up as quilting designs on additional fabric.

Twin-Needle Quilting

If your machine comes up in left-needle position when you turn it on, write yourself a note and post it over the turn-on switch. If you forget, you'll break the twin needle with the first stitch.

A fast way to bring the excitement of quilting to a plain area is to quilt with twin needles. Remember that there is only one bobbin thread underneath and that unless you loosen top tension, an unwanted ridge may be quilted into the fabric. For this reason, always check your stitching on a test cloth first, because you may also need to loosen bobbin tension. I had trouble stitching with rayon thread, using the walking foot and my serpentine stitch. Stitches were loose in some places on one line of thread. Loosening top tension did not help but changing to the wide open-toed appliqué foot did.

Most decorative stitches can be worked with the twin needles. The serpentine stitch is particularly effective in machine quilting. Since the presser foot follows a straight line, even though the needle snakes back and forth, it's convenient to use in a diamond grid.

Zigzag Methods

Zigzag Quilting

One of the complaints often heard about machine quilting is that it gives a "hard line." A way around this is to quilt with a narrow zigzag. You will have to experiment on your machine to see which width you like best. I like a 1 width, 2 length.

Be sure to check the thread tension on a test cloth when zigzag quilting, particularly when using both light and dark threads on top and bobbin. If tension is not balanced properly, loops of one color or the other show on the opposite side of the quilt, which is not always desirable. (A way around this is to use invisible thread on the top.)

On large areas, like quilting a sheet, learn to guide the fabric with the left hand spread around the needle area and the right hand stuck through the machine head opening, grasping the material behind the needle and gently coaxing it through the needle. Otherwise your zigzag stitches may be uneven, even if you're using a walking foot. Using zigzag, you will have better results setting your machine at the slow speed and using the needle/down feature if you have it.

On large quilts that hang over an edge or large items that will be washed many times, use polyester thread. It stretches with stress and stitches will not pop.

Appliquilting—Zigzag

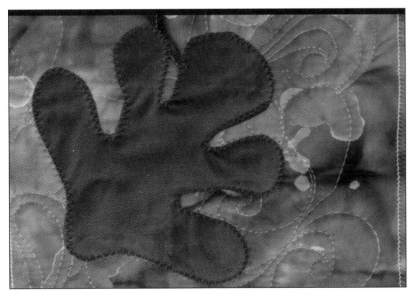

For nonfrayable fabrics like doubleknits, Ultrasuede, and Fabu-Leather, you can appliqué and quilt in one step with a zigzag stitch. This is called "appliquilting." Double-knits look particularly puffy in quilts because of their stretchability.

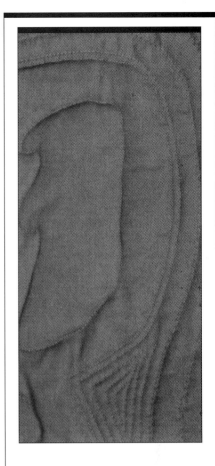

Use a narrow, short zigzag for a softer quilting line. Close-up of Kali's Koala Quilt by the authors.

Left: *Appliqué and zigzag quilt at once on nonfrayable fabrics like Fabu-Leather. Hoffman fabric, Clearly Cotton batting (bleached), smoke monofilament, background stitched with Signature Metallic in bobbin stitched underside up.*

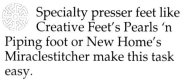 Specialty presser feet like Creative Feet's Pearls 'n Piping foot or New Home's Miraclestitcher make this task easy.

See page 182 for more information on stabilizers.

The same principle as appliquilting is used in couching ribbon, trim, or thread to the top. The zigzag stitch couches the trim and quilts at the same time. If you use monofilament thread, the zigzag stitches are almost invisible. (You can also use decorative stitches or utility stitches like the blindhem.)

Appliquilting—Satin Stitch

As with zigzag appliqué/quilting, you can appliqué and quilt with satin stitch all in one. However, the satin stitch tends to draw in the backing fabric. (If you're experienced, you can sneak by with spray-starching a lightweight backing.) Counteract this tunneling and shrinkage in several ways.

1. Use a heavier-weight backing fabric than is normally used for quilts—poplin, denim, or pillow ticking.

2. Put typing-weight scrap paper or tear-away stabilizer behind the squilt, to be torn away after satin stitching (any left-over bits of paper caught in the stitches wash away with the first machine-washing).

3. Design modules not too large to be put into your hoop while satin stitching. This keeps the backing taut while stitching, but it does compress the batt so that it doesn't puff up as much. Try using a double batt.

4. Break the quilt down into manageable modules, but cut 1" – 3" extra of the three layers. When you're done stitching, trim the module to the correct size for the quilt. Use the lines on your cutting board (assuming you have checked them for accuracy) for precision in measuring, and add borders to the block to fill it out to the correct size. (If you don't add borders, you are limited in how you join blocks by how close the satin stitching comes to the edge of the block—see joining methods on page 246.)

5. Make a lap quilt that doesn't require an accurate mattress-top measurement.

Satin stitch does not have to cover edges. You can design frayed or fringed edges or take advantage of the fabric design to create extra texture.

Here a plaid design woven into the fabric (not merely printed on the surface) is backed with a lightweight fabric. Then a squilt is made with batting and backing. Plaid squares at intervals are satin-stitched. The fabric between is cut and fringed, letting the lightweight fabric show through.

Have an old machine with no way to adjust for a fine satin stitch? Do what ingenious Peggy Bendel, prolific writer for *Sew News*, did. She used the buttonhole setting in the forward position only, not reverse, to get a satin stitch.

Left: *Maggie Backman of Things Japanese quilts with satin-stitch lines of white silk thread on white silk fabric. She then paints the quilt with VisionArt Instant Set Silk Dye, which requires no additional heat setting.*
Photo by Lee Lindeman.

Below: *Use the design of the fabric to create texture. It works better if the plaid is woven in, not printed. Mission Valley Textiles fabric, Warm & Natural batting, DMC on top, Coats Extra-Fine Dual Duty Plus in bobbin, RinsAway stabilizer underneath.*

Decorative Stitch Quilting

If you can machine quilt with straight stitch and you can machine quilt with zigzag, you can obviously machine quilt with built-in decorative stitches, including the alphabet and stitches you program. Start by using the straight-stitch grids on page 64 but use the serpentine or multiple zigzag stitch. Another easy design is a vest with straight lines quilted by decorative stitches. However, it is essential that you experiment on a test cloth first. Some stitches are temperamental and you'll want to know that *before* you start on something important.

If you can't make the stitches behave, quilt with a straight stitch first. Then cover the stitching with decorative stitches. Be sure to check the underside of your test cloth; sometimes the heavier bobbin thread looks better than the top. If so, work underside up.

For close-quilted patterns, you'll want the decorative stitches lined up (as with serpentine) or whole. The newest sewing machines have a "begin pattern" button. If you do not have this feature on your machine, you'll have to count on the test cloth how many stitches comprise one motif and make sure you begin quilting with the needle in the correct position.

The New Home educators showed me a pretty wine carrier made with pre-quilted fabric quilted with twin needles. They added a decorative stitch between the lines of stitching and stitched on each side of the carrier one of the large built-in motifs stored on a memory card.

One caution about decorative stitches: If there are many tiny stitches to each design, it takes a long time to stitch. If you were to stretch the stitches end to end, you would finish the quilt in straight stitches days before you finish with decorative stitches.

Above: *Quilt with decorative stitches, including the alphabet. Linnette Whicker of Pfaff programmed machines with this message on our quilting cruise to Mexico.*

Right: *Close-up of Ann Boyce's Hawaiian quilt.*

*Ann Boyce, Littleton, CO,
Hawaiian quilt completely
machine-appliquéd and -quilted.
Technique explained in Ann's*
Appliqué—The Ann Boyce
Way *(Chilton, 1993).
Photo by Lee Lindeman.*

*Pat Whittemore, Saratoga,
CA,* Old Fashioned Rose,
*41" square, 1994. Invisible
machine appliqué with
monofilament on a Pfaff 7550,
Hobbs Heirloom Cotton
batting, made in honor of
Pat's mother.
Photo by Lee Lindeman.*

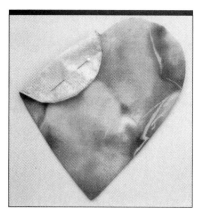

Above: *Evelyn Crittenden of Magalia, CA, stitched this heart in the Hidden Appliqué method with Do-Sew, a pattern tracing material. You could also use water-soluble stabilizer.*

Appliquilting—Decorative Stitch

As with other forms of appliquilting, you can fasten appliqués to the surface with decorative stitches and quilt at the same time. A favorite stitch is the blanket stitch or if your machine doesn't have that, the blindhem stitch. There are four ways to handle the edges of the appliqués:

1. Fuse appliqués to top fabric with paper-backed fusible web. Layer squilt. Stitch around shapes with decorative stitch. You don't care about the raw edges. See next page.

2. Sew a second lightweight fabric to the appliqué, rightsides together, all around the edges. Clip curves and trim seam allowance to 1/8". Cut a slash in the facing fabric only and turn rightsides out. Press edges. *Optional:* Trim facing to rim the shape about 1/4". This is called Hidden Appliqué.

Place the shape on the squilt, secure with gluestick or pins, and quilt around the outside edge with a blanket, blindhem, or decorative stitch.

If you use two layers of water-soluble stabilizer for the facing fabric, it will disappear in the first wash, leaving no bulk. Pat Jennings of Everett, WA, a Bernina educator, uses this technique for all-machine Hawaiian quilting.

3. Lay appliqués on the squilt or directly on the batting. Cover the edges with bias or straight-grain binding. Stitch each edge of the binding with a blanket, blindhem, or decorative stitch. Margaret Rolfe of Curtin, Australia, author of *Australian Patchwork*, was the first to show me this technique. Jackie Dodson also uses it in *Quick Quilted Home Decor With Your Bernina*, only she turns tubes with Fasturn (see Resource list) and uses these to edge the appliqués.

Speaking of turning tubes, Beki Biesterfelt of Tripoli, IA, put fleece behind her Fasturned tubes, then turned them rightsides out. She connected the tubes with decorative stitches for a vest front.

4. Your way. What will you discover, as you play? Have fun with the decorative capabilities of your machine. Quilt messages into your work; hold down bindings with pretty stitches; design your own motifs.

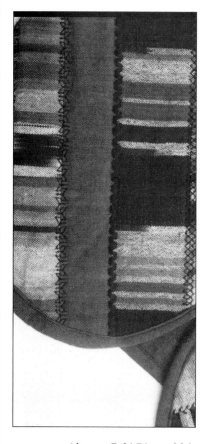

Above: *Beki Biesterfelt's Fasturned vest. The tubes are connected by decorative stitches.*

Facing Page: *Susan Parker Beck calls this layered quilting in* Second Stitches, *her book about recycling and sewing (Chilton, 1993). Piece scraps; then unify them by fusing small squares at the intersections. Layer the squilt; then quilt around small squares with decorative stitches.*

Other Ways to Quilt With the Presser Foot On

There are three other ways to quilt with the presser foot on:

1. One-step quilting
2. Tying
3. Your way

I'll discuss the first two; you discuss the third and let me know.

1. One-Step Quilting

With planning, you can combine piecing and quilting in one operation, thus avoiding the time it takes to join modules. This is sometimes called quilt-as-you-go, which can be confusing to machine quilters. Several other techniques are also referred to as "quilt-as-you-go," so we will try to avoid confusion by consistently using this terminology:

Quilt-as-you-go: The process of making several squilts that are smaller than the whole quilt and quilting each one before joining them together. See page 246 for ways to join modules.

Finish-as-you-go: Making quilted "pillows" with finished edges which, when joined, make a whole. The Great Batting/Wheel Cover Test on page 174 uses this technique.

One-step piece-and-quilt (for short, one-step quilting): The piecing and quilting of the fabric is done in one operation. Sometimes the entire project is one-step quilted, and sometimes a block at a time is one-step quilted (in which case it is also quilt-as-you-go—do you see the distinctions now?). Let's look at both.

Teaching the first quilt-as-you-go class.

Whole Quilt One-Step Quilting

This is a great way to make a simple reversible quilt.

1. Cut long strips of top, batting, and backing. If you want, machine quilt the strips first. This can call to mind the traditional English strippie quilts. (If the strips are wider than 4" – 5", the quilt will hold up longer through many washes if you do machine quilt.)

2. Rightsides together, place another top strip against the existing top strip and another backing strip against the existing backing strip. Underneath, place a batting square. Sew or serge together. (This is not rocket science, so don't worry about an exact 1/4" seam allowance. Use the edge of your walking foot.)

The serger is ideal in three ways for this quilt: A) You don't have to rewind bobbins; B) the layers feed evenly, even without differential feed; and C) the seam allowance is compressed so you don't have to trim out the batting.

It's also a good technique for tree skirts, and you can buy batting ready-cut in that shape. Work in pie shapes rather than strips.

3. Flip the strips out and repeat. Finish the edges with binding or decorative thread serging. If you serge, stitch a straight stitch or zigzag about 1/4" – 1/2" inside the entire edge. This will take the strain off the serged edge, so nothing will pull loose.

4. *Optional:* Add additional quilting.

Block One-Step Quilting

We will demonstrate one-step piece-and-quilt with a log cabin square.

1. Starch your fabrics. The center of the log cabin is 2" square with 1/4" seams. If you are doing many blocks, cut one long strip 2-1/2" wide and slice off each center when you need it. All the "logs" of the log cabin except the outer logs are 1-1/2" wide, cut in long strips. For simplicity, we are using two solids and two prints, one set dark and one light. The outer logs are cut 2" wide.

2. Cut a backing fabric the size of your block + 1/2" all around for seam allowances. Cut a batting square the same size.
Optional: Machine-baste the two together 1/2" in from the edge, using the zipper, roller, or no-snag foot so it won't catch in the batting. (This step is not necessary, but makes joining the blocks more precise and discourages the backing from shrinking and/or puckering.)

Make long squilts.

Add elements of the second squilt to the first.

Flip out the second strip and continue to build the quilt.

Trim the batting close to the stitching. Find the center of the square by laying a ruler diagonally from corner to corner and either drawing lines with a water-erasable pen or marking where the diagonal lines cross with pins. (If you use the pen, be sure to soak your quilt in cold water when you finish it, to remove the pen marks. Otherwise, the first time you wash it in hot water, the pen marks may seep to the surface and be set.) Center a 2-1/2" square of fabric in the middle; pin-baste in place.

3. The next step is simple, but calls for craftsmanship. Place a light print along one side of the center, rightsides together and top and sides even. Pin across the strip 1/4" in from both ends. If you cannot gauge 1/4" by eye, use a small piece of masking tape or cut yourself a gauge from graph paper. (See illustration for why to do this—the backside looks terrible if you don't.) Stitch with a 1/4" seam, either backstitching at both ends, lockstitching by setting your stitch length at 0 for the beginning and ending stitches, or taking tiny stitches for 1/4". Cut off the strip even with the center square. Flip out the fabric and finger-press. Pin down the fabric securely, but don't flatten the batting completely. If you make no allowance for the loft of the batting, the backing will shrink in. If you've never done this before, turn your square over after each seam and check the back for tucks and creeping. Place another piece of light-colored material along the bottom long edge, rightsides together. Stitch, using pins, a graph paper strip, or masking tape, to start and stop 1/4" from each edge. Continue spiraling around the center, using light colors on two sides and dark on the other two sides.

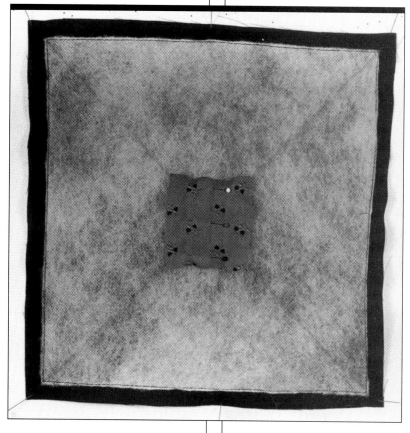

Above: *Find the center of the square.*

Right: *Sew a light print to a dark.*

4. Now examine the backing side of your one-step quilting. How does it look? If you didn't pin each fabric down as you worked, thinking you could eyeball it, the backing often creeps and puckers, although pin-basting helps. So does using a stiff backing fabric such as denim or interfacing or using spray starch to stiffen a light-weight fabric. If you sewed from raw edge to raw edge, the inter-section seamlines on the back are often a mess.

To compensate for shrinkage of the backing because of quilt-ing, I sometimes add a 1" seam all around the backing and cut the outer logs an extra 1/2" wide. When I finish, I pin a graph paper pattern of the finished block including 1/2" seams to the fabric block and trim to exact size.

Color, Wheels I on page 58 and the *Wigwarm* on page 130 use one-step quilting.

Above: *Continue spiraling around the center, stopping 1/4" from each edge.*

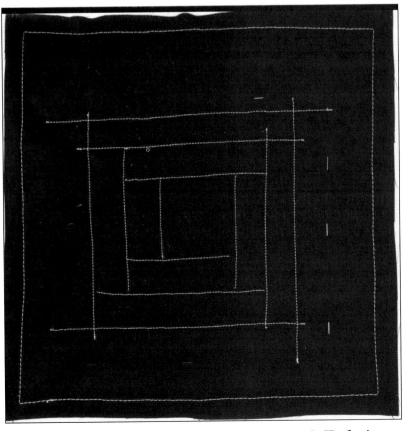

Left: *If you sewed raw edge to raw edge, the back is not pretty.*

A word of warning: Combining the piecing and the quilting in one operation is so ingenious that it's easy to run amok with the idea. However, it doesn't always look good or wear well. If the strips being quilted are less than about 1" apart, one-step quilting flattens the batting and you lose the puffy look of quilting. (The experienced can use a double batt to counteract this.) If the strips are huge and there is no further surface quilting, the quilt can look poorly made and the batting may shift around in the wash. Always make a sample first, to be sure you like the look. Also decide what your personal standards are. For quilts (not always for smaller items), I lay my fist on the block and if there aren't quilting lines nearby on *all* sides, I add some. (See page 214.)

General Guidelines for One-Step Quilting

One-step quilting adapts well to many quilting techniques and patterns: Nine-Patch, Flying Geese, crazy, and string quilts. For best results:

1. Baste the batting to the backing fabric on the seamline and then trim batting close to the stitching. If you don't do this first, you may later have to rip out one-step quilting lines that extend into the seam allowance before you can trim away the extra batting.

2. Use your most exciting fabrics for one-step quilting because the actual puffiness of quilting does not show up unless additional lines of quilting are added. (You may want to use a double batt.)

3. If you insert strips of batting into one-step quilting strips or between one-step quilted blocks, plan to add quilting lines along or across the strips, or the batting will pull away from the seamline.

4. Watch the backing fabric carefully. It wants to pull in and pucker, usually because the fabric on the top has been flattened too much between seams, not allowing for the loft of the batting. The backing fabric also puckers because it is too light-weight for the technique. Either spray-starch the fabric or use a medium- to heavy-weight backing fabric.

5. Use your quilting gauge as a 1/2" seam guideline when you are one-step quilting in the middle of a batt and cannot use the guidelines inscribed on the needle plate. Or draw the guidelines on each block.

6. Keep a small square of scrap paper near the machine. Before pulling the one-step quilting in progress away from the needle, slip the paper under the presser foot. Pull the fabric away to the left, holding the paper under the foot. This way the foot does not catch in the batting as you work. Use the paper to reposition the fabric under the needle.

7. If you have a low-shank machine and do a lot of one-step quilting, buy a no-snag foot, which does not catch in the batting. Otherwise, use a roller or zipper foot.

8. Consider adding selected lines of hand quilting. Your piece is technically quilted and can be used while you add lines of hand quilting (slowly, in my case) on other areas.

2. Tying

For quilted projects of heavy materials (corduroys, some denims, washable wools) and for fillers that won't shift (flannel, mattress pads, pre-quilted fabric remnants), the squilt may be connected by tying through the layers. There are three ways to tie on the machine:

1. Single decorative stitch
2. Mock tying
3. Machine-applied buttons

Single Decorative Stitch

Use the "single pattern" button on your sewing machine or if you don't have one, practice on a test cloth so that you know exactly how many stitches comprise one motif. If it's not clear where to tie on your project—usually the intersection of major seams—mark it before assembling the squilt. I like to poke holes through transparent graph paper (available in office supply and art stores), which is then placed against the quilt top and is marked through the holes with a pencil dot. The transparency makes it easy to reposition the graph paper for the next marking.

Another possibility is to mark the design on lightweight interfacing. Then punch small holes along the design lines.

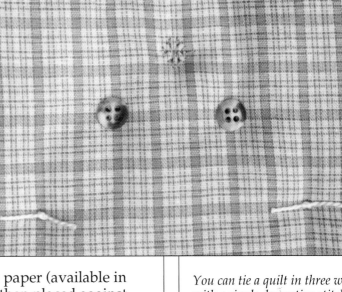

You can tie a quilt in three ways: with a single decorative stitch, with buttons, or by mock tying (zigzagging over yarn or ribbon). Mission Valley fabric, Putnam Special Edition batting.

Left: The Cambridge Marking System uses mock tying in large patterns. Photos courtesy of Cambridge Marking Systems. See the Resource list.

The ties should not be farther apart than about 8" or they may break over the years. You need not end off the thread for each decorative stitch. Simply lift the presser bar lever, hold the thread down behind the presser foot with a finger, and gently pull the fabric to the next position. When you're done with a row, preferably working parallel to the rolled-up bulk of the quilt under the head, cut the threads on front and back halfway between each stitch. Draw the top thread to the back and tie off ends in a square knot (see Chapter 2).

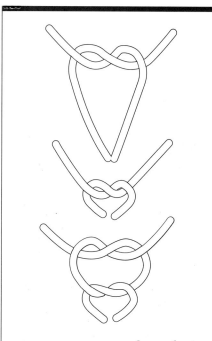

Square knot.

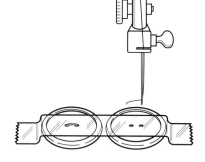

Putting buttons on by machine is easy.

Mock Tying

Mock tying imitates the traditional method of tying. Lay a 4" length of washable yarn or ribbon on top of the squilt and perpendicular to the satin stitch you are about to use. Set stitch length at 0 and (only for beginning and ending) stitch width at 0. Press the top thread against the fabric behind the presser foot so the thread won't be drawn down into the bobbin case. Pierce the yarn with the needle, taking three or four stitches. Then set the stitch width control to whatever you choose, after having experimented on a test cloth (always). Satin stitch in place about four to six times (what you're doing is bar-tacking). Set the stitch width control back to 0 and lock the threads.

After you've attached all the yarns to the squilt, tie them in square knots.

Some people prefer using cotton yarn for the ties because each time the quilted project is washed the knots shrink tighter.

You can also use ribbons. To tie a perfect bow, make a loop with the tail of the ribbon on top and hold it securely between your thumb and forefinger. Wrap the remaining ribbon over your thumb and around the back of the loop. Pinch a second loop with your other hand, with the tail of the ribbon underneath. Insert the second loop through the first and pull tight.

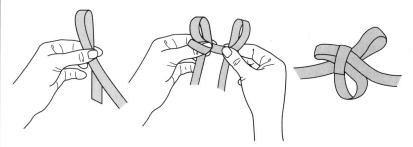

Tying a ribbon.

Machine-Applied Buttons

Wallhangings and decorative objects that no one will sit or lie on can be tied with buttons put on by machine. Using removable tape or gluestick, tape or glue the button in place. The tape tears off easily after stitching. Set your machine to stitch width 0, stitch length 0 and lower the feeds. If you can, decenter the needle on your machine either to the left or right. Holding the top thread securely, carefully lower the needle into one hole of the button. Stitch in place several times to lock threads. Then set the stitch width lever to make a zigzag. You will have to try several settings, moving the needle by hand on the handwheel (not foot pedal) to find the exact position for stitching each button. Satin stitch several times. Then set the stitch width lever back to 0 and lock threads again.

Some machines have special button-sewing feet.

When you quilt by machine, you have two choices for what to do with the presser foot. You can leave it on, for the good straightforward bread-and-butter quilting techniques described in the previous section. Or you can take it off when you quilt. This is called free-machine quilting.

Oh, the freedom that comes with free-machine quilting! You can stitch in and out of tiny little corners and around intricate curves without turning the quilt around, as you must when the presser foot is on. It's fast. It's easy. It's exhilarating.

But for success, you must put in a few playful hours of practice. And you must understand how a stitch is formed on the machine, so re-read Chapter 1, particularly page 5.

How to Free-Machine Embroider

Setting the stitch length control on your machine determines how much the feed dogs move back/forth; the longest stitch setting (baste) activates the greatest movement in the feed dogs. The presser foot works with the feed dogs to move the fabric straight through in a smooth line.

When you take off the presser foot and set the stitch length to 0, you are freeing the fabric to be moved sideways, backward, diagonally, in fact in any direction you want. This is called free-machine embroidery and it is especially useful to the machine quilter struggling to handle large amounts of fabric.

Here we'll explain how to do basic free-machine embroidery with a straight stitch and a zigzag. Then we'll explore free-machine quilting. We will practice on a solid-colored medium-weight cotton or cotton-blend scrap big enough to fit in your hoop. If you work on a portable machine, put on the flat-bed extension. Otherwise the hoop will tip over the edge.

Since there is no presser foot to hold the fabric taut against the needle plate, you must take precautions against skipped stitches. The easiest way is to put the fabric in a screw-type embroidery hoop. This is done in an opposite way from hand embroidery—i.e., the outer ring is set on a flat surface (with the carved half-moon up if your hoop has one). The fabric is spread topside-up over the ring and the inner ring is carefully pressed into place.

To adjust your machine, take off the presser foot, lower or cover the feed dogs (optional), loosen pressure on the presser foot (depends on brand of machine), loosen top tension slightly, and set both stitch width and stitch length on 0. (On some machines 0 equals the place between "fine" and reverse.) For best results in the beginning, use 100% cotton extra-fine machine-embroidery thread and a size 10/70 or 11/75 needle. Choose a color that contrasts with the fabric. Any color and type of thread can be used in the bobbin, but if you use a thinner thread, like lingerie nylon,

Free-Machine Quilting

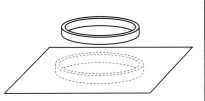

Put the outer ring on a flat surface. Press the inner ring in until the fabric is taut.

If your brand doesn't have a flat-bed extension, stack up phone books to the right height. If they wiggle, tape them to the tabletop.

Spring hoops are easier to take off the fabric than screw-type hoops, but it's difficult to use spring hoops with any bulk, like the three layers of a squilt.

Don't panic if you can't lower the feed dogs. Cover them with masking tape—or do nothing. I stitched miles on my old Elna Super only setting the stitch length at 0 to reduce the movement of the feed dogs. This works even on old machines, like the beloved Singer Featherweight.

Darning feet vary greatly: Bernina, Pfaff, Big Foot, New Home, Brother.

Hold the top thread securely in your left hand and bring up the bobbin thread.

you can get more onto the bobbin and won't have to rewind bobbins as often.

For an extra precaution against skipped stitches and against running a needle through your finger, use a darning foot, darning spring, or spring needle—but this is optional. The foot comes down with the needle as it enters the fabric and holds the fabric flat against the needle plate as a stitch is formed. When the needle goes up, so does the foot, which allows you to move the fabric in any direction.

If you choose to use no foot, your fingers must act as the presser foot, holding the fabric down against the needle plate. Be careful not to pull the fabric off-grain.

Slide the fabric and hoop under the needle. (The underside of the fabric is now flat against the needle plate.) For thick hoops and on some machines, you may have trouble fitting the hoop under the needle. Try sliding the hoop on its side and tipping it under. In drastic cases, you may have to take the needle off to fit the hoop under. (A slender machine-embroidery hoop is worth owning.)

Hold the top thread securely in your left hand. Turn the handwheel toward you one revolution so that the needle enters the fabric to the left of center hoop. Bring up the bobbin loop. Use a pin or tweezers to pull the bobbin thread to the surface of the fabric.

Lower the presser bar lever!

This is easy to forget but important! You have no top tension at all unless the presser bar lever is down. Take about three stitches in one place to lock the threads. You could theoretically cut off the threads now because they are locked, but to keep from cutting the actual sewing thread, wait to trim thread ends until you've stitched away from the area.

Now place your pinkies and thumbs on the outside of the hoop and your middle fingers on either side of the needle, pressing down lightly. Pretend that your name is written in script on the fabric and that you are tracing it with the needle. Slowly and carefully stitch your name. Take your time; there's no need to hurry or to stitch your nose to the fabric. To dot i's or cross t's, either:

1. Lock threads at the end of your name, raise the presser bar lever and gently draw the hoop into the new position, lower the presser bar lever, lock the threads again, and stitch (cut off excess threads when you're all done); or

2. Stitch around and over to the needy letter in a continuous line.

The worst thing that can happen: you'll break a needle. Big deal—who cares? If you pull or jerk the hoop, the thread will pull the needle which will bend, hit the needle plate, and break. Stitch more slowly—you have lots of time.

If you run the machine too fast without moving the hoop, the needle will pierce the thread and it will then fray and break. Using extra-fine machine-embroidery thread is a precaution here. Slow down; there's no need to rush.

If you allow the hoop to lift up as the needle enters the fabric, the bobbin hook cannot catch the top thread loop and a stitch is skipped. Keep your fingers on each side of the needle, pressing the fabric against the needle plate.

Free-machine embroidering is fun, easy, and exciting. It can be done by anyone of any age (past about four years old) on any machine. Although your first attempts may be laughable, keep practicing—it's especially worth learning for machine quilters. One expert has said it takes about ten hours (cumulative, not in a row) of practice to be proficient.

If you're borderline-scared, practice at first with an unthreaded needle. You'll learn the movements. When you're ready, thread the machine. Practice these maneuvers on your test cloth (don't bother to transfer the designs—just eyeball it):

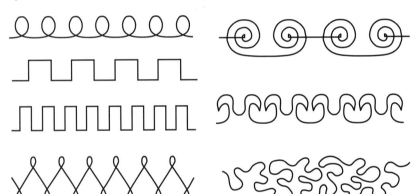

Then when that becomes easy (or boring), try drawing simple shapes: a square, a circle, a triangle. When that seems a breeze, try drawing something near your machine: scissors, pincushion, thimble.

Don't worry about how it looks. You're only practicing. Enjoy the freedom, don't worry about results, and perfect your skills.

When you feel more confident, practice on small items that are not earthshakingly important, like a message for the Message Board (page 18), making a nametag, or filling in a third color on a two-color printed fabric.

Now you are ready to free-machine quilt. The methods are the same as for quilting with the presser foot on.

Holice Turnbow was not interested in machine quilting for a long time because he thought you had to run the machine fast and he didn't like monofilament nylon thread. But when he was able to machine quilt Spartex's Canna Lily with Sulky rayon in six hours, he became a convert.

When he is demonstrating machine quilting on the designs he develops for Spartex, Holice's three pieces of advice are:

1. Use Tacky Finger, the fingertip moistener used by office workers, to help control the bulk.

2. Remember the ovals you practiced in penmanship class? That's the movement you want in machine quilting.

3. Find a balance between the speed of the motor and the speed of your hands. Holice does not like to run the machine fast.

Holice suggests a good learning project is a sampler using machine-quilting stencils from daughter Cindy's company, The Stencil Company (see Resource list).

Experiment with the speed of the machine you're most comfortable stitching. Some people like to run the machine fast and move the fabric slowly; others prefer to stitch at a moderate speed and move the fabric very slowly.

You'll find that your style of stitching is as individual as your handwriting. If you're uncomfortable, deliberately stitch "wrong." Make large, jerky stitches. Now you know what *not* to do.

You don't have to use a hoop, but if you're new to free-machine quilting, it makes it easier to move the fabric. When you're more experienced, you can abandon the hoop. I usually spread my left fingers around the darning foot and grab a handle of fabric on the right.

If the bobbin thread appears on the surface, loosen top tension. Sometimes it happens anyway, when you go around corners. Learn to lock the threads when you change direction—and don't be afraid to color the offending thread with a permanent marker.

Below: Put a squilt made of scrap fabrics in the hoop to practice free-machine quilting with a straight stitch.

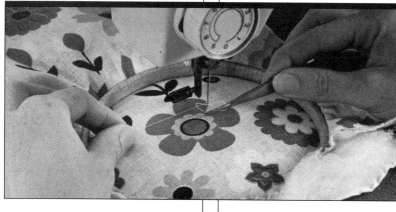

Above: Outline the design motif for practice.

Straight Stitch

For your first attempt at free-machine quilting with a straight stitch, start simple on something not important. Choose a scrap of fabric with some medium to large shapes on it, such as flowers. The scrap should be bigger than your hoop; the flowers, smaller. Make a squilt, pin- or thread-baste it together, and put it in the hoop (you may have to loosen the screw quite a bit). Set up for free-machine embroidery as usual, but use a size larger needle than you normally would for the top thread. You're going through three layers, all of which saw at the thread, so you need a needle that will make a larger hole for the thread.

I like to use 100% cotton, but I've seen people use all kinds of thread with success. If you're a beginner, stay away from monofilament nylon and rayon, for now.

Bring up the bobbin thread and lock the threads, as usual. Be sure the presser bar lever is down. Stitch around the shape of the flower and any inner details you want. Lock threads and remove the hoop. Are you happy with the quality of your stitches? If so, you're ready to free-machine quilt a larger project. If not, practice more until you're satisfied. Usually you will just need to go slower and move the hoop more smoothly.

In planning free-machine quilting, here are some considerations to keep in mind:

1. If you want to free-machine quilt a length of printed fabric, don't make it larger than about 54" (1-1/2 yd.). The bulk and weight of the quilt sometimes make it difficult to maneuver the hoop. An alternative on larger quilts is to free-machine quilt blocks, to be joined later (for details on quilt-as-you-go, see Chapter 5).

2. If you want to use a hoop, does the motif you want to quilt fit into it? You can always move the hoop mid-design, of course, but it's annoying. You can also free-machine quilt without a hoop, but it takes lots of experience to do it well. An 8" hoop is about as big as you can use without bumping into the head of the machine. Of course you can turn the material around and continue stitching, but if you're working with a lot of bulk, this, too, is annoying and awkward.

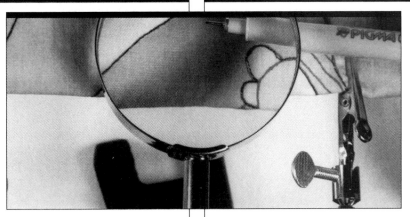

3. Baste well, as you do for quilting with the presser foot on, although correctly putting the fabric in a hoop helps eliminate puckers. (See Chapter 7 for basting methods.)

4. If you choose to quilt-as-you-go and if you will be joining two blocks directly together with no lattice strips in between, you must leave *twice* the seam allowance unquilted all around. For example, for a 1/2" seam allowance, don't quilt closer than 1" to any raw edge, so that the seam allowance can be pressed open and lie flat without any interference from quilting.

5. There are two ways to ensure that the hoop can be moved freely around the squilt, without falling off the edge:

A. Cut the squilt about 2" larger all around, to be trimmed to size after stitching. Since quilting shrinks in the overall size somewhat, you can lay the block on a cutting mat or graph paper and cut it precisely to size (including seam allowances, of course). The disadvantage is that you waste fabric—but these leftovers are perfect for string or crazy quilts.

B. Machine-baste strips of an old sheet to the outside edge of the squilt, so that the hoop can be moved partly off the squilt for free-machine quilting. To make it easy to remove the basting stitches, loosen top tension drastically. Then pull the bobbin thread when you're done quilting and it will easily slide out.

6. To mark the pattern for free-machine quilting if you are not quilting a print, use either pencil or transfer pencil (or possibly a water-erasable pen) on the top, or pin tracing paper to the back of the squilt and stitch underside up, so that what you see on top is the bobbin thread. Don't forget to test this on your test cloth. Think twice about stitching through tracing paper on the top—parts of it tear away easily but parts remain locked under piles of free-machine stitches. If you know you'll wash the piece before displaying it, there's no problem because the paper disintegrates.

7. Choose the color of your backing fabric carefully. Since the top thread tension is loosened, you will see tiny loops of the top thread on the back. Where you lock stitches, there will also be a little lump, usually unnoticeable...unless you use a light, solid-color fabric on back and a dark thread on top. For backing, I recommend using either print fabrics or the same solid-color fabric as your top thread.

For small free-machine quilted items using special fabrics on which hoop marks might show, make yourself a protective fabric ring. Put a square of muslin into your hoop. Free-

I like to use the Extra Hands With Magnifier by X-ACTO from PS Uniques to fix places where the bobbin thread shows on the surface, coloring the bobbin dots with a Pigma Micron pen. Photo by Larry Brazil.

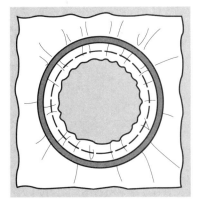

Protect special fabrics with a ring of muslin. Put the muslin in the hoop and baste the special fabric to the muslin. No ring marks will be left on the good fabric.

For free-machine designs like echo, stippling, figure 8, and more, see Chapter 4.

Mock trapunto compresses the batting around the shape.

A quick fake trapunto, which will not puff out as much as trapunto stuffed by hand, is to make a squilt, stitch the shape, and cut away the excess batting outside the shape. Comfortloft by Mountain Mist is perfect for this, because you can stack layers.

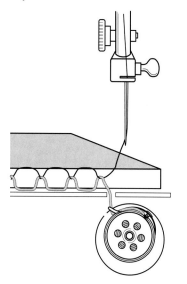

When using heavy threads in the bobbin, stitch underside up.

machine stitch around the inside near the edge of the hoop three times. Remove the hoop from the needle but don't remove the fabric from the hoop. Cut out the center circle. Now you can pin-baste the special fabric to the protective fabric without putting the special fabric into the hoop.

Mock Trapunto

Compressing the batting around a shape by stitching several concentric lines of free-machine quilting raises the shape from the background, making it look like it's been trapuntoed. Mock trapunto is considerably faster than traditional trapunto and on small pieces, like this Santa ornament, can be stitched through a double batt for extra height.

On small items like this, finish and stuff before stitching. You don't need a hoop for these little projects. Simply take your time in stitching, use a darning foot if possible, and keep your fingers in close, pressing the fabric against the needle plate. The shinier the fabric, the richer the effect.

For full-size quilts, don't use a double batt. It makes the quilt too heavy and it won't fit easily under the head of your machine.

The way you baste can make a difference, however. Deb Wagner told me that her quilt on the cover of the Singer book *Quilting by Machine* had a backing stretched tauter than the top. When the piece was washed, the backing shrank in slightly, forcing the top unstitched areas to puff up nicely like traditional trapunto.

Heavy Threads In The Bobbin Quilting

We machine quilters are fortunate in being able to use almost any washable thread in quilting. If we can't get it through the needle, we put it in the bobbin and stitch underside up.

Most threads can be wound onto the bobbin the usual way. If not possible, handwind the thread. Unlike decorative machine stitchery, which uses thread as unusual as knitting yarn, we limit ourselves to washable thread in a size compatible with the fabric—thread like cotton or polyester buttonhole twist, crochet or pearl cotton, and such.

Be sure to experiment with tension settings on a test cloth. You want to *tighten* top tension slightly, so the heavier thread will lie snug against the surface. If you can loosen bobbin tension on your machine, you may need to do so. Use an extra-fine machine embroidery thread on the top and a size 12/80 needle.

For a test cloth put the squilt in a hoop, backing fabric up. Practice free-machine quilting the design. Check the thread underneath. Does it look OK? If not, adjust the tension until you're satisfied.

One problem with using heavier threads is how to handle beginnings and endings without having ugly bumps. Solution: Either design stitched lines to run into the seam allowance, to be crossed by another line of stitching that anchors the first; or make the bumps look intentional or by pulling the threads to the underside and tying off.

Using the pattern of a print fabric for the quilting design is an easy way to make a reversible quilt—e.g., use a bandanna on one side and denim on the other. Be sure the pattern is a fairly continuous line and that it's centered on the block.

Don't forget: when you finish quilting, reset your machine to normal tension.

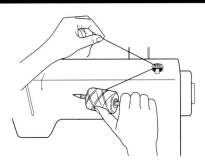

Winding heavy threads onto the bobbin.

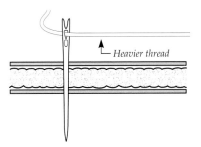

A self-threading hand needle is helpful to pull heavy threads to the back.

Janet Rostocki of Summa Design, author of Sashiko for Machine Sewing, *used flannel as batting and ribbon floss in the bobbin for this sashiko bag, stitched underside up. Photo courtesy of the artist.*

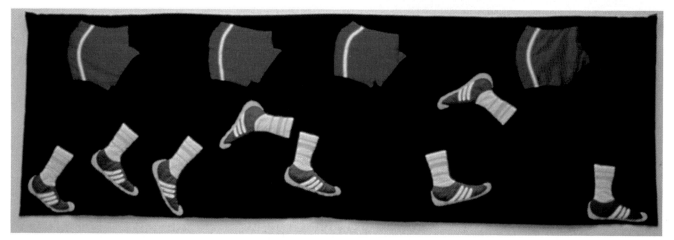

Above: *Ann Bird, Ottawa, ON, Canada, Runner, 10' x 3', 1981. Cotton, satin, machine-appliquéd, machine-quilted. Photo courtesy of the artist.*

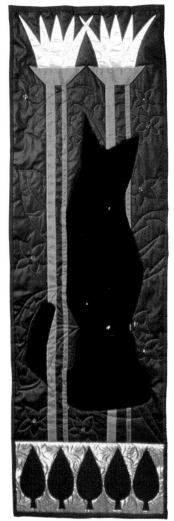

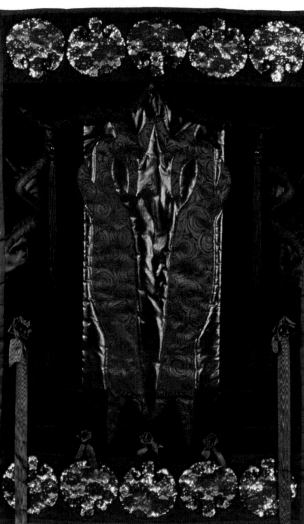

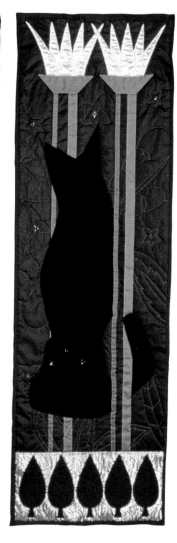

Roxy Ross Mosteller, Marco Island, FL, Vashti, 1991, 5' 3-1/2" x 6'. Manipulated images of Marlene Dietrich's clothes interpreted in glass, beads, ribbon, upholstery vinyl, panné velvet, corduroy, knits, metallic brocade, all on a Bernina 1130. Photo courtesy of the artist.

Special Loft

Putting the squilt in a hoop and free-machine quilting compresses the three layers a lot. Using a double batt circumvents this compression somewhat, but you don't always want to use a double batt. On a full-size quilt, for example, it is too heavy.

The technique of putting only the backing fabric in the hoop and pinning the batting and top onto it, then free-machine quilting, gives the puffy effect we all love in quilted objects. (This can be done with the presser foot on, too.) This technique is limited, of course, to blocks the size of your hoop, which means for an entire quilt you'd spend more time joining blocks than free-machine quilting.

Zigzag

The same maneuvers you practiced with a free-machine straight stitch can be done with a zigzag stitch. The only difference is setting the stitch width control between 1 and your widest zigzag. By running the machine fast and moving the fabric slowly, you can pack in stitches closely, yet still have the freedom of stitching off in any direction. If you think the stitches are skimpy in some places, back up and fill them in.

One good use for free-machine zigzag is to sign your name and date your quilt. You can add messages, too. Caryl Rae Hancock once stitched into a quilt "For Heidi, with love from Mommy" and the date.

The tops of letters are usually stitched without rotating the hoop, so that all the stitches are roughly parallel.

To use high-loft batting, put only the backing in a hoop. You can barely see the handles of the hoop sticking out of this squilt. American Homestead Appliqué fabric from Concord Fabrics, Fairfield Hi-Loft batting.

Decorative Stitches

Not many people have explored the use of decorative stitches in quilting, other than to enhance seam edges, as in crazy quilting, but I think this has the greatest potential of all for machine quilting. Part of the reason these have been ignored is the scale of the machine stitches to the whole piece; the stitches are dwarfed by the rest of the quilt.

In this sample, Carla Lopez of New York City uses twin needles and a free-machine decorative stitch to surround built-in stitches on her Pfaff 1475.

Yet the decorative stitches are useful in many ways: to change the value of a color you're not satisfied with (light stitching on a dark fabric, for example, makes it appear more midgray); to perk up dull or ordinary materials; to create centers of interest; and to actually quilt or tie the squilt (see page 45).

Choose the background color you stitch on carefully, so that it will contrast with and show off the stitching, not swallow it. White backgrounds, for example, are difficult unless you're using strong colors—black, brown, purple, charcoal. I once stitched a rainbow of decorative stitches on white and for all the hours of work, compared to how little the stitches showed up, I might just as well have drawn the rainbow with felt-tipped pens on the fabric.

In *How to Attract Attention With Your Art* (see Bibliography), Ivan Tubau lists these color combinations as the most striking (in order of most impact): black on white, black on yellow, red on white, green on white, white on red.

For decorative stitching, use extra-fine machine-embroidery thread in the top. Rayon is a good choice because it catches the light like silk yet is long-wearing and washable. Use any thread in the bobbin and loosen top tension slightly. Use a topstitching needle or one of the needles developed for metallics (or use a 14/90 H-J). Practice on a test cloth to be sure the stitches are not pulling in the fibers of the background material. If so, back the fabric with stabilizer (see page 182) or typing-weight scrap paper (to be torn away later). You may want to starch the fabric heavily, too.

Try double needles with free-machine decorative stitches, as Carla Lopez has in the photo. Be sure to handwalk the first stitch to make sure the needle clears the needle plate.

Computer machines often have a twin-needle setting to prevent the needles from being used in a too-wide stitch, thus hitting the needle plate and breaking.

Most of us use both kinds of machine quilting—with the presser foot on and with it off. On large items, save yourself some grief by putting in anchor lines with the presser foot on. Divide the object into quarters or more and use a walking foot to stitch. Then you can free-machine embroider within the quarters without the squilt twisting or puckering.

Now you know your choices in techniques. In Chapter 4 we'll look at possible designs. But you don't have to know any more than you do today to machine quilt. Let's practice on a wallhanging that also is a lesson in basic color.

Combination Quilting

Yvonne Perez-Collins, San Diego, CA, Monkey Doodles. *Birthday gift for Brittany Collins, appliqués on pre-quilted fabric, edges couched with rayon yarn, braided rickrack couched with monofilament. Yvonne is author of* Soft Gardens *(Chilton, 1993). Photo by Lee Lindeman.*

Color, Wheels I

The first step in learning color theory is to experience viscerally the six basic colors (called hues)—by selecting them with help, cutting strips, quilting them to a backing, then quilting on top of them. When you are finished, you will know true red, true orange, true yellow, and so forth.

First you will cut strips of the colors and set up the batting and backing. As you stitch strips together the long way, you will simultaneously quilt through the batting and backing. Next you will add double-fold binding, all stitched by machine. Then you will quilt wheels. Finally, you will add stipple quilting in the background (optional).

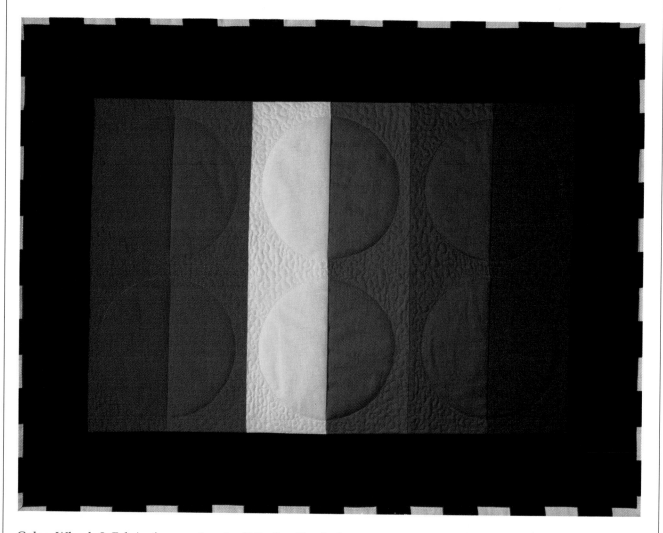

Color, Wheels I: *Fabrics from a color wheel kit offered by Quilts and Other Comforts, Glory Bee I batting, Sulky Sliver on top, Metrosene Plus in bobbin, Metafil 80 needle. Quilted on an Elna Diva. Photo by Lee Lindeman.*

Wall Hanging Size: 30" x 22"

Techniques: One-step quilting (page 40), free-machine stippling (page 73), double-mitered binding (page 234)

Materials

- 1/4 yd. each of red, orange, yellow, green, blue, violet (this is enough for two hangings)
- 30" x 22" rectangle of light-colored denim cut on-grain
- 1/2 yd. black-and-white fabric for binding
- 1/2 yd. black fabric for border
- 9" x 30" strip of muslin or any fabric
- 31" x 23" rectangle of low-loft polyester batting (I used Glory Bee I)
- strong thread in bobbin (can be cotton, polyester, or cotton-covered polyester since you're using a denim backing) in a color to match denim
- any color thread in top for piecing, as long as it is not too fat—it will not show (I used Thread Shed gray)
- extra-fine monofilament nylon
- 12/80 H-J or 14/90 H-J needle
- walking and darning feet
- black permanent pen like Sharpie or Pigma Micron
- 3" x 5" card or similar size scrap of paper
- pins, scissors, rotary cutter, mat, long plastic ruler (mine is the Omnigrid 6" x 24")
- thumbtack and tape to make circles
- soap
- Sewing Notebook

Directions

1. Set up an 8" test square of batting and denim.

2. On the side of the full-size denim that will hang against the wall, write your name, title of piece, and date with permanent pen (I used a black Pigma Micron). I wrote it twice, parallel to both long edges, in case I ever wanted to flip the piece.

3. On the side of the denim that will be inside the hanging match the two 22" ends of the denim and press-mark the center on the edges. Connect the marks with the black Sharpie permanent pen. It helps to have a full-size cutting mat with a grid. Use your plastic ruler to mark parallel lines on both sides of the center line, about 6" apart. These are alignment guides to keep your piecing lines straight.

4. Mark 3-1/2" from the top and bottom long edges.

5. Spread the batting over the backing. Cut it slightly wider and longer than the backing. If it is wrinkled, hold a steam iron above it and steam mightily, but don't touch the batting. You should be able to see the marked lines through the batting.

Work with a good quilt or fabric store to select true colors. You will have fun comparing close colors and choosing the truest one. Alternately, order a color wheel kit from a mail-order source (see Resource list).

Use a couple of Post-it Notes on the underside of the ruler to mark the 3-1/2" line. I learned this from Blanche Young.

Use the 3" x 5" index card under the foot and over the batting to keep the foot from catching on the batting.

See page 138 for more information on rod pockets.

6. Starch the undersides of the colored and black fabric yardage. Use a plastic ruler and rotary cutter or scissors to square the ends of the color strips. Cut 4-1/4" strips from all six colors across the width of the doubled fabric. Cut each strip in half at the fold (you have enough strips for a second hanging).

7. Cut three 4" strips of black across the width.

8. Arrange the color strips on a surface like an ironing board in this order: red, orange, yellow, green, blue, violet. Pick up yellow and green. With rightsides together and green on top, align the long edges with the center mark on the denim and the top short edges with the drawn line. The strips will be longer than the hanging.

9. Stitch a 1/4" seam, using the walking foot and gray thread on top, light-colored on bobbin. Start 1/4" inside the top horizontal line you drew on the backing. When you are three-quarters of the way down the seam, stop and draw a horizontal line on the green fabric even with the bottom horizontal line on the backing. Stop stitching 1/4" inside this line. Trim the two fabrics on the drawn line.

10. Flip green fabric to right and pin in place. Don't squish the batting, but don't let the fabric be too loose, either, or it will pucker when you do the circle quilting. Place blue strip on top and sew right edge as you did in Steps 8 and 9. Continue with violet. Then turn the hanging upside-down and stitch orange to yellow and red to orange.

11. Sew a black strip on each side. Before you flip them out, draw horizontal lines with soap connecting what you can still see on the backing. This will be the alignment line for the top and bottom black strips. Flip out side strips and pin. Then sew a black strip along the top and bottom, aligning the edge with the drawn lines. Flip out and pin. Your hanging is almost done.

12. Make a rod pocket. Cut a piece of muslin 9" wide by 30" long. Turn in the short ends 1/2" and press. Turn in again and topstitch to hold. Fold strip in half the long way, wrong sides together, and press to mark the center. Open up flat. Align one long end with top back of piece. Zigzag it to the top edge.

13. By hand, stitch the pocket to the backing along the pressed fold. Make sure your stitches do not show on the front of the hanging.

14. Fold the remaining half of the pocket to the top and straight stitch it at the edge of the previous zigzag stitches. The raw edges will eventually be covered by the binding.

15. For 1/2"-wide double-fold binding, cut straight-grain strips of the black-and-white fabric 3-1/4" wide. Be sure to test that this covers the edge on your test square before cutting long strips. Follow the instructions on page 234 for double-mitered binding. You could quit at this point and hang up the hanging.

16. *Optional:* On the color bars, measure 3-3/4" in from the top and bottom edges on the first, third, and fifth seam lines. Place a pin or make a dot.

17. For circle quilting, set the tack 3" to the left of the needle. Use a walking foot and monofilament thread to quilt six circles. I used a short, narrow zigzag. Be careful where the foot crosses seam lines.

18. *Optional:* Free-machine quilt the background with stipple quilting.

19. Make notes in your Sewing Notebook about batting used, thread, needle, tension settings, what you wish you'd done better.

20. Return tension settings to normal. Throw away needle. Clean out lint and oil machine if necessary. Then hug it.

Jackie Dodson, LaGrange Park, IL, Appliquéd Wallhanging *and* Sampler of Stitches *book. Reprinted with permission from Jackie's* Quick-Quilted Home Decor With Your Bernina *(Chilton, 1994).*

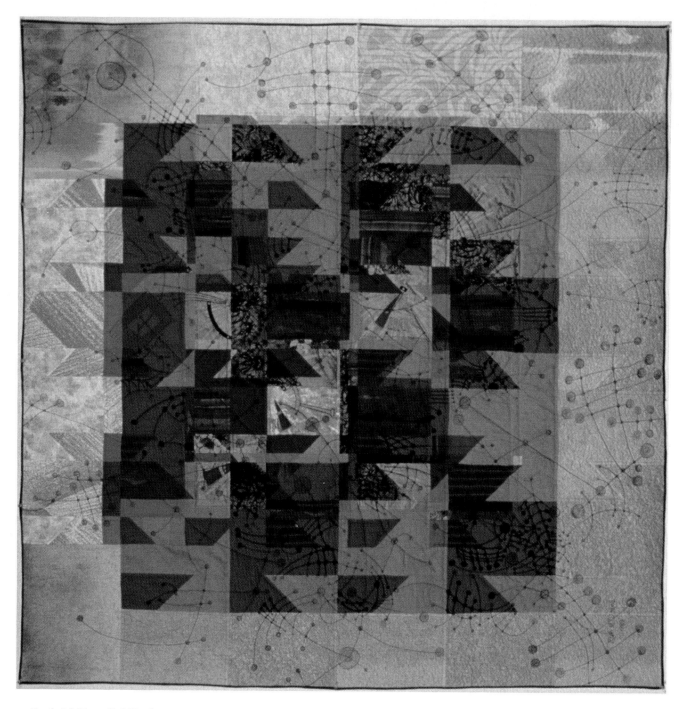

Ruth McDowell, Winchester, MA,
Double T, *71" square, 1989.*
Cottons, paint, polyester batting,
free-machine quilting adapting a
design from one of the fabric
prints. Reprinted with permission
from Pattern on Pattern *by Ruth*
B. McDowell (Quilt Digest Press).
Photo courtesy of the artist.

Chapter 4

Design

When you emphasize machine quilting rather than piecing, the world begins to resonate with line. You become sensitized to lines in the environment—telephone lines, wire fences, grillwork, ropes, garden hoses, plowed fields from the air, topographic maps, wheel covers on cars. Study the way modern artists like Vasarely, Miro, Klee, Kandinsky, and others use line.

What do you see?

"As a child, I injured my forearm while playing. I was confined to bed for a day or two…an eternity! The wound was dressed with some organdy, a light, plain, even-textured fabric that changes with the slightest movement. I pondered this micro-universe, always the same and yet different, as I played with it, pulling the crossed threads of the weave one by one."

Victor Vasarely

First we'll talk about designs for presser-foot and free-machine quilting. Then we'll discuss how to make templates.

Presser-Foot Machine Quilting

To design your own quilting patterns for whole quilt tops, remember to keep the quilting line continuous and straight or broadly curved nearly all the way across the quilt. Angles that involve turning the whole quilt to stitch invite problems.

Straight-Line Grids

Aside from following a pieced top design with stitch-in-the-ditch, you can quilt any grid. The advantage is that you usually stitch from side to side of the quilted object, omitting tying off threads. Here are some traditional grids:

Cable, slant, tri-grid

Channel, hanging diamond

Double-grid, mixed grid

Two pioneers of machine quilting have perfected different grids: Ernest B. Haight and Barbara Johannah.

Ernest B. Haight's Whole-Cloth Method

Below: *Detail of one of Ernest Haight's quilts. In 1978 he said, "I have always been intrigued with puzzles where the pieces intersect from three directions yet fit completely and perfectly. To me, every quilt pattern is a puzzle, a challenge, to choose agreeable colors or prints, to work out an order of assembly, to make corners meet as they should."*

Ernest B. Haight of David City, NE, began quilting 60 years ago when he kibitzed over his wife's shoulders about a poorly matched cross-seam. Mrs. Haight gracefully said, "Why don't *you* do it?" and he did. Soon he'd enlisted the aid of his father, who offered to quilt a top for each of the grandchildren if Ernest would piece it (on a treadle machine).

When the elder Mr. Haight died, Ernest's wife began hand quilting the tops, but there were too many, so Ernest experimented with machine quilting a whole quilt top. By then, he was working on a zigzag machine. Each year before he was permanently slowed down by Alzheimer's Disease, he made eight to ten quilts, one for each of the grandchildren, plus several more quilts to give away to the pastor, the organist, and for wedding and anniversary gifts.

Ernest B. Haight died in 1992. His son, Aubrey, estimates he made 300 quilts. Because his methods will live on, I've continued their explanation in the present tense.

See page 209 for more on quilting frames and basting.

Squilt = Quilt sandwich before quilting

When he first entered a machine-quilted quilt in the Butler County Fair in the early 1960's, it was almost refused as "*not* art" until a sympathetic official stepped in and said "we must create a new category." The quilt won a First Premium Blue Ribbon, as have many of Ernest's original-designed, machine-pieced and -quilted quilts.

In 1971 the Stuhr Museum in Grand Island, Nebraska, held a retrospective of Ernest B. Haight's work.

In 1973 the Superintendent of Needlework at the Nebraska State Fair urged Mr. Haight to write a booklet explaining his methods in order "to get machine quilting accepted as an art form." *Practical Machine-Quilting for the Homemaker* (see ordering information in Bibliography) is highly recommended to all machine quilters for its excellent and comprehensive instructions and for its collectible value—first-hand advice from the patron saint of machine quilters.

This is Ernest B. Haight's method. Read through the explanation carefully before attempting it.

1. *Mark the quilt top.* After piecing, Ernest B. Haight marks his quilt top with a diagonal grid of parallel lines about 1-1/2 to 2" apart (he uses cotton batting so his lines must be close). Notice that his quilt-top designs are usually geometric with diamond or square shapes predominating. The quilting therefore echoes and integrates these shapes, instead of being slapped on top of any old design. The diamond grid is also perfect for machine quilting, as you are stitching on the bias and can manipulate the fabric as you quilt to eliminate puckers.

An easy way to find the first diagonal line from the top left corner is to fold that corner down along the opposite long edge, making a square, with a rectangle extending below it.

Mark where the corner hits the side. Connect this mark with the corner (or iron it in lightly). Do the same for the opposite corner and you have the two main quilting lines.

2. *Baste in a frame.* This is the secret to pucker-free machine quilting. Ernest B. Haight straight-pins the lining to the quilting frames, stretches it taut but not overly so, makes the squilt, and bastes it together with about 200 safety pins for an 80" x 96" quilt. As he works, the quilt is rolled onto the short frames; the whole basting process takes him three to four hours. When done, he removes the straight pins holding the lining to the frames and machine-bastes around the perimeter of the squilt.

3. *Machine quilt.* Haight uses a straight stitch of regular length. He changes to the straight-stitch needle plate so the squilt is not dragged into the slot, causing puckers. (You can also use a left-needle position on a zigzag plate, for the same reason.) He also uses a narrow presser foot and advises *tightening* the pressure so the squilt will feed smoothly. If your presser foot pressure is adjustable, you can do this too.

Be sure to work in an open area with lots of support for the squilt behind the machine (see Chapter 1). If it drags over the edge, it will pull against the needle, causing uneven stitches, possibly puckers, and lots of impolite language.

Start at the upper left-hand corner, backstitching two or three stitches to lock threads. Stitch across the squilt, following the marked line, and taking your time. Your left hand spreads on either side of the presser foot to keep the working area smooth, your right hand guides the rolled-up bulk of the squilt under the head of the machine, and your left elbow wrestles the rest of the squilt into position. When you reach the opposite side, leave the needle in the fabric, raise the presser bar lever, pivot the fabric, lower the presser bar lever, and continue to stitch until you run out of lines to pivot toward (upper right-hand corner). Your first lines of stitching look like this:

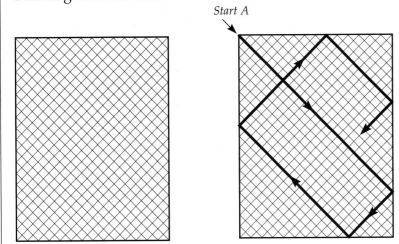

Start A

Above and Right: *Ernest B. Haight's Whole-Cloth Method.*

The beauty of Ernest B. Haight's quilting method is that except for the two long diagonal lines, the bulk of the squilt is always to your left and not underneath the head of the machine.

The second pass mirrors the first, by starting in the lower right-hand corner of the foot end, except that when you've turned the squilt upside-down, it becomes the upper left corner again.

Each new spiral is stitched twice, once from the head end of the squilt and once from the foot end. All starting points move down a long side from a corner. This is quite clear as you're working, although your mind may boggle looking at the overall quilting diagram. With experience, the machine quilting of a full-size top can be done in 8 – 12 hours, and a crib-size quilt can be finished in under two hours.

4. *Bind the edges.* Ernest B. Haight cuts fabric 2-3/8" wide along the *straight* of the grain (he prefers this to bias binding), seaming fabric together the long way until he has a long enough strip to go entirely around the quilt (about 30'

You will use this method in miniature for the Machine-Quilting Sampler on page 78. Barbara Johannah taught me that to be able to make the quilting lines ricochet perfectly, the proportions of the quilt must be 4:5, 3:4, or 7:9. The latter proportion would translate to a quilt that is, say, 84" x 108". You can use the method on any size quilt, but you will have to put in more lines of quilting and stop/start more often for other proportions.

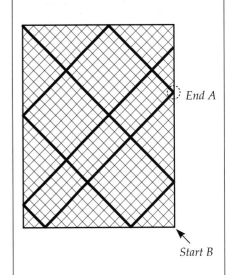

End A

Start B

for an 80" x 96" quilt). Fold the strip in half lengthwise, wrongsides together, and seam to the **underside** of the quilt, using a 1/4" seam. Bring the fold edge to the seamline on the topside, miter the corners, and stitch the fold down by machine. You now have a quilt made entirely by machine.

Barbara Johannah's Continuous-Curve Method

After changing the course of quilting in the 1970s with her quick-piecing methods, Barbara Johannah then devised an easier way to quilt, using the advantages of the machine: continuous line, minimal starts and stops, and speed. The key is to arc through the corners of a design. This method is stronger on designs with a definite figure/ground or light/dark relationship.

Instead of completing one motif at a time, you track a course through an area or complete quilt. A motif may not be completed until you've made two or more passes through it.

To plan the design, overlay parts of the quilt top with tracing paper and lightly draw the path of the quilting stitch with a pencil.

Sashiko Grid

The Japanese word *sashiko* means "tiny stabs" or running stitch. The stitches, worked through several layers in a variety of grids, used to reinforce the shoulders of peasant jackets. Sashiko was traditionally worked with white thread on indigo-dyed cotton. (Incidentally, it is pronounced "saw-she-co," either with equal emphasis on all syllables or a slight emphasis on the first syllable.) See the Bibliography for books on sashiko.

On lightweight clothing, the batting can be as light as cotton interlock or silk.

You can machine quilt sashiko designs in three ways:

1. Use heavier thread like cordonnet, buttonhole twist, topstitching, or silk through a topstitching needle, with a slightly longer stitch length. If the bobbin thread color matches the top fabric, the top contrasting thread becomes more pronounced. You can also use two regular or fine threads in the needle.

2. Use heavier thread like pearl cotton in the bobbin, using a color to contrast with the fabric. In the top, use two strands of regular thread that matches the fabric in color. Sew underside up.

3. Use monofilament nylon in the top and contrasting thread in the bobbin. Tighten top tension until the bobbin shows on the surface. The effect from a distance is like hand quilting.

Small quilt from Barbara Johannah's Crystal Piecing, *showing her Continuous-Curve method. Quilt worked by Pat Whittemore. Crystal Piecing is an ingenious way to get intricate pieces without cutting them out individually.*

Barbara Johannah often worked with quilt-as-you-go modules or rows because of the difficulty of turning a whole quilt when quilting with the presser foot on. Along came Harriet Hargrave, who simply used free-machine quilting on continuous curve designs—and the quilting world changed again.

For in-depth information on continuous curve and original piecing ideas, see *Barbara Johannah's Crystal Piecing.* For many machine-quilting techniques, see Harriet Hargrave's *Heirloom Machine Quilting.*

Right: A bag worked in sashiko designs. From Alice Allen's excellent book, Sashiko Made Simple. *Photo courtesy of Bernina of America.*

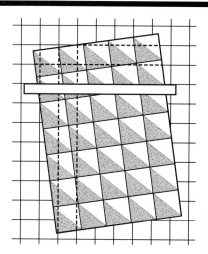

The skewed grid developed by Ruth McDowell. Illustration based on a similar one in Ruth's outstanding book, Pattern on Pattern *(Quilt Digest Press).*

A good way to design is to drop ribbons, string, or pickup sticks on your worktable. Do you like what you see? What happens if you blow on the arrangement?

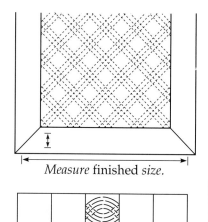

Measure finished size.

One cable unit

To fit a cable into an existing space, cut paper the finished length of the border, divide it into units, and make the cable fit one unit.

Skewed Grids

One of the most innovative machine-quilting artists is Ruth B. McDowell, author of *Pattern on Pattern*. She came up with a skewed grid by putting her quilt top at an angle on a large grid and drawing quilting lines. If your quilt top were not large, you could use the lines on a cutting mat.

Any of the straight-line grids can be stitched with the machine's built-in wandering lines, such as the multiple zigzag or a scallop. Also try them with twin or triple needles. Double the grid lines or make the spaces between lines irregular.

Experiment—find your own way and then let the rest of us know about it.

Traditional Linear Designs

You have lots of help in using traditional linear quilt designs such as cables. Almost any handquilting book is filled with designs. See the Bibliography for some good books. You can also use purchased stencils, available in craft, fabric, and quilting stores, or look to other fields for appropriate designs, like fabric painting or "liquid beads."

Be sure when you choose a design, however, that you aren't signing up for lots of stops and starts that are easy to handle with handquilting, but are a pain with machine quilting. Don't be afraid to modify the stencil to fit your methods.

If you're designing the quilt on paper, it's far easier to design the height of the border according to the given cable pattern instead of trying to manipulate the cable to fit a space.

But if you need to fit a design, such as the cable, into a certain existing space, such as a quilt border, measure the length of the *finished* border. Cut it out of freezer paper. Fold the paper in half, quarters, or thirds to find a pleasing size unit for one cable. Blow up the cable pattern to fit the space using any of the five methods shown in Chapter 7.

Don't be afraid to quilt a large rectangle or square in a traditional design and then cut it up and insert other quilted strips in it.

Your Own Linear Designs

Explore the potential of built-in stitches on your machine for linear designs. On the next page, for example, Agnes Mercik has used the simple scallop stitch in clever ways.

If you have one of the new computer sewing machines, you may be able to stitch diagonally or sideways. Use it to quilt complex lines without turning the squilt.

You can make a linear design out of almost any outline. You may have to stitch it in two or more passes, but as long as you can get into and out of the shape, you can make it

linear. Often, however, these designs are better stitched with free-machine quilting.

Isolated Motifs

On the whole, large isolated motifs are better stitched with free-machine quilting, but some of the newer computer machines can stitch huge outline motifs suitable for quilting. Here, for example, is a crest outline from a New Home memory card. The Brother Pacesetter and the Tacony Esanté also stitch wide motifs.

Computer Design

The personal computer allows you to easily repeat lines and shapes, erase, overlap—in short, to play. It frees you up from rigid thinking, too. See page 74 for more information on programs and bulletin boards.

Above: *A pillow by Agnes Mercik of Enfield, CT, worked on one of her Berninas.*

Below: *One of the outline stitches of the New Home Memory Craft 8000 that is suitable for machine quilting an isolated motif.*

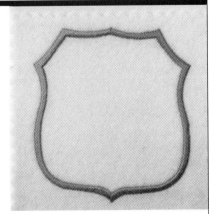

Designs For Free-Machine Quilting

The main reason you would choose free-machine quilting over presser-foot quilting is that the quilting line involves many turns, angles, stops and starts. As for finding designs for free-machine quilting, all you have to do is start looking—and record what you see:

ringed by lines of stitches

Stuffed

- meander (from watching the pattern of children moving through a playground)
- freely interlaced (designed from dropping ribbons on a table)
- sketches of buildings
- wheel covers on cars
- traditional quilting designs
- wicker and grillwork

A few suggestions for free-machine quilting designs

In the last 15 years, helped by artists like Harriet Hargrave, Caryl Bryer Fallert, Deb Wagner, and Ruth B. McDowell, some free-machine quilting designs have become standard. They are:

1. *Echo.* Surround the motif—pieced, appliquéd, or quilted—with radiating lines of free-machine quilting. The lines can be any distance apart, but are usually 1/4".

2. *Stipple or meander.* Mat down the background with a meandering free-machine straight stitch that resembles a drunk puzzle piece. Some people try never to cross quilting lines, but that isn't a rule from above.

3. *Repeated shape.* You can use little script e's, a Greek key, a figure 8, or any other continuous shape. I like the figure 8 to fill in shapes, like the heart on page 81. Wander back and forth between two lines in a figure 8 motion.

4. *Dense quilting.* Named by Nancy Moore, author of *Machine-Quilted Jackets, Vests, and Coats,* this method defines a shape by stitching parallel lines about 1/4" apart around it.

5. *Doodling.* Again, study artists who use line imaginatively, or pay attention to the design in your fabrics. Both Charlotte Andersen and Ruth B. McDowell have used free-machine quilting designs that remind me of Miro's work.

6. *Your way.* The field is wide open. Plunge in.

Computer Designs

If you're computer literate, you can design lines and shapes for both kinds of machine quilting on your personal computer. Tony used Vellum on a Mac to design the wheel cover shown on page 1 and others. You could also use Adobe Illustrator or MacDraw. On a PC, he uses Corel Draw. These are not for amateurs, however, so we're still waiting for a program expressly for machine-quilting designs. In 1994, the programs available are for quilt-top design. (See Resource list.)

At the time of writing this, the only machines capable of being hooked up to a computer are the Pfaff 1475 and the 7550. Other companies are scrambling to do the same. You can design on the computer monitor, then stitch the design on your sewing machine.

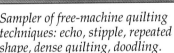 Try free-machine echo quilting with twin needles.

Sampler of free-machine quilting techniques: echo, stipple, repeated shape, dense quilting, doodling.

Worried that you don't have enough room to add a computer to your work area? Linda Shogren of San Mateo, CA, uses a laptop. Gail Brown, author of *Quick Napkin Creations,* uses a 60' serial cable, thus putting her sewing machine far from the computer.

The computer bulletin boards like Prodigy, GEnie, and others have "chats" between enthusiasts. The Pfaff people vigorously exchange designs for machine embroidery and quilting. (See the Resource list.)

Linnette Whicker, a Pfaff educator, stitched these quilting samples from their Design Collection #2. The sewing machine hooks up to the computer and you can design on screen, then stitch it out through the sewing machine.

Linda Shogren of San Mateo, CA, uses her laptop computer next to her sewing machine. On this table runner she has stitched a computer design first, then echo-quilted it with metallic thread.

Since we are not discussing piecing in this book, our discussion of templates refers specifically to machine-quilting designs.

Some companies have done the work for you. You can buy either stencils, designs to be copied onto fabric, or paper that you stitch through, tearing it away later. You can also stamp designs with fabric ink. (See the Resource list for all of these.) For information on transferring designs, see Chapter 7.

Above: Stitch-through stencils: *EZ Quilting Stitch-Thru, Pelle's bear paw stamped fabric and sewing stamp, Beautiful Publications' Continuous-line Quilting Patterns (Dimensions Collection), All-Occasion Designs for Machine Quilting from Leman Publications, Pattern Pack from Silkpaint Corporation (Comical Cats, a favorite).*

Right: Ready-made stencils: *Small feathered heart and double cable corner by Bettina Havig for American Traditional Stencils (brass); Liquid Beads by Plaid's Shape Maker Template (plastic); Ann Colvin stipple pattern, heart, and feathered wreath from Stencil Company (plastic); large meander pattern from StenSource (plastic); mystery stencil from LeeWard's (plastic).*

Templates

Whenever you repeat the same maneuver over and over, step back and ask yourself, "How can I do this easier?" For example, I taught the Machine-Quilting Sampler on page 78 on our 1994 Creative Machine Cruise in the Caribbean. Instead of having each student measure and mark the outline on her fabric, I decided to take a large template that could be traced (measure once, cut endlessly). Template plastic was too big to ship, so I prowled the hardware store and found heavy ribbed plastic shelf liner that could be cut with scissors. It proved so successful that I now have basic vest and pants patterns that I often use cut from the same plastic.

You can also design your own templates. Anything you trace along or around to mark quilting lines for the quilt is a template.

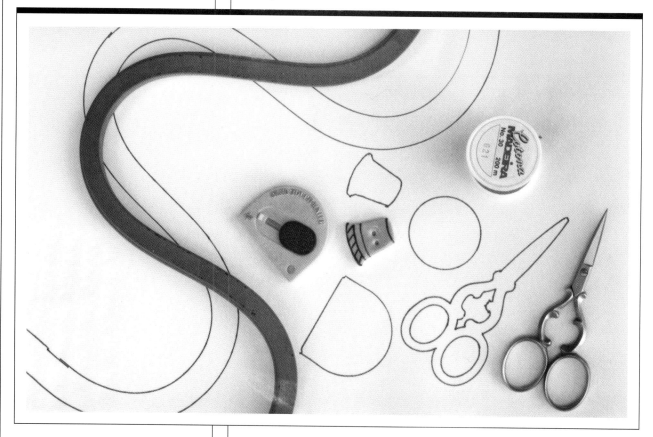

Any shape can become a template.

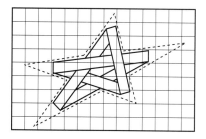

I learned to make this happy star from Janet Kime's Log Cabins/ New Techniques for Traditional Quilts.

For straight lines, use a plastic ruler, yardstick (make sure it's really straight by laying it on graph paper), artist's T-square, the edge of a book, or a right angle. (These supplies are available in fabric, art supply, and hardware stores.) Another handy template for straight lines is masking or white artist's tape in the widths you need. You can mark along both sides of it and then pick up the tape and reuse it.

You can mark shapes, as well as lines. Here's a happy star made with short lengths of 1/4" masking tape.

For wavy edges, use a scallop sewing guide, a dressmaker's French curve, or a flexible ruler (see illustration). The last can be bent into interesting shapes, repeated, and overlapped. You can also use it to round off the floor edges of quilts. (This useful tool is inexpensive and available in art supply stores.)

For marking shapes, use household items like cookie cutters, teacups, glasses, plates, and sewing supplies like thimbles, embroidery hoops, scissors handles; and any object that is the right shape for your design. For precise geometric shapes, draw them with a straight edge on graph paper; then spray-glue the back of the graph paper to template plastic, acetate, styrofoam meat trays, cardboard, used X-ray film, or sandpaper. Cut out the template shapes, using a straightedge or plastic ruler and an X-ACTO knife. Paper can be cut in quilting shapes, pinned to the squilt, and machine-quilted around. This includes freezer paper and Sulky's Totally Stable, which can be ironed to the top fabric, then later moved.

You can buy whole sheets of pressure-sensitive label paper at stationery stores. Photocopy your quilting designs and shapes onto the paper; then cut it out and stick it to the top. Shapes can be reused several times before they wear out.

The same idea of using repositionable templates applies to cutting shapes out of clear sticky shelf paper or painting repositionable glue on the back of paper templates (e.g., Clotilde's Sticky Stuff or Zig 2Way Glue—see page 183 and Resource list).

Store these sticky-backed templates on waxed paper or, as I do, inside wax sandwich bags torn partly open.

Your own stencils for marking quilting lines can be made by rubber-banding two X-ACTO knifes together or using a double-bladed knife. These are available in art supply stores—while you're there look at all the interesting templates that draftsmen use in their work. Some are suitable for quilting. If you are making a stencil for an enclosed shape, don't forget to skip cutting from time to time so the shape doesn't fall out of the stencil. Quilting stores sell a lightweight plastic suitable for this. Also check the hardware store for plastic.

For the advanced, you can buy a woodburning or stencil-cutting tool and sheets of Mylar to cut your own designs. Be sure to leave periodic bridges (uncut areas), or the shape will fall out.

See the Resource list for suppliers.

Now you know the techniques and designs available to you. In the next chapter, we'll examine your choices of where to apply them. But first, let's make a sampler of what you've learned so far.

Don't leave these templates on the quilted object overnight. I don't know for sure, but I suspect they would begin to draw the batting from the inside to the outside if left on.

Searching for design motifs can be wet and dangerous.
Photo by Larry Brazil.

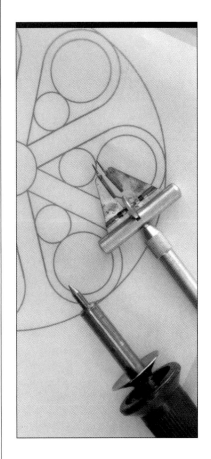

Tools for making your own stencils: *A doubled-bladed X-ACTO knife from the art store, The Creative Woodburning tool from Walnut Hollow, and stencil plastic from Inglish Publications.*

Machine-Quilting Sampler

Make a simple sampler of machine-quilting techniques that's also a portable pressing pad and a flannel design board—perfect to tuck into your bag for class. First you will mark the outside fabric, back it with batting (but no backing), and make our machine-quilting sampler. Then you will layer it with the Teflon-coated fabric inside, covered by the flannel, and bind the whole project. Finally, you can fold the sampler and carry it to class with you, then press piecing on the inside (the gridded fabric helps maintain squareness) or hang it up as a small design board.

Sampler Size: *19" x 25"*

Machine-Quilting Sampler: *Chintz from stash, Pellon Fusible Fleece, DMC Size 50 thread on top, Thread Shed on bobbin, 12/80 H-Q and 3,0/90 twin needles, Iron Quick from Nancy's Notions inside, gridded flannel (not visible). Quilted on a Pfaff 1475. Photo by Lee Lindeman.*

Materials

- 19" x 25" shiny fabric (chintz, polished cotton, silk, etc.)—do not preshrink; also do not rip the fabric because the finish often makes it off-grain and you'll end up with a skewed piece of fabric
- 1/2 yd. for binding and test square
- 19" x 25" Teflon-coated fabric (I used Iron Quick—see Resource list)
- 19" x 25" 100% cotton flannel for ironing side (plain or printed with a grid)
- 20" x 26" batting—you will need extra for testing (I used Pellon Fusible Fleece)
- 100% cotton extra-fine machine-embroidery thread for top in color to match fabric (I used DMC size 50)
- extra bobbin wound with top thread
- slightly heavier thread for bobbin, any color (I used Gutermann all-purpose)
- 3.0/90 twin needle, 12/80 H-J or 14/90 H-J (or the Schmetz quilting needle, 75/11 H-Q)
- walking foot, open-toed embroidery foot, darning foot
- long ruler, marking device (not disappearing—I used Multi-Pastel Chalk Pencil), freezer paper or Totally Stable, paper scissors, iron, pen, large paper clips, safety pins
- *Optional:* Spray-on repositionable glue, like KK 100 or Sprayway 22.
- Sewing Notebook

Directions

1. Set up a test square of chintz and fleece. Test stitch length and width, tension settings, and needle size.

2. Mark the outside fabric: First mark a 1/2" seam allowance all around. This line is the finished edge. Mark points on the finished edge 6" apart. You should have two marks on the short ends and three marks on the long sides. Now we will mark diagonally so we can use Ernest B. Haight's Machine-Quilting Method (see page 65). Barbara Johannah pointed out to me the importance of the ratio of length to width. This one is 3:4 (18" finished to 24" finished). Start in any corner of the *finished* edge and mark diagonally until you hit the opposite *finished* side at the marked point. Use the end of your ruler to mark a 90° angle and continue the line to the next finished edge. You should draw six lines and end up in the finished corner on the same long edge where you started. Make sure your lines are parallel to each other. If they aren't, you've connected the wrong dots. Now repeat the diagonal line on one of the remaining corners.

If you have a large cutting mat already marked in squares, use that as a guideline, even though you may discover that your cutting mat is not accurate in one direction. I trust my Omnigrid ruler and it revealed that my cutting mat was inaccurate in the 25" direction, but I used the markings on the cutting mat anyway because it was easier to mark the long diagonal lines.

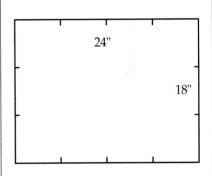

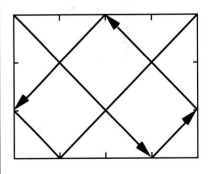

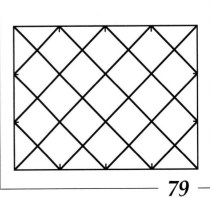

3. Back the top fabric with batting cut 1/2" larger than the outside fabric. If you are not using fusible fleece, secure the batting to the fabric, either with safety pins (can leave holes in some fabrics) or by spraying repositionable glue to the back of the fabric and pressing it to the batting. We are not using a backing for this project.

4. With the H-Q needle and the walking foot, straight stitch around the outside edge on the seam allowance. This stabilizes the quilt before you do the diagonal stitching.

5. Set up the machine for a narrow, short zigzag (I used 1 width, 2 length). Test on your practice square to see if you need to loosen top tension slightly. I worked the entire project with the top loosened; however, since we are using slightly heavier thread in the bobbin, the top thread will be pulled slightly to the back, which is what we want. Starting at one corner, follow one marked line until it runs out, ricocheting off the sides. Pivot when the needle is in the righthand position of the zigzag. If the bulk of the fabric between the needle and head bothers you, roll it under so the batting is inside and secure it with safety pins or large paper clips. Be careful not to push or pull the fabric on the bias or it will distort. Reset the machine for straight stitch, center position.

6. Change to the twin needle. Put the bobbin filled with top thread on top of the spool or on another spindle if you have it. Make sure the threads wind off in opposite directions, to prevent tangling. Thread the two threads through all tension disks as if they were one, but separate them in the thread guide immediately above the needles. Use a straight stitch about the length you use for sewing garments (I used 10 – 12 stitches per inch or 2.5)—test on the extra square. Now stitch the remaining long line. At corners, stitch until the left needle touches the finished edge. Lift the needles and pivot the fabric. Lower the right needle into the same hole and continue to stitch. You have now marked off the main squares, where you will practice other forms of machine quilting. The squares should be about 4-1/2" square.

Before we continue, look at what you've done. We could have stitched the straight lines with a straight stitch. I like a narrow, short zigzag better; the eye seems to skip every other zig, giving a softer look. The twin needles give a more pronounced look. If you were to tighten the lower tension and loosen upper tension, you could produce an even more Italian-cording look this way.

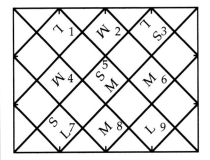

7. Trace the three heart shapes on freezer paper or Totally Stable. Cut them out. You can position these hearts anywhere you wish. For simplicity, I've placed the largest heart on the outsides, both the small and medium heart in the middle, and repeated the medium heart around the middle. Lightly fuse the hearts where you want them or use the diagram. Trace around them. Heat the paper lightly to pull it off. You will be able to reuse it.

8. Change to an open-toed embroidery foot and the quilting needle. Using a straight stitch, stitch around the four medium hearts (positions 2, 3, 7, and 8) and the smallest heart in the center. The open-toed foot allows you to see easily where you need to pivot. Overlap by several stitches to lock threads. Cut the top thread first, then the bottom thread. This pulls the top thread end into the batting.

9. Choose four decorative stitches on your machine. They should be fairly simply, without a lot of thread put into each stitch. I used a serpentine (or multiple zigzag), a stretch stitch, a briar stitch, and a straight-stitch scallop. Practice on the test square for stitch length and width. Draw about three parallel diagonal lines in each of the four medium-heart squares (positions 2, 3, 7, and 8), slanting them toward the half-heart below. Now stitch lines of decorative stitches from the center marked line to either side, using the edge of the presser foot as a guide to space rows and the guidelines to keep the rows parallel. When you reach the stitched heart, lift the presser foot and pull the fabric behind the needle until you reach the other side. Continue to stitch.

If you have been sewing steadily, this is a good time to take a stretching break.

Don't worry about locking threads. When you have finished with all four squares, cut the floating top threads in the middle. Turn the work over and cut the bobbin thread in the middle. Pull top threads to the back and cut them off about 1-1/2" from the surface. Since this sampler will not get a heavy workout, you do not have to knot the threads (unless your conscience bothers you). I like to do this job sitting at the ironing board, so my neck doesn't get sore bending over my lap.

10. Now for the fun. The rest of the sampler will be stitched free-motion, without feed dogs. Review page 47. On the test square, practice running the machine at different speeds without varying the pace at which you move the fabric. When you feel confident, free-machine quilt the remaining five squares in this way (in each type, practice first on the test square):

A. *Echo quilting*—Trace half the large heart in positions 1 and 9. Pull up the bobbin thread and lock threads at the top of the heart. Roll under the edges of the sampler so you have some handles to hold as you maneuver. Free-machine quilt the half-heart shape. When you reach the tip of the heart, stitch away about 1/8" and echo the half-heart shape. Continue to radiate out, increasing the distance from the previous line of stitching for each line.

B. *Dense quilting* (developed by Nancy Moore, author of *Machine-Quilted Jackets, Vests, and Coats*)—In the center square, draw a vertical guideline in the middle of the heart. This will help you keep your lines of stitching straight. Start at one side and stitch vertical lines about 1/4" apart. When you run into the outline of the outside heart, stitch along it until you start the next vertical line. You will stitch this square in two passes, one defining the lower part of the heart, one defining the upper part. Make sure that the heart is sufficiently defined at the sides; if it is not, add some stitching along the outside curve to define the heart.

Above: *Nancy Moore, Wake Forest, NC, pink jacket of 100% cotton with colored threads, dense quilting, and trellis design. 1988. Reprinted with permission from Nancy's* Machine-Quilted Jackets, Vests, and Coats *(Chilton, 1991).*

C. *Repeated shape*—You can use any shape you want, from small e's to a Greek key to the figure 8 used here in position 4. Stitch back and forth between the two heart shapes, doubling up shapes on the top curves and making sure the bottom of the heart is well-defined, by tiny stitches along the outside outline, if necessary. If you don't like some of your stitches (never could crayon inside the lines?), remove them, pulling the ends to the back, and restitch. There is great freedom in free-machine quilting.

D. *Stipple*—Define the inner heart in position 6 with the meandering brain-coral look of the stipple stitch. Run the machine fast and move the fabric slowly. Don't worry if your stitches must cross here and there, no matter what you've read elsewhere. You're doing this to have fun and to learn, remember? On the outside of the heart, make the stippling slightly larger and make sure it touches the outline frequently enough to define the heart. Hold the fingers of your left hand parallel to the grain to make sure you don't stretch the fabric on the bias.

You can either leave the remaining squares plain or practice other forms of machine quilting on them shown in this chapter and the last: channel quilting, large isolated decorative motifs, sashiko, free-machine or programmed messages (about batting used, date, jokes, life—whatever), or something you invent for yourself.

11. The quilting will have shrunk in the fabric somewhat. Trim away the outside batting. Turn the sampler over, batting side up. Then cut rectangles of Teflon-coated fabric and flannel to match the size of the sampler. The Teflon side should face up, with the flannel rightside up above it. Turn the sandwich over and stitch around the outside edge slightly to the right of the previous line of staystitching. I like to hold the layers together with large paper clips. To reduce bulk, trim Teflon and flannel close to stitching.

12. For the binding, cut straight-grain strips of fabric 3-1/2" wide across the fabric (or about 92" long). Seam the strips if necessary (see page 238). Change bobbin to match top thread and equalize tension between top and bobbin threads. Bind the edges, using the double-mitered method (see page 234). Start from the flannel side and wrap to the front, so you can do it all by machine. If you have extra time, use a decorative stitch over the edge of the binding.

13. Make notes in your Sewing Notebook about batting used, thread, needle, tension settings, decorative stitches, what you wish you'd done better.

14. Return tension settings to normal. Throw away needle. Clean out lint and oil machine if necessary. Then hug it.

Don't let yourself get tense while you're learning free-machine quilting. I overheard Mary Lou Rivera of Sun City, AZ, say on Doreen Speckmann's quilting cruise to Mexico to a fellow student: "Relax: We're not getting paid or graded."

Marti Michell, Chamblee, GA, One-step quilting on a Log Cabin quilt, pioneered by Marti in 1977 in a Woman's Day *article. When Marti owned Yours Truly, she published wonderful quilting books that helped spread the word about machine quilting. Now she has authored many books herself, including one on machine quilting due in 1995. Photo courtesy of the artist.*

Jane Hall, Raleigh, NC, Chroma II, 30" x 30", 1990. Silk pieced to foundation. Jane is co-author with Dixie Haywood of Precision-Pieced Quilts Using the Foundation Method *(Chilton, 1992). Photo courtesy of the artist.*

Applications

The previous two chapters showed you types and designs of machine quilting. This chapter explores your options for four applications: quilts, clothing, interiors, and crafts. It also discusses special considerations for fabric, thread, batting, techniques, and care. Each section includes two simple learning projects.

 Kandinsky's first abstract painting was a landscape that he inadvertently hung on a wall upside-down.

Quilts

Batting is not discussed in depth in this chapter. See the discussion of batting on pages 179 and 220, which gives particulars for each category of machine quilting.

Standard Bed Sizes

Over the years of making quilts, I have found that there really is no "standard" bed size and that every bed should be measured before making a quilt for it. Besides the dimensions of the mattress top, the other two important measurements are:

1. the drop, which is the distance from the top of the mattress (with sheets and blankets on) to the floor, and

2. the tuck, which is the amount of extra fabric added to the mattress length so the quilt can be tucked under the pillows and still cover them.

These two measurements vary widely, depending on whether people sleep on box springs, platforms, water beds, folding foam beds, or read in bed with eight pillows total, as we do.

See the Mini-Encyclopedia on page 228 for Standard Bed Sizes.

If you don't need the quilt to go all the way to the floor—say, the bed has a dust ruffle—here are suggested drop sizes:

Comforter: add 7" on each side of mattress size (used over a bedspread)

Coverlet: add 8" – 12" on each side of mattress size (used with a dust ruffle)

Make a Sloper

Once you've decided a particular bed needs a quilt, make a sloper for the bed. (Sloper, pronounced *slow-purr*, is a term borrowed from sewing, meaning a master pattern.) On graph paper (1/4" is useful; use centimeter graph paper if you're metric), draw the dimensions of your bed, making either 1/4" = 1" or 2".

If it's 1/4" = 1":

1" on the graph paper = 4" of the quilt.
10" of the graph paper = 40" of the quilt

Using this scale, you will need to tape graph paper together. If the scale is 1/4" = 2":

1" on the graph paper = 8" of the quilt
10" of the graph paper = 80" of the quilt.

Add drop and tuck to the mattress rectangle. Label all parts and whose bed it is. Now you can design for this bed by putting tracing paper over the sloper and trying out various blocks, colors, and layouts. Don't ever draw on the sloper itself; keep it flat in a file or drawer and you can use it for years. It isn't difficult to keep one sloper for each bed in your house. When the time comes to whip out a machine quilt, you can pull them out and go right to work, designing.

Blanche Young, author of many wonderful speed-piecing books, makes a smaller size, which she calls "cat quilts"—just the right size for cats.

To make life easier for you, we've put bed sizes on a graphed sloper on page 228. Overlay it with 1/4" graph paper and copy off the size you need.

If you're computer-handy, you can create the forms in a drawing program like MacDraw or Adobe Illustrator. Use "Save As" to create a new file from the basic sloper. Do your designing on the new file. That way the basic sloper is never compromised.

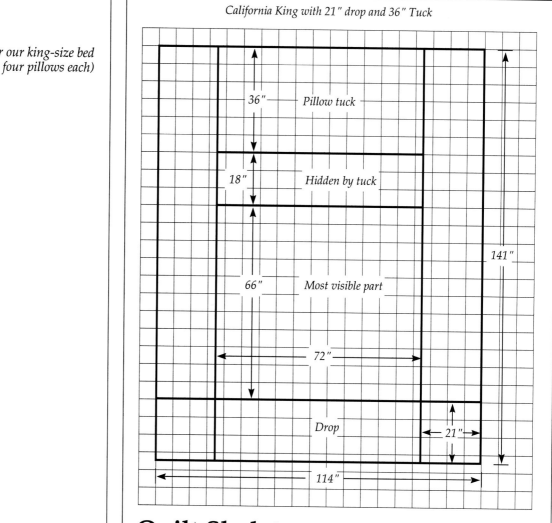

California King with 21" drop and 36" Tuck

36" — Pillow tuck

18" — Hidden by tuck

66" — Most visible part

72"

141"

Drop

21"

114"

Quilt Skeletons

While we are not covering piecing in this book, you may end up designing machine-quilted blocks. Here are ways to set the blocks together attractively.

Whole cloth,
channel,
adjoining blocks

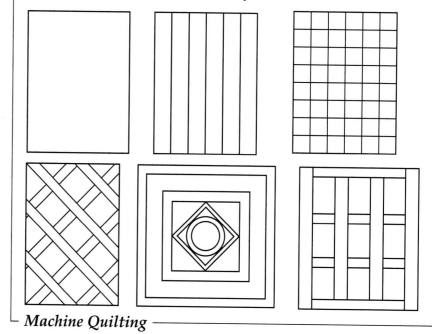

On point with sashing
medallion,
rectangular blocks with sashing
and borders

If you find a quilt you want to make, but the directions are for a double-size bed mattress top when yours is queen-size, you will need to know what changes to make. Don't change the basic block size; change the total number of blocks and add or subtract borders around the blocks to make adjustments. See the Block Chart on page 233 for planning.

Fabric Selection for Quilt Tops

Although traditional handquilters use only 100% cotton, we can use anything washable. For more information, see page 171.

If you are quilting a printed motif, as for the dinosaur baby quilt on page 105, and there will be areas with little quilting, you may be happier using a cotton/poly blend. It will not wrinkle when the quilt is washed.

If you're giving the quilt away, be sure to ask whether the lucky people have allergies. Some people can tolerate only natural fibers. Consider top, batting, backing, binding, and thread.

Whatever fabric you choose, starch it heavily before you cut, sew, or quilt. It makes quilting much more manageable.

If you have light solid colors in the quilt-top design, be careful in choosing the batting fiber and the backing color. Dark colors filtered through polyester batting may change the appearance of top fabrics—e.g., with a 1/4" polyester batt, a navy-blue backing will make top white fabric grayer and yellow fabric greenish. Sometimes, however, the effect is pleasant. When I hold up the dinosaur quilt shown on page 105, the colorful small dinosaurs on the back shine through like watercolors.

Estimating Quilt-Top Yardage

How much fabric and batting you need obviously depends on the size and complexity of your quilt. Most of us rarely go out and buy fresh yardage all at once for an entire quilt. We may buy the backing and some important color, but we add bits and pieces from our overflowing stockrooms for the rest of the quilt.

Therefore it's tricky to estimate accurately. If you are browsing in a fabric store and see something you would like to combine with other fabrics, buy a minimum of three yards; five to six yards would be better. If you want to use the fabric for an entire top or backing, see the Standard Bed Size Chart on page 228. You'll want closer to ten yards than three.

To estimate yardage for a traditional pieced-top quilt, there is an easy way and a harder way. The easy way is to refer to *Speed-Cut Quilts* by Donna Poster, which has pages of calculations and templates for 400 traditional blocks in

Thank you, Deb Wagner, for teaching me this. I have become a starch fiend—for straightforward garment sewing, too.

three sizes, telling how much fabric to buy for different block sizes.

The harder way is to draw a sample block on graph paper and measure each component of the block, including seam allowances. Multiply each component by the total number in the quilt; then use a pocket calculator to figure out how many components will fit across your fabric width. Don't forget that the usable width and length are each 2" – 4" less than store-bought, after cutting off selvages and straightening the ends. Divide the number of components per width into the total components needed; multiply *that* number by the number of inches your template stretches along the length of the fabric.

For example, if you can get 10 components out of each 42" and you need 100 components, you need 10 lengths of fabric. Each component is 4" long. Therefore, you need 40" or 1-1/9 yds.

For contemporary quilt designs, the calculations are even more complex. If there are many seams in your quilt, you will need more yardage. For insurance, always buy one yard more than your calculated amount. Paying a few dollars extra is little compared to the pain of running out of fabric in the middle of a quilt.

Most yardage calculations are based on 45"-wide fabric. If your chosen fabric is wider or narrower, use the Yardage Conversion Chart on page 254 to figure out how much yardage to buy.

If you are making a large F.A.S.T.* quilt, use a laundromat to preshrink the fabric. Eleven yards is too much for your machine.

Fabric for Backings

One important factor to remember about machine quilting is that it shrinks in proportion to the loft of your batting. **Therefore, always plan the batting and backing to be at least 2" per side larger than the top.**

On larger quilts, add 4" per side.

Backing fabric is generally a light- to-medium-weight cotton or cotton-blend fabric. If you are new to machine quilting, choose a small print for the backing (glitches and gremlins are less noticeable this way). And if your backing is poly/cotton, be sure the top and batting are preshrunk. Test, too, to be certain you like the look of the quilted test square after it's washed. The top and batting may draw in more than the backing. (See the Great Batting/Wheel Cover Test on page 174.)

Think about what thread colors will be in the top before choosing the backing. For example, if you must use a dark thread on top but a light thread on the back, you may not be happy if one or the other shows on the opposite side. (You can sometimes fix offending thread by coloring it with a permanent fine-tipped marker.)

* F.A.S.T. Quilting is used throughout this book in sympathy for working people with lots of ambition but little time. The acronym means Fabric-Aided to Save Time.

Turn the backing over the batting and pin on the topside. Otherwise, the batting will shred as you work.

Some fabric stores and mail-order places sell 90"-, 108"-, or 120"-wide fabric, which is ideal for backing quilts. Usually this wide fabric is white or natural, but it is easily dyed. If your favorite store doesn't have it, ask them to order it for you. If time is precious to you, as it is to me, it is worth it in hours saved to spend more for extra-wide fabric.

Sheets are also a good candidate for backings because they are wide. If they are poly/cotton, be sure to use the safety-pin method of basting with a helper like the Kwik Klip (see pages 195 and 208). Otherwise, your fingers will get sore.

Sheets on sale or seconds/irregulars are a good buy, but be sure to buy enough for the entire project. The backing fabric will shrink in with the machine quilting.

The Flat Sheet Yardage Chart on page 254 shows you how many yards of fabric are in each size when turn-overs are opened out.

To decide whether a sheet is a good buy, divide the sale price of the sheet by the number of yards for the price per yard (use your calculator)—example, a king flat sheet opened up is the equivalent of 8 yards of 45"-wide fabric. If it were on sale for $35, it would be $4.50/yard, a good deal when 45"-wide fabric is currently more than $6/yard.

For quilts, if you do not have a dust ruffle on your bed, the mattress or box springs may show, unless you piece two sheets together. For everything but king-size beds, buy the next largest sheet (e.g., buy a king sheet for a queen-size bed). For kings, buy a king and a twin sheet and piece the twin. (You'll have lots leftover for pillow cases.)

Unless you buy extra-wide fabric or use sheets, you will need to piece the backing. In calculating how much yardage you will need, remember that you lose about 2" when you trim the selvages.

Divide the width of your quilt by the width of the fabric (minus selvages) and round up to the nearest whole number. That is the number of lengths of backing you will need.

Multiply the length of your quilt in inches by the number of lengths you need and divide by 36" to get the number of yards needed.

Always plan for the batting and backing to be at least 2" larger per side than the top, to allow for machine-quilting shrinkage.

Anita Hallock, author of *Fast Patch*, once quilted a queen-size quilt which shrank from 95" x 105" to 84" x 96".

For example, our California King bed with big enough pillow tuck to cover four pillows each is 114" wide and 141" long. 45"-wide fabric yields a usable width of 42".

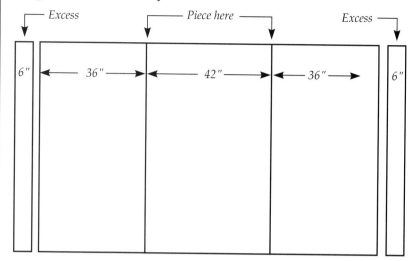

114" wide divided by 42" = 2.7
rounded up to 3 lengths needed

141" long times 3 lengths needed = 423"
divided by 36" = 11-3/4 yds.

Don't think of the excess yardage as "waste." You may be able to use it as binding or to piece it to other leftovers to make a new fabric for a top or backing. Make the back as interesting as the top!

In fact, if you're willing to put in the extra time, you could make the quilt reversible. Use the machine miter on page 234 for the binding.

If you're using a thin batting and tying it, try using pre-quilted fabric as backing, to add an extra loft to the quilt.

Estimating Binding Yardage

In order to buy enough yardage for binding, you have to answer four questions:

1. What method of binding, single or double fold?
2. Straight-grain or bias binding?
3. How wide a finished edge on the front?
4. How wide is the fabric you're buying/using?

The tables on page 232 will help you. For a survey of edge-finishing choices, see page 215. For details on binding construction, see the Mini-Encyclopedia.

Incidentally, if your binding is picking up a color in the quilt top, try to buy from the same manufacturer, if you know it. I find bindings made from mystery fabric fade differently from the rest of the quilt over the years.

Piecing a backing. Who says all the fabrics have to be the same?

How Much Thread?

It's simple. A king-size quilt with straight-forward quilting can take 1300 yards or more of thread. Buy lots.

Handling Bulk

Below: *Handle bulk by folding the quilt and supporting it with aids like this movable computer table on the left. Don't let your shoulders hunch up, and support your left elbow or you'll get a terrible neck ache. Photo by Larry Brazil.*

The key to wrestling the size of large quilts is more in your working surface than in anything you do to the quilt. You must work so that the quilt is supported behind the machine. Even better is to have additional support to your left as you quilt.

You can sidestep the issue by planning one-step quilting (page 40), using quilt-as-you-go methods to join smaller units into a large quilt (page 247), or by using Ernest B. Haight's diagonal grid (page 65), which puts most of the quilt bulk to your left.

Nevertheless, there will be times when you have a monster squilt between the needle and the head of the machine. You have several choices to tame the monster, depending on the method of machine quilting you've chosen:

Deb Wagner has another clever idea. She cuts the batting into thirds and quilts one part at a time, joining the parts with a hand stitch (see page 181).

Squilt = Quilt sandwich before quilting.

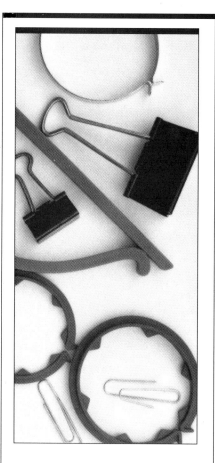

Above: Tools for handling bulk: *Dritz bicycle clips (old round ones—mine have been replaced by oval ones), EZ Quilting Quilt Clips, Lynn Graves' Jaws.*

New gadgets appear all the time. EZ International has Quilt Clips with a flat bottom and arched top. They can also be used to hold a small quilt against a surface for basting.

Lynn Graves' Little Foot has Jaws Clips in two sizes, since as you work, one roll gets bigger and the other, smaller.

Jean Botkowsky of North Babylon, NY, wears jersey garden gloves with rubber dots on them. She says, "The dots grab the fabric magically and the quilt moves almost effortlessly."

Holice Turnbow of Shepardstown, WV, uses the fingertip moistener used by office workers to sort paper. It is available in office supply stores.

1. Use oval bicycle clips for straight-line quilting with the presser foot on. Harriet Hargrave pioneered this method. Roll the area to the right of center tightly and attach many clips along the roll. (Round bicycle clips fly off the quilt, amusing only to cats.) Harriet also folds the left side and accordion-pleats the whole bundle in her lap.

Deb Wagner prefers to accordion-pleat the bulk under the head of the machine, letting it fan out behind the machine.

2. For a diagonal grid, throw the folded quilt over your shoulder. This may not work if you have arthritis or bursitis or are short.

3. For free-machine quilting, Deb Wagner has developed a thoroughly unique posture. She angles the machine so the needle is at 10 o'clock and the handwheel at 4 o'clock. Then she reaches around the right side of the machine with her right hand. She used to gets aches in her shoulders until she began free-machine quilting this way.

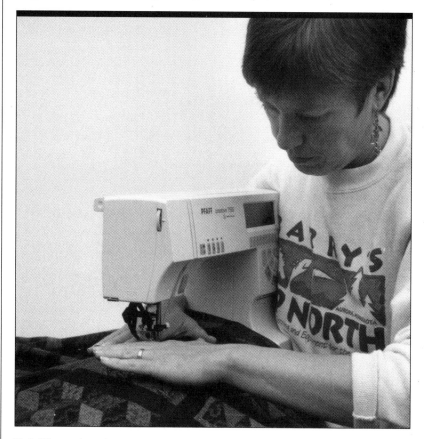

Deb Wagner's unique position for free-machine quilting to avoid shoulder aches. (It may not work on machines where the needle is positioned to the back of the head.)

4. Use safety pins. I often fasten the roll under the head of the machine to the middle of the quilt with safety pins. This is slower, but sometimes I spend more time chasing stray quilt clips than I would pinning and unpinning safety pins.

5. Your way. What have you invented?

Whole Quilt Construction Methods

You have two choices for constructing quilt tops that are already in one piece:

1. Finish edges first; then quilt. This is called the Envelope Method.
2. Quilt first; then finish edges.

Envelope Method

This method allows you to construct a complete quilt before you quilt it. It does not allow you to stretch the backing tautly, so your chances of ending up with a perfectly quilted piece are lessened. Often, this doesn't matter. The parents who were the given the dinosaur baby quilt on page 105 never noticed the imperfections. They were thrilled.

You can help the odds by starching the top and backing heavily and pressing them as one. Use a low- or regular-loft batting. I prefer to reserve this technique for smaller quilts—too many chances for Pucker to visit on large quilts.

The edges do not have to be straight. Try scallops, curves, or triangles. Be sure to clip carefully.

1. Stack the top and backing rightsides together and place them on top of the batting. If the piece is not large, spray a temporary glue like KK100 or Sprayway 22 on the batting to help hold it in place without shifting. (Be sure the spray glue won't activate allergies in the giftee.)

2. Sew around 3-1/2 sides, leaving a 12" opening. Take two or three tiny stitches across each corner. At the opening, stitch on and off the quilt.

3. Trim the batting close to the stitching. Trim corner fabrics.

4. Press the quilt top seam allowance back on itself.

5. Turn quilt rightsides out. Close the opening by hand or edgestitch all around the quilt.

6. Tape or clip the quilt to a tabletop to hold it as taut as possible. Baste with thread or safety pins (see page 206).

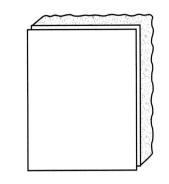

The Envelope Method: *Stack top and backing rightsides together, with batting behind.*

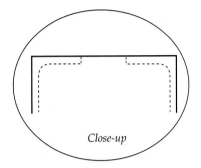

Close-up

Sew around 3-1/2 sides, taking a few tiny stitches across corners and stitching on and off the quilt at the opening.

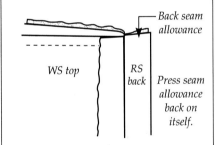

Back seam allowance

WS top

RS back

Press seam allowance back on itself.

Press the quilt top seam allowance back on itself.

Linda Denner, author of *Baby Quilts*, says, "Since machine quilting is derivative of hand quilting, we often assume common methods work when in fact, they do not. Like most machine quilters, I safety-pin baste my quilts with #0 or #1 brass safety pins. I secure the three layers at a minimum of 2" intervals. Pinning frequently is an absolute necessity, but admittedly tedious. After I have pinned, using a low-loft batting, I find no reason whatsoever to quilt from the center of the piece out. With the volume of pins I use, there is no shifting.

"I begin quilting from the outside edge into the center, rolling out of my way the quilted areas. The completed sections roll quite flat, without the need of bicycle clips. Once half the quilt is completed, I rotate the quilt to the opposite side and repeat the process.

"Order of operation is important. Quilt the background filler first, stabilizing the layers, and finish with any free-motion patterns. This minimizes shift and provides a better layered surface for manipulation."

Quilt First; Then Finish Edges

For large quilts, quilting first, then finishing edges is most common. Any of the quilting techniques discussed in the last chapter can be used. I am fond of mixing presser-foot quilting with free-machine quilting. The lines of presser-foot quilting stabilize the quilt. Then I can add accents of free-machine quilting.

It's also worth learning Ernest B. Haight's method of machine quilting (see page 65). If you've never quilted before, it's easiest to practice on a sheet. Be sure to baste properly (see Chapter 7).

Finishing Edges

These are discussed on page 215 and in detail in the Mini-Encyclopedia.

Quilt-As-You-Go

The term "quilt-as-you-go" isn't a new concept. The idea is to break a large quilted project into manageable blocks, make a squilt for each block, quilt each block independently, and then re-assemble the blocks into a full-size item like a quilt.

This method allows the quilting to be intricate and noticeable. As each unit is finished, we feel satisfied, as if in these busy times we've finally accomplished something. You also don't have to fight the bulk of a large quilt. Ultimately, however, there is more work in joining the blocks than there is in quilting a whole top at once.

Joining Quilt-As-You-Go Blocks

Choose from nine methods of joining finished quilt-as-you-go blocks. This shows you your options; the construction details for the first eight are in the Mini-Encyclopedia starting on page 2465. In all cases, I prefer to use 1/2" seams for durability. Often, then, you must stop quilting within 1/2" of the edges. Whenever possible, I finish seams on the topside so that everything can be done by machine.

1. Handle each block as if it were one layer, not three, and cover the seam with something. If you sew undersides together, putting the seam on the top, you can sew the strips down by machine. If you have quilted too close to the seamlines, you must use this method or #6.

2. Sew the backing seam without catching in the batting and top. Trim the batting even with the seamline, turn under one top seam and lap it over the other, and edgestitch or stitch with a decorative stitch. You can't use this method if you've stitched too close to the seam allowance. Leave two times the seam allowance free all around the unfinished block (e.g., don't stitch closer than 1" with a 1/2" seam allowance). You can always add more quilting afterwards.

3. Sew the backing and batting seam, fold back one top, stitch in the ditch to secure the one top, and edgestitch the remaining top.

4. Seam all layers as one, backing sides together, except for one top fabric. Finish by lapping remaining top and edgestitching.

5. Line quilted modules with one large backing and cover the joins with strips.

6. Join one-step quilting by sandwiching both top and backing with strips of fabric laid rightsides together against the blocks.

7. McRee Hickman of Southmayd, TX, came up with a wonderful all-machine sashing idea. She cuts the backing and batting about 4-1/2" larger than the top. After quilting, she puts the backings rightsides together and sews a 1-1/2" seam allowance. She trims away the batting, presses the seam open, turns under the raw edges, and sews them in place. They look like quilted sashing. To order McRee's booklet, see the Bibliography.

8. Include ribbon or tape on the sides or corners of finished modules. Then tie the modules together. You can rearrange the design, if you wish. See the Great Batting/Wheel Cover test on page 174.

Close-up of McRee Hickman's clever quilt-as-you-go joining technique. In this example, she folded back the sashing and inserted a second color, similar to Cathedral Window. See the Bibliography for her book.

9. Your way. Have you come up with something clever?

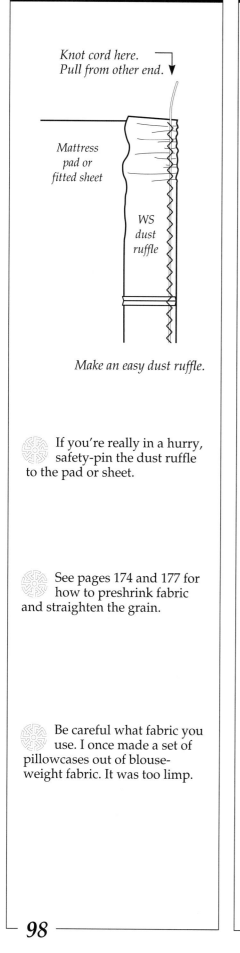

Knot cord here.
Pull from other end.

Mattress
pad or
fitted sheet

WS
dust
ruffle

Make an easy dust ruffle.

If you're really in a hurry, safety-pin the dust ruffle to the pad or sheet.

See pages 174 and 177 for how to preshrink fabric and straighten the grain.

Be careful what fabric you use. I once made a set of pillowcases out of blouse-weight fabric. It was too limp.

An Easy Gathered Dust Ruffle

This dust ruffle covers three sides of the bed. You will need an old mattress pad (the size of your mattress) or a fitted sheet, two old flat sheets (the size of your mattress—dye them if they're the wrong color), string or cord or #5 pearl cotton measuring the mattress width plus two times its length, and safety pins (optional).

1. Measure the distance from the bottom of your mattress (where it hits the box springs, if you have them) to the floor. Add 1/2" turn-under and 1/2" seam allowance. Cut off the bottom and top hems of your flat sheets (unless you have extra time—then you can open them out). Cut strips as wide as your mattress to floor measurement off the length of both sheets. Rightsides together, seam strips together across widths in 1/2" seams, making one long strip. Press seams open. Turn under two crosswise ends of long strip so no raw edges show. Stitch close to edge. Turn under 1/4" on one long raw edge and press. Turn another 1/4". Stitch close to edge of hem.

2. Lay cord or string on underside of strip along 1/2" seamline of raw edge. Run a line of wide zigzag over the cord, being careful not to pierce the cord. Gather dust ruffle by pulling cord.

3. Rightsides together, lay ruffle on mattress pad. (If you're using a fitted sheet, put it on the bed and pin the ruffle where the sheet meets the top edge of the mattress.) Distribute ruffles evenly around three sides of mattress pad. Pin. Straight stitch 1/2" seam. Put dust ruffle on bed.

How To Make A Standard Pillowcase

You will need 7/8 yd. medium-weight 45"-wide fabric per case. Buy good quality, closely woven fabric or cut up old sheets. After preshrinking and straightening fabric, turn under 1/4" across the fabric and stitch. If you are adding any decorative work, sew it on now, leaving 2-1/2" free on the end you just stitched. Fold fabric in half lengthwise, rightsides together. Stitch or serge across the unstitched end and down the side in a 1/4" seam. Clip across corners.

Turn open end inside 2-1/2" and stitch close to edge (your bobbin thread will show on right side). Turn rightside out, poke out corners gently, and press. This whole process takes less than 20 minutes. You also can make more beautiful cases than you can buy. Ours are all different colors.

For king-size pillowcase, measure length of pillow and adjust length of fabric accordingly. The rest of the procedure is the same. They are longer, but not much wider, than standard pillowcases.

How to Make a Pillow Sham

Pillow shams echo the design of the quilt and hide pillows. They have a center-back opening into which you insert the pillow. They usually have a ruffle or fabric flange. For the former, see Inserted Edges on page 236. For the latter, add 6" to the length and width of the dimensions that follow.

1. Make a paper pattern for the sham. For the front, add 1" each to the pillow length and width. For the back, use half the front measurement plus 4".

2. Cut or piece one top. Cut two backs.

3. To hem the raw edge of the center back opening, press under 1" twice on one short edge of each back piece. Topstitch.

4. Overlap the back pieces until they fit the front piece. If you are inserting a ruffle, do so now.

5. Sew around all sides, taking several tiny stitches at the corner or wrapping the corner (see page 142). Finish the edges with zigzag or serging.

6. Turn rightsides out through the opening. If you are making a flange, straight stitch 3" from the edge.

How To Tame A Slippery Quilt

Quilts made of satin, tricot, and some knits (and all quilts slept under by children, regardless of fiber content) tend to slide off the bed at night as you move in your sleep. Stitch the cut-off end of a contour or flat sheet or of an old blanket to the bottom underside of your quilt. Then tuck the extra flap over and under the mattress and you'll have no more problems.

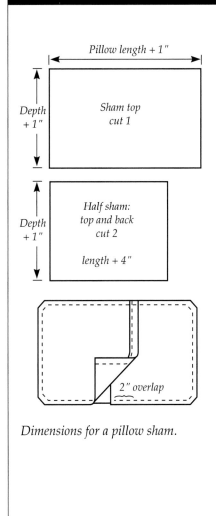

Dimensions for a pillow sham.

Gail Brown's All-New Instant Interiors is my constant reliable source for this kind of information.

How To Take Care Of Machine-Quilted Quilts

As you finish each quilt, make a muslin or fabric sack for it, so that each unused quilt can be rolled and stored in the sack in a dark, cool, dry area.

The enemies of quilts are dirt, creases, damp, some chemicals, and direct sunlight. Keep your quilts clean—no problem with machine-quilted quilts, which can be washed and dried in home machines. Use a gentle wash cycle and cool rinse. Harse detergents will fade fabrics, so use one of the special quilt soaps found in quilt and fabric stores. (Otherwise, use liquid dishwashing soap or shampoo.) When the quilt is wet, threads can break, so treat it carefully. Dry it on low or air. Alternately, if you have room, spread the wet quilt on sheets on the floor.

Try to roll your quilts. If necessary to fold, try to do so on a seamline. Put a note on your calendar once a month to unfold, hang out for airing, and reroll stored quilts (I can't think of a more pleasant household task). Try to refold stored quilts a different way each time.

Don't store quilts in plastic bags. Moisture may collect inside and rot your quilt. Plastic bags pose other dangers: I was once told about a woman who stored her quilt in a large green plastic bag which was mistakenly picked up and carted off to the garbage dump.

Most tissue papers and newsprint are acidic and will destroy the quilt fibers over a number of years. (See the Resource list for the address of acid-free tissue paper.)

If you have wall space, hang the quilts you're not using. Alternately, if you have a spare bed, stack them up on it. But be sure direct sun does not fall on them because some of the fabrics will fade.

To remove dust, batting, lint, or dog and cat hairs, pin netting over the quilt and vacuum the whole thing. This protects the quilting stitches from being sucked into the vacuum cleaner and possibly broken by the strain.

The Serger General says: You can never buy enough fabric.

The Quickest Full-Size Quilt Of All: The Duvet

This quilt can be made in less than four hours because to avoid piecing, you use extra-wide yardage for backing or sheets and you don't care about workmanship: the quilt itself is hidden inside a fabric envelope. The duvet (pronounced doo-vay) or Continental quilt doubles as a top sheet and a bed cover. As you sleep, it snuggles around you. In the morning, you simply smooth it out without tucking it in. On laundry day, you untie the hidden ties of the duvet, remove the outside envelope, and wash it. The inner quilt is never washed or seen, which allows you to space the quilting lines as much as 10" apart. It's also a perfect opportunity to experiment with the handling of thick batts.

You can use the same idea to hide down and dacron sleeping bags for bed use (or old quilts, mattress pads, electric blankets, ugly blankets).

In my hotel in Germany, each person had his or her own duvet—no more fighting for covers!

Duvet: *VIP fabric on top, Spartex 90"-wide Doubleglaze on underside, Dritz Snap Tape, Metrosene Plus in top and bobbin, 12/80 H-J needle; inner quilt made of old sheets and Mountain Mist Fatt Batt. Constructed on a Pfaff 7550. Photo by Lee Lindeman.*

Duvet Size:
Varies according to bed size
Technique:
Straight-stitch quilting

For the duvet cover, try to use two sheets made by the same manufacturer. Otherwise, no matter what measurements are given on the package, the sheets will differ in turned allowance. Also if the outside sheets are light-colored, don't use darker colors on the inner quilt, as they will show through.

If you'd like to piece the outside cover, this is the perfect opportunity to use a serger. It will overcast the edges, keeping them neat when you wash the duvet cover.

Materials

- two no-iron decorator flat sheets to fit your bed (see Flat Sheet Yardage Chart on page 254) or yardage (I used VIP for the top and Spartex Doubleglaze for the back)
- two old flat sheets for inner quilt or yardage
- batting the size of inner sheets minus 1/2" all around (I used Mountain Mist's Fatt Batt)
- regular sewing machine thread
- 12/80 H-J or 14/90 H-J needle
- walking foot
- 6-2/3 yds. polyester tape to make 24 ties, each 10" long (cut ends at an angle to prevent raveling)
- snap or Velcro tape
- clothespins, bulldog clips, or bicycle clips
- Sewing Notebook

To make the duvet cover

1. This is the one time when you don't need to make a test square. Wash all sheets to remove finishes. Open out hem on sheet that will be top. Although not held any longer by thread, 1/4" at the edge is still turned under. Sew one side of the snap or Velcro tape on the underside of the top sheet over the 1/4" turn-in, starting and ending tape 1" from the sides of the sheet. Sew the other side of the tape to the rightside of the second sheet over the stitched hemline. When the two sheets are later lined up at the sides, the snap positions should match.

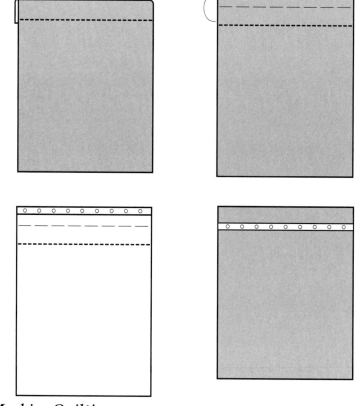

2. To mark the other tie locations, fold one sheet into half lengthwise and iron in the crease. Fold folded sheet to the seam allowance of the long edge and iron. This creates four lengthwise sections. Open out.

3. For the ties at the top edge, align the ends with the original fold line on the vertical press-marked lines. Add a tie at each outer edge slightly inside the seam allowance. For the ties at the bottom, place raw edges of ties even with the edge of sheet on the fold lines (see cartoon). Add a tie at each outer edge, as at the top end. This makes a total of five ties each at top and bottom. Sew 1/2" in, stitching back and forth several times for each tie.

4. Sew ties on each side under the fold line. Sew two more ties at the side bottom, as shown. The exact placement is not important. Pin all the ties in place.

5. Turn top hem of top sheet to rightside on fold line. Pin fold in place at sides. Rightsides together, place the two cover sheets together. Sew 1/2" side and bottom seams. Be careful not to catch loose ends of ties in seam. Trim corners and turn rightside out. The outside envelope of the duvet is done and can easily be removed for washing.

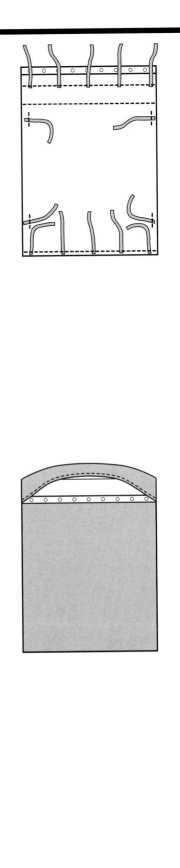

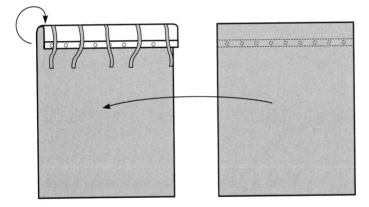

To make the inner quilt

1. Make sure the inner sheets are not larger than the outer sheets. If so, trim to the same size. (If they're slightly smaller, it doesn't matter.) To mark the quilting lines, fold one sheet in half lengthwise and iron in the crease. Fold folded sheet into lengthwise thirds and iron. This creates six lengthwise sections. Open out.

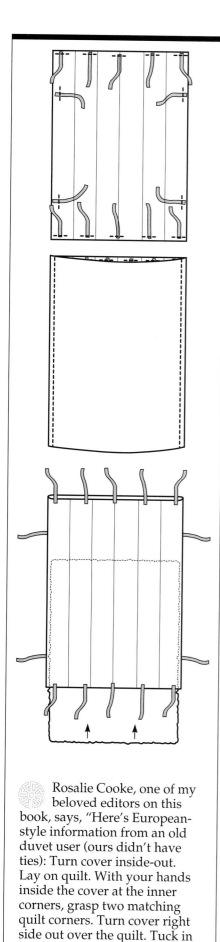

2. Securely sew 14 ties to rightside of marked sheet in same position as outside fabric envelope, always matching raw edges of ties to edges of sheet. Place two sheets together, rightsides together, and sew side seams only, in a 1/2" seam. Turn rightside out, ironed sheet on top.

3. Pull batting through this fabric tunnel until it is 1/2" from the two open edges. Fold in ends and zigzag or straight stitch shut, letting ties hang loose. Pin along five ironed lines through all layers. Stitch down them with a straight stitch and walking foot (or regular presser foot), using any thread you wish. Sew from right side of quilt to center, rolling and securing the finished rows with clips as you work. Then rotate quilt 180° and sew again from side toward center. It doesn't matter if your fabric puckers or creeps or the thread skips or frays—no one will see it. Stitch all around the quilt about 1/2" from the edge, to secure the batting at the edges.

4. Gather outer fabric envelope like you're putting on a nylon stocking. Push inner quilt to bottom inside of enve-

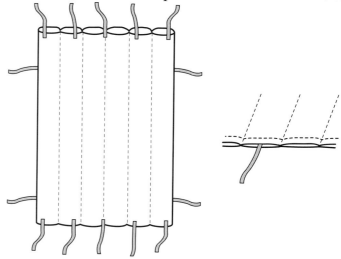

lope. Match ties and tie in bows. Tie side bows. Tie top bows. You're in business.

5. Make notes in your Sewing Notebook about batting used, thread, needle, tension settings, decorative stitches, what you wish you'd done better.

6. Return tension settings to normal. Throw away needle. Clean out lint and oil machine if necessary. Then hug it.

Rosalie Cooke, one of my beloved editors on this book, says, "Here's European-style information from an old duvet user (ours didn't have ties): Turn cover inside-out. Lay on quilt. With your hands inside the cover at the inner corners, grasp two matching quilt corners. Turn cover right side out over the quilt. Tuck in the other two corners."

Machine Quilting

F.A.S.T.* Baby Quilt

Use a pre-printed panel with matching yardage for a quick baby quilt. This uses the Envelope Method of finishing the edges first, then quilting. Lower your standards a little. You will never have as perfect-looking a quilt with this method, because the backing is not stretched taut for basting—but the baby won't notice and the parents don't mind.

Quilt Size: *33" x 42"*
Techniques: *Free-machine straight stitch (page 50)*

* F.A.S.T. Quilting is used throughout this book in sympathy for working people with lots of ambition but little time. The acronym means Fabric-Aided to Save Time.

F.A.S.T. Baby Quilt: *Springs Cozy Prints Glaze (50/50 cotton/polyester) top and underside, Mountain Mist Glazene batting, Gütermann Sew-All in top and bobbin for making squilt, DMC in top and Mettler in bobbin for free-machine quilting. Quilted on a Bernina 1530. Photo by Lee Lindeman.*

Remember to unfold the batting the day before, so wrinkles will relax. If you forget, hold the iron over it, without touching the batting, and gently steam it.

Materials

- pre-printed fabric panel about 44" x 35" or 1 yd. 45"-wide fabric (poly/cotton so it won't wrinkle) (I used Springs Cozy Prints Glaze)
- 1-1/8 yd. 45"-wide fabric for backing (gives you enough extra to make a test square)
- 44" x 35" low-loft batting (I used Mountain Mist Glazene)
- polyester or cotton thread to match colors (I used Gütermann Sew-All, Mettler, and DMC Size 50 cotton)
- 12/80 H-J or 14/90 H-J needle
- darning foot, walking foot
- spray starch
- template material (quilter's plastic, cardstock, freezer paper)
- Sewing Notebook
- *Optional:* repositionable spray glue like KK100 or Sprayway 22, newspapers, shirt cardboard, Zig 2Way Glue or anything to make template repositionable

Directions

1. Set up a test square of two layers of backing and batting (I am assuming you have no extra top fabric). Test stitch length and width, tension settings, and needle size.

2. Wash the fabrics to remove chemicals and sizing. If the pre-printed fabric panel forces you to use the selvage as a seam allowance, clip it diagonally before washing.

3. Before putting the fabrics rightsides together, spray them both heavily with starch. Press them as one fabric. Pin them together around the edges.

4. Lay the fabric on the batting and pin around the edges. Put a few pins inside the edges so nothing will shift as you carry it to the machine.

Optional: Spread newspaper on the floor. Lay the batting on the newspapers and spray it with a repositionable glue. Fold the pinned fabrics in half and lay them on the batting. Unfold the fabrics. Smooth the fabrics against the batting. Pin edges.

5. Stitch around 3-1/2 edges, following the instructions for the Envelope Method on page 95. Your fabric may dictate the seam allowance. If you have a choice, use 1/2". Be sure to trim the batting close to the stitching and to press the seams open.

6. Close the opening by hand or machine.

7. Tape the squilt to a surface. Safety-pin or pin-baste.

8. Quilt in whatever way the design speaks to you. I used a walking foot on straight lines and free-machine quilted others.

9. Turn the quilt over and use the Closed Fist Test (see page 214) to see if you need to add any quilting. I copied the small star in the panel onto shirt cardboard, put Zig 2Way Glue on the back, let it dry so it would be repositionable, and moved it around the quilt. I pinned around the star to form a tiny hoop, then free-machine quilted around the star. (You could always trace around the template with a water-soluble marker.) Don't leave the template on overnight.

10. Check the back and front at an oblique angle for loose ends to trim. Run your hands over the quilt to be sure all pins are removed.

11. Sign your name and date (see page 216).

12. Make notes in Sewing Notebook about batting used, thread, needle, tension settings, what you wish you'd done better.

13. Return tension settings to normal. Throw away needle. Clean out lint and oil machine if necessary. Then hug it.

Barbara Johannah, Northern California, Grandmother's Sky, *72" x 46-1/2", pieced and quilted by Sharon Hose. Instead of piecing hexagons, Barbara figured out how to strip-piece equilateral triangles and sew them into hexagons. Photo reprinted with permission from* Barbara Johannah's Crystal Piecing *(Chilton, 1993). Photo by Lee Lindeman.*

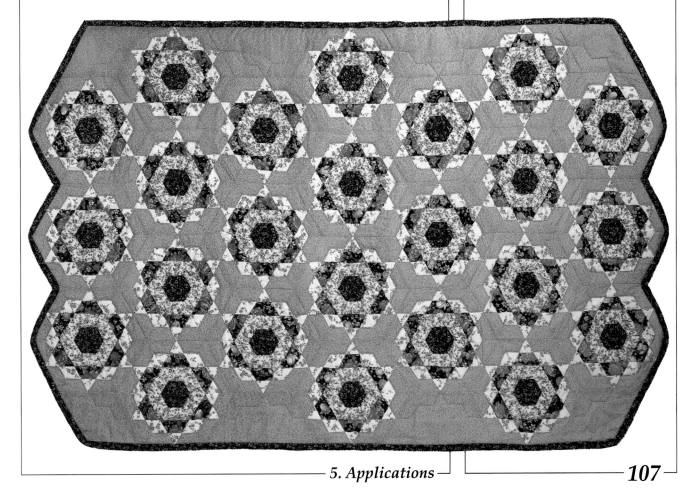

*Annrae Roberts, Rio Rancho, NM,
Earthsong…Opus I, a Green
Quilt to wear, with 2,000 yards of
decorative threads, worked on a
Pfaff 1475CD.
Photo courtesy of the artist.*

*Mary Stori, Prospect Heights, IL,
Sulky Savvy vest, 1993. Quilted
with satin stitch and a narrow
zigzag on a Pfaff 7550. Photo
courtesy of the artist.*

Clothing

"When I teach, I constantly tell my students to 'S.T.O.P.' and with a critical eye, check their work for Shine, Texture, Opposites, and Pattern...Once, I realized the polished cotton's shine in a piece was not enough, so I added beads and sequins."
   Annrae Roberts via *Pfaff Club Magazine* #1

Caryl Rae Hancock, Indianapolis, IN, Blue on Blue. *Jacket and skirt of polished cotton with air-brushed design outline-quilted with rayon in bobbin. Low-loft batting in jacket removed from non-quilted areas to reduce bulk. Skirt batting is half layer of Cotton Classic not preshrunk, later washed to give soft, antique look. Photo courtesy of the artist.*

Lynn Lewis Young, Houston, TX, Gemini I, *1994. Collage of satins, lamés, cottons, and taffetas pieced to batting, then lined. Lynn is publisher of* Art/Quilt Magazine. *Photo courtesy of the artist.*

W hile more and more people are enamored of quilted wearables, the first big question to ask yourself is: Why am I doing this?

I have seen people put in hours piecing a vest or jacket, layering it over batting, then quilting for even more hours, and when they are done, they feel like they're wearing Japanese armor, they die of the heat, and worst of all, the quilting does not show.

Why Quilt?

So again, why quilt a garment?

1. *You want 3-D texture:*
• Make an outer garment, like a jacket, coat, or cape, rather than a more close-fitting garment, like a vest.
• Either use a fabric with a sheen, so the texture will be highlighted by the play of light, or use metallic threads.
• Use a regular-loft batting (1/4" – 1/2" height), so the quilting will show.

2. *You want warmth:*
• Make a garment you can remove, like a jacket or coat, rather than a more close-fitting piece integral to your look, like a vest.
• Use any of the battings discussed in the Mini-Encyclopedia on page 220.

3. *You want a pieced but drapeable garment:*
• Use extremely low-loft battings like muslin, flannel or flannelette, or cotton interlock; battings designed specifically for clothing, like Thermore; or the battings that can be split (e.g., Cotton Classic).

How to Choose Patterns

Try to find patterns with few darts or design details, like notched collars or extra seaming. The trade-off is boxiness, but depending on where you will wear the garment, it may or may not matter. If you run in quilting circles, you could wear a beautiful quilted tent and we'd still admire your garment. If you work in a conservative office, you may prefer to keep the fabric classy and the quilting subtle.

If you are busty or large, you will be happier if you have a dart or two in the garment or some way to shape your bumps—gathers, tucks, easing, or princess lines. This is not the right book to teach you how to add a dart to anything, but I recommend the information in Nancy Moore's *Machine-Quilted Jackets, Vests, and Coats.*

You may be attracted to ethnic patterns based on rectangles or which are one-piece, without set-in sleeves. Before you put a lot of work into the piece, be sure to test-fit the pattern (see below). These garments were not designed for

For spring and summer jackets, Jasmine Hubbel of Birch Street Clothing buys used silk blouses in large sizes for $1 or $2. She cuts them up and uses them as batting, so that the resulting garment is warm, but extremely lightweight.

The quilting in this case merely stabilizes the many seams of the piecing and adds a nice weight to the garment. It also prevents wrinkling when you've pieced with cotton fabrics. The quilting line does not add 3-D texture. If you do not want to quilt the garment at all, use a serger for piecing the outside, if possible. Finished seam allowances will hold up better over the years.

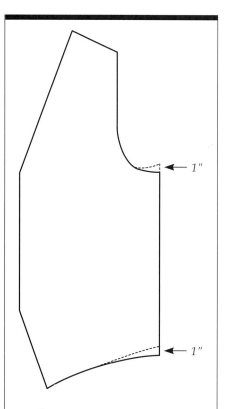

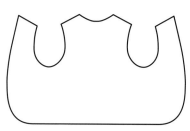

the modern woman. For one, we wear undergarments meant to push us up and out. With no darts or shaping in the design, you are going to see a lot of diagonal wrinkles and hemlines that rise in the front, as the fabric struggles to get over your bustline. Wrinkles usually make you appear larger. Is that what you want? If you persist in embellishing these garments, be sure to make them loose-fitting, use a lightweight batting, and wear shoulder pads.

For commercial patterns, you may be able to eliminate straight seams in the center back or side. This allows you to quilt in freely flowing lines, but may constrict how you finish the garment. You can't, for example, use the Easy Vest Lining on page 125 if you eliminate the side seams.

Eliminate side seams

Don't be seduced by the attractive model in the sketch on the pattern. Instead, study the line drawings on the back of the pattern. These will give you a better preview of the fit and design lines. Pay special attention to the neckline, depth of armhole, number of seams, darts, amount of ease in the sleeve cap, and where the garment hits the body. Read the pattern notations, too. If it says "very loose fitting," buy one size smaller. Otherwise, there will be so much design ease that you will be swimming in the garment.

Gale Grigg Hazen sometimes puts a hook shape in the armscye of vests for large-busted women. In this example, she raised the underarm and bottom front side 1". The side seam length remains the same after the alteration. When you match up the side seams, the hook forces extra fabric into the underarm, like a phantom dart for the bust, but the vest ends up hanging straight across the bottom.

Right: Julie Nodine of Julie's Quilting Services made this Misty Meadow Vest from Timber Lane Press (available from Log Cabin Dry Goods). She machine-quilted the lining to an old flannel sheet with her professional quilting machine (see page 258).

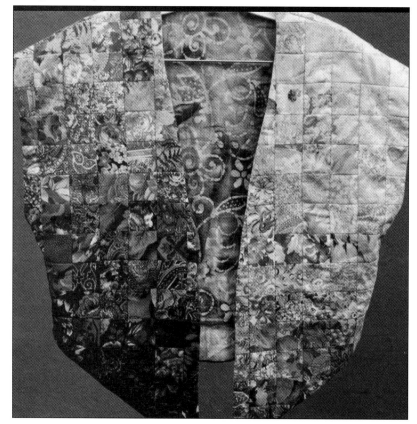

How to Test-Fit

While this book is not an appropriate place to discuss fitting techniques, we'll give some suggestions because you don't want to spend hours on a piece, then discover it doesn't fit. The first challenge is to buy the right size pattern. If you have been discouraged from sewing because nothing you make fits right, you have probably been buying a pattern too large. For tops, take your high bust measurement, not your full bust measurement, and buy the pattern for that measurement.

Then test the fit of your pattern before you make it, by taking two steps:

1. Measure yourself against the pattern. This can be done in two ways:

   A. Compare your measurements to those on the back of the pattern envelope. The difference between your measurements and theirs is the amount you need to alter. And here's the good news: once you know these alteration measurements, *you can automatically make them on any pattern from that company* and be guaranteed that the garment will fit you. It will look the way the designer intended. Of course, you may not like the design; Step #2 will help prevent unhappiness.

   B. On patterns from independent companies, useful measurements are usually not given on the pattern envelope. Measure across the pattern at the bust, waist, and hip lines, excluding the seam allowances. Make sure there is at least 8" – 12" more than your measurements at bust, waist, and hips for outer garments like vests, jackets, and coats, depending on how loose a garment you want. If the garment has straight sides, alter for the bust and hips; then draw a line in between. Don't worry about the waistline.

   Now learn to alter for bust, waist, and hips—which is not difficult (see books in the Bibliography on page 266). I prefer the pivot-and-slide method used by Sew/Fit and by Nancy Zieman.

2. Make a mock-up from one of three materials:

   A. Alter the pattern on wax paper, using a tracing wheel. You will need to lay the paper over a spongy surface, like a length of wool yardage, in order for the tracing wheel markings to show. You can also use a felt-tipped pen. (To make a larger surface, you can easily fuse two or more pieces of wax paper with an iron heated to low.) Cut away the neckline and center front opening seam allowances and the hem. Overlay the seam allowances of the front and back shoulders and side seams and fuse with an iron. Spot-fuse the underarm seam of the sleeve and cut off the hem allowance.

   Try on the pattern, pinning center front and back to your blouse and pinning the sleeve to the body only at the top. Do you like the fit? Do you need more room

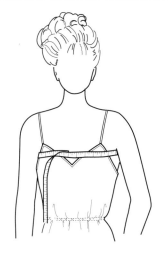

Are you buying a pattern too large? Buy the pattern by your high-bust measurement (but get enough fabric for the full-bust measurement).

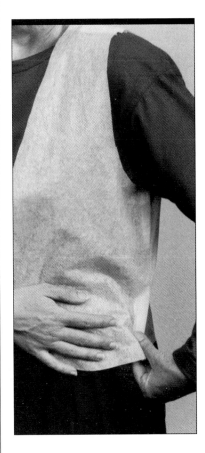

I used Mönster paper to make a quick mock-up of the vest shown on page 127 It showed me that I didn't need to add as much at the hips as I thought. (Paper from The Sewing Place—see Resource list.) Photo by Larry Brazil.

anywhere? Is the center back length long enough? As we age, we tend to stoop forward slightly. If your garments pull toward the back, you need a longer center back. I routinely add 1" to the center back, except on Burda.

B. Buy muslin in 10-yard lengths when it is on sale or use old sheets. Make a fitting model from the muslin, cutting off the neck and center front seam allowances and all hem allowances. Baste the garment together, but don't bother to set in the sleeve. You will be able to judge fit from pinning on the sleeve. This method and the next are better than wax paper because they are full-size, not half-size, and because they drape as fabric will. But they both take a little longer. Loosen top tension when basting. It makes it easy to remove the stitches.

C. Use nonwoven interfacing or one of the materials specifically meant for pattern tracing (Do-Sew or Mönster paper—see Resources). Cut and sew the pattern as in B.

While all of this takes time, it ensures that you will be happy with the final results. You will also be able to reuse the pattern confidently.

Quilting Designs for Clothing

My assumption is that we are emphasizing quilting, not piecing, on the garment. Here are five ways to design:

1. *F.A.S.T.* Quilting:* Take advantage of a fabric designer's expertise by using interesting fabric on one side of the squilt with plain fabric on the other. Quilt with the interesting fabric up—but it will become the inside of your garment. Be sure to practice on a test square to be sure that bubbles of the top thread used to follow the design aren't showing on the plain side. If so, use monofilament nylon. This is the method used for the vest project on page 127.

In this case, you will bind the edges (see page 121), so be sure to cut out the pattern with no seam allowances at the neck, front, or armscye.

You can either quilt a length of fabric first, then cut out the patterns, or cut out the three layers with generous seam allowances (at least 1"), quilt, and then lay the patterns over to recut the outlines. I prefer to quilt yardage with a presser foot on and quilt pattern pieces free-machine with a hoop.

After you quilt the main outlines following the fabric design, you can always turn the piece over and add other quilting lines from the plain side, perhaps with metallic threads, ribbons, etc. Remember, though, that the more stitching you do, the more shrinkage there is and the more stiff the fabric becomes.

2. *Projector (slide or opaque):* Trace your pattern pieces on fabric. Put the fabric on the wall, project a slide or design or magazine page, and trace the design on the fabric. Be sure that you are happy with where motifs fall on your body. A bust encircled by wheel cover designs may not please you.

* F.A.S.T. Quilting is used throughout this book in sympathy for working people with lots of ambition but little time. The acronym means Fabric-Aided to Save Time.

114

Machine Quilting

3. *Templates:* Use precut quilting stencils, machine quilting paper you stitch through (see page 75), or homemade stencils to trace designs. The template method makes sense when you are repeating one or more motifs. I like to cut designs out of pressure-sensitive paper (like uncut label paper) and move them around the garment, tracing shapes. Sometimes I dispense with the tracing and quilt directly around the shapes, moving them to a new location when I finish each section. (Don't leave the templates on overnight.)

If you have made a mock-up of the pattern, make lots of paper copies of the templates. Pin them to the mock-up, moving them around until you are pleased. Then take the mock-up apart and trace the shapes onto the outer fabric.

4. *Directly:* Some intrepid people can plunge in. They see a design on the fabric in their heads, they point the machine, and off they zoom. Periodically, they hang the piece on a wall or dress form, study it, and add more quilting. I envy this talent, but I don't have the time to develop it.

5. *Your way:* There is no one right way to do anything. Have fun as you work and invent the methods you need.

Yvonne Perez-Collins, author of *Soft Gardens/ Make Flowers With Your Sewing Machine*, uses 3-M Photo Mount on cardstock. She stitches around the shape and moves it to a new position. "If you accidentally sew through the template, tear it out and continue. Using templates allows you to make/change your composition—not so easy if it were drawn."

Many new glues make paper or fabric repositionable. Look for Sprayway 22, Insta-Tack, Zig 2Way Glue, KK100, Sticky Stuff, or Stikit Again and Again. See page 183.

Peggy Bendel of Bogota, NJ, used Sulky rayon thread to machine quilt this jacket. She drew three sizes of leaf on freezer paper, then ironed them onto the surface of each garment section. She reused the leaves many times and didn't have to mark the design on the fabric.

Ways to Break up Space in Clothing

We seem to like dividing the population into two parts: Type As or Bs, red or white wine drinkers, hand or machine quilters. Here's another one: asymmetrical or symmetrical. Decide for yourself, but remember that if you choose a garment with an asymmetric closing, you must wear it closed.

You can break up the lines on garments any way you want, but some will be more flattering than others. Most of us are trying to appear slimmer, so keep with lines that are vertical or slanted to make the shoulders wider than the hips. Be careful about emphasizing parts of your body you're less proud of. For example, a jacket that ends at the widest part of your hips may not be flattering.

Vertical lines are attractive.

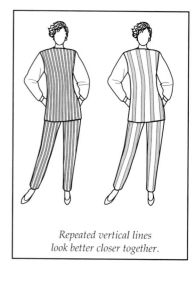

Repeated vertical lines look better closer together.

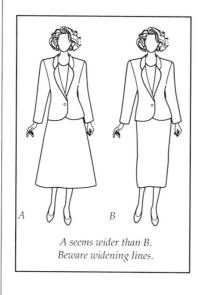

A seems wider than B. Beware widening lines.

Are raglan sleeves flattering to you? Lines tapering in, not out, are more flattering.

Choosing a Batting:
The Great Vest Experiment

In my Madame Curie mode, I decided to test specifically for clothing some of the many battings available. I would use the same type of fabric on the outside, the same vest pattern, the same thread and needle. Then, when I wore the vests, I would be able to feel the subtle differences between the battings.

I prewashed the 100% cotton fabric, layered the outside fabric over the batting with no backing, and quilted straight lines 1-1/2" apart, using an 12/80 H-J needle and DMC size 50 gray thread in top and bobbin. I used the with-nap layout in Burda 4441 because in some cases I had to match motifs across the princess seams in the front later when I cut it out. This required 7/8 yard and to quilt that much took about 1-1/2 hours, with plenty of time to cheer on the 49ers. Because I never intend to wash the vests, I didn't bother to preshrink the batting when suggested by the manufacturer.

On ribbons backed with paper-backed fusible web, I used the built-in alphabet of a Pfaff 1475 to stitch the name of the batting, and fused it as a label to the inside, knowing that otherwise, I would never remember later.

After quilting, I laid the pattern pieces over the quilting, checking for any needed design motif alignment, and cut out the pieces. I used the Easy Vest Lining (see page 125), trimming the excess batting out of the seam allowances. This involves loosening the quilting stitches in the seam allowances, but does not take much time. I like to use a small awl for this task. I gently pressed all seam allowances open, using the point turner side of my tailor board when I could. When I couldn't, I pressed the allowance back on the body of the garment.

What did I learn? That I'm not a scientist. After the second vest, I got bored with making the same pattern. I will keep testing for myself, but I'll vary patterns (which makes this "test" invalid).

For more specific information on battings, see the Mini-Encyclopedia on page 220.

Madame Curie tests the same vest pattern until she quits in extreme scientific boredom.

Nevertheless, this is a good way to find out which batting feels better to you. If you're not sure which batting to use, make a simple garment at least twice. I suggest making one in a poly-blend batting and one in an all-cotton. If you're ambitious, make a third in Thermore, which is expressly designed for clothing.

Constructing the Garment

Decide before you stitch how you will care for the garment—wash? dry-clean? It will make a difference whether or not you preshrink the fabric and batting, what kind of closure you choose, and how you finish the edges.

Remember, you do not have to follow pattern instructions slavishly. For example, Jacqueline Querns of Phoenix, AZ, prefers to break the garment into modules and quilt each separately, using a hoop. This makes it much easier to handle bulk.

Care of the Garment

If you want to be able to wash the garment, make sure everything you use in it is preshrunk, from fabrics and battings to cording used in piping to zippers. Otherwise, you may have unhappy surprises after the first wash.

Think about what will happen to the unquilted areas and to seam allowances of pieced areas—are they secured by quilting?

Closures

Other than buttons and buttonholes, which terrify many people, some of your choices are:

• *Snap tape.* This is a way to use special buttons on the outside. While it sidesteps buttonholes, it also means you must wear the garment closed. Snap tape comes in colors. For the top vest shown on page 117, I was putting the tape on late at night and only had white (is this not the universal condition for make-do invention?), so I colored the tape red with permanent fabric marking pens.

• *Snaps.* I particularly like the gadget from Prym Vario Plus (see Birch Street Clothing in Resource list) because it works, it comes with lots of pretty choices of snaps, and the snaps make the garment reversible.

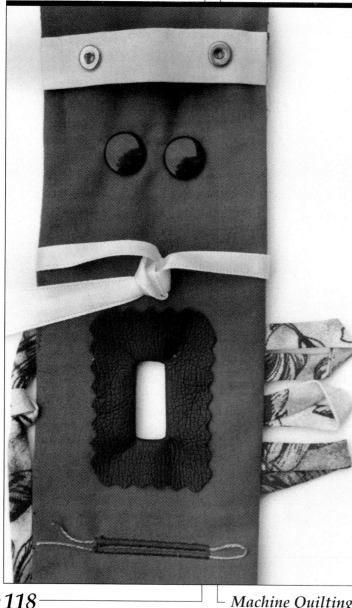

Closures (top to bottom): *Snap tape, Prym Vario Plus snaps from Birch Street Clothing, ribbon ties, opening faced with Fabu-Leather trimmed with Fiskars' wavy cutter, three kinds of loops, and Lois Ericson's technique for piping gaps. (Crowning Touch's Miniturn makes turning tiny tubes easy. P&B fabric.)*

• *Ties.* This is the age-old way to close garments. Be sure to sew the ends securely onto the garment. I like to use a box of stitching. See the Bibliography for books that cover frog and other elaborate closures.

• *Piping gaps.* Clever Lois Ericson has come up with many ways to close garments. For this one, handsew corded piping to the edge of the front opening, leaving gaps for buttons or other closures.

• *Loops.* Turn narrow tubes of bias fabric, cut them apart for the loop size you want, and sew them to the front edge before finishing it. Test to be sure the loops are long enough to close over the button easily. I like to use the Miniturn tube turners from Crowning Touch (see Resource list).

• *Faced openings.* Sandra Betzina showed me how to sew a shape (square, rectangle, circle, triangle, odd-ball) of fabric to the underside, cut the opening, turn the fabric to the outside, and secure it. If you use a nonfrayable fabric like leather or Fabu-Leather, you do not have to worry about the edges. If you use something else, finish the edges of the shape first by sewing organza to it all the way around the rightside. Clip corners. Then make a slice in the organza and turn the piece rightsides out. Press. Sew this finished shape organza side up to the underside of the garment, cut the opening, and complete as before.

If you want buttonholes, I suggest you cord them and use tearaway stabilizer underneath. Then when you cut the buttonhole open, trim out all the batting you can and color any remaining wisps with a permanent marker.

A way to change the look of the garment is to make buttonholes in both sides, then choose one of two ways to close the garment.

1. Put the buttons on a strip of grosgrain ribbon and button through both layers of garment. Be sure to sew the buttons on the ribbon with a thick shank so it will pass easily through two quilted layers. If you can sew the buttons on by machine, use the tailor-tacking foot, leaving long thread ends at the end. Then pull the button to the top of the shank and wrap it with the thread ends, knotting to finish.

2. Sew a hidden smaller button behind the decorative button, leaving an adequate thread shank. Button both layers from the topside with the smaller button.

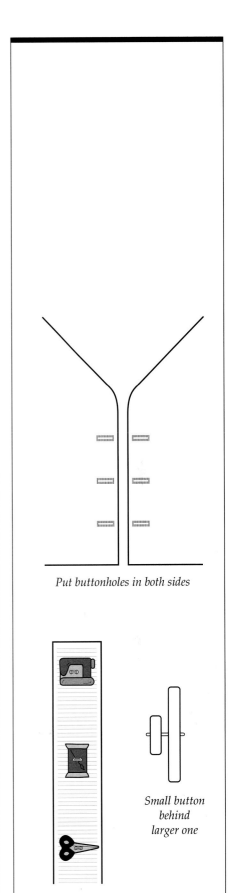

Put buttonholes in both sides

Small button behind larger one

Buttons sewn to grosgrain ribbon

Edge Finishes

Your choices depend on whether you choose to quilt first, then line the garment, or quilt the outside to the lining.

Edge Finishes on Lined Garments

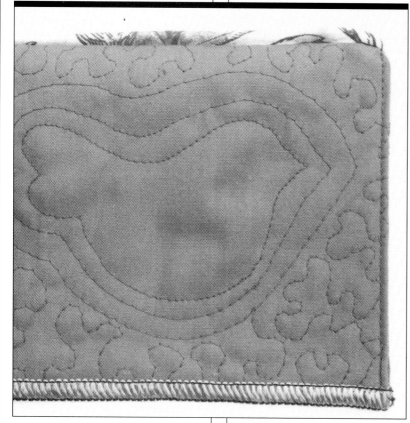

Edge finishes: (right) edgestitching, (top) piping inserted, (bottom) serging with Designer 6 from YLI.

• *Edgestitching.* If you choose the Easy Vest Lining on page 125, you may want to edgestitch the entire vest. You can also use decorative stitches or trim at the edge.

• *Seam insertion.* You can pipe, trim, or insert anything into the seam (see quilt choices on page 215). If you choose something that sticks out, be sure it will be comfortable under your arm. See page 238 for joining ends neatly. Fill the piping with something proportionate to its width—pearl cotton in size 3, 5, or 8 for dainty edges and cotton or polyester cable cord for wider widths. Kenneth King likes rayon rattail cord as a filler. If the garment will be washed, be sure to preshrink the trim. I put it in a lingerie bag and wash and dry it with the laundry. Others wet the cord in hot water and dry it in the microwave.

Ask your sewing-machine dealer if your machine has a cording foot. It makes applying the cord to an edge an easy one-step procedure. Or try Claire Rowley's Pearls 'n Piping foot, which fits almost any machine (see Resource list).

• *Serging.* You can further embellish the finished edge with decorative serging. Put heavier thread like pearl cotton, rayon, or metallics in the upper looper. Test with a wide, balanced 3-thread stitch that covers closely. Serge slowly and make sure the thread feeds smoothly off the cone. Start in an inconspicuous place, like under the arm, and raise the knife if you can. If not, take care not to cut the edge.

Tammy Young and Naomi Baker taught me this hidden lapped serger technique for joining stitches in *Know Your Serger*. Overlap the stitching for 1/2", taking care not to cut the original stitches. Raise the presser foot and needles. Clear the stitch finger by pulling some thread loose above the eye of the needle; then gently pull the fabric and threads behind the needle. Serge off to form a thread chain. Either secure the thread by putting a spot of Fray Check on the overlap end and later cutting the thread tail, or thread the tail into a tapestry needle, bury the stitches in the previous stitches, and trim the tail.

Edge Finishes on Quilted-to-Lining Garments

You will not need seam allowances at bound edges. Remember to **cut the pattern pieces at the finished edge**. For single- or double-fold binding, use the same cutting widths shown on page 232, but be sure to cut a small extra length of binding first. Stitch it to the edge of your test square, checking that the binding has been cut wide enough to stretch over the edge. If you've miscalculated, you can still cut the binding wider or narrower. Here are a few of your choices in edge finishes.

• *Fabric binding:* Edges can be finished with single- or double-fold binding. Techniques depend on whether the binding is woven, knit, or is of nonfrayable fabric.

If you are going around curves using *woven fabric* for binding, be sure to make it bias binding, not straight-grain binding, or the binding will wrinkle. To connect the ends attractively, see page 238. For single- or double-fold binding, I prefer to stitch from the underside to the topside, so it can all be done by machine. Be sure to use your steam iron to shape the bias around curves.

Consider rounding corners on center front of the garment for easier binding. Use a pocket former template, circle template, coffee cup, or edge of a saucer. To miter corners, see page 237.

On inside curves, gently pull the outer edge of the binding to make it stretch. On outside curves or corners, ease a little extra binding by placing your finger behind the

Your machine and technology can help you with binding. I like to use a walking foot when sewing binding so it doesn't become skewed. I sometimes use fusible thread in the bobbin. Then I can lightly press the binding into place and the fusible thread holds it. Otherwise, I use dabs of gluestick to hold the binding in place.

Nancy Zieman does not recommend clipping the edge for bindings less wide than 1/2". It weakens the edge and sometimes shows through, giving a less than professional look.

Round corners by using circle or oval templates, a pocket former from Clotilde, or a teacup.

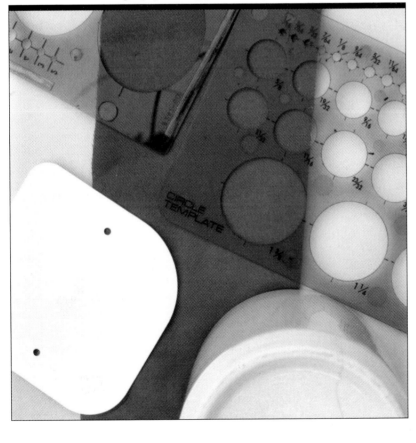

Bird Ross finished the edges and inside seam of this art jacket made of maps and fabric with scribble stitching over raw edges. Map Jacket *collection of Robbie and Tony Fanning.*

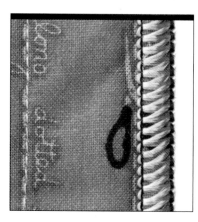

On thin edges, you can serge the edge with decorative thread. Fabric Traditions fabric, Thermore batting, Decor 6 thread, stitched on a White Superlock.

presser foot to impede slightly the flow of the binding or using a pencil or other improvised tool to push in a little extra fabric. Otherwise, it will pull the edge up.

On straight edges like fronts and hems, you can use anything. I once saw the front and bottom of an attractive vest bound with the fringed selvage of China silk turned to the outside.

Another attractive method of woven binding has been popularized by Bird Ross. She stitches 1" – 2" squares of fabric on the diagonal over the edge, using a simple Singer Featherweight and a back-and-forth stitching movement. The raw edges are part of the charm. Her method is described in the April/May 1992 issue of *Threads* magazine.

You can use many knits as binding—jerseys, doubleknits, even ribbing. Treat double-fold *knit bindings* exactly the same as woven. Single-fold binding looks good only on a beefier knit, like doubleknit, unless you are turning it completely to the inside.

If you are using a *nonfrayable fabric* like suede, leather, or synthetic leather like Fabu-Leather, pull on it to see if there is more give in one direction (crossgrain, lengthwise grain, or bias). If so, cut strips parallel to the stretch. Keep your binding width narrow (e.g., 1/2") for inside curved edges like a neckline or armhole or you will have wrinkles. Cut strips three times the finished binding width plus the loft of the batting—e.g., for a finished 1/2" binding with a low-loft batting, cut the strips 2" wide. Test on your test square.

For nonfrayable fabric, I prefer to work from the topside, as in the Wigwarm on page 130. Rightsides together, sew a seam the same width as you want the finished binding. Join ends as shown on page 238. Fingerpress the binding over the edge and pin in the well of the seam. Stitch in the ditch from the topside. If the binding on the underside is not parallel to the stitching, trim it where necessary.

• *Serged binding.* I would use this only when the batting is extremely thin, like flannel. Again, I learned this technique from Tammy Young and Naomi Baker in *Know Your Serger.* Use a decorative thread like pearl cotton or rayon or metallic thread in the upper looper. Experiment until you have a wide, balanced, short 3-thread stitch. Serge slowly. Be sure to trim something off. The loops will look better. Cut a 2" section of the seam allowance to the serger cutting line. Position the cutting line against the knife and serge slowly. Overlap the final line as described on page 120.

Construction

Quilted-to-Lining Garments

I don't recommend quilting to the lining if you have darts in your piece. There is no pretty way to handle the dart on the inside and you end up with too much bulk in that area.

Order for vests:

1. If the side seams are straight with no darts and handling bulk does not frighten you, you may want to overlap and eliminate side seams in the pattern (see diagram on page 112). This, however, allows no chance for adjusting too tight or too loose a garment. Make sure the pattern fits. Cut the front and back as one unit for outside, batting, and lining. Remember to flip one front pattern piece. Leave generous amounts around all pieces—at least 1"—to allow for the shrinkage that machine quilting causes.

2. Stitch a label on the lining before layering.

3. Quilt, but stay at least 1-1/2" away from the shoulder seams. It helps to draw a line with a removable marker.

4. When you are done quilting, reposition the pattern and trim garment to actual size. Join the linings, battings, and one outside shoulder seam to the outside. Trim the excess batting away from the seam allowance. Press open the seams, using a light touch with the iron.

5. Press the remaining shoulder seam allowance under and lay over the other. Edgestitch, zigzag, or handstitch. Now you can quilt over the seamline and everyone will think you're a genius. Finish the side seams the same way, if you have them.

If that's too much trouble to remember, sew the seam allowances rightsides together. Choose one of these all-by-machine methods to finish the seams.

• *Serged.* You can use regular thread with a balanced 2- or 3-thread overlock or use decorative thread in the upper looper. Either serge the seams together and press with the upper looper thread showing, or serge seam allowances separately and press open. You can topstitch to hold the seam allowance in place, unless straight lines of quilting are incompatible with your design. If so, add or stitch over some quilting lines from the topside near the seam that will hold the seam allowance in place

Tammy Young and Naomi Baker, co-authors of *Know Your Serger* and many other books, recommend either using fusible thread in the lower looper, so no topstitching is required, or using the blindhem foot on the sewing machine to topstitch the serged edge accurately.

Diane Tucker of Cicero, IN, unscrews the base from inexpensive trophies and uses them as weights. I use 3" square lineoleum tile samples.

Seam finishes (top to bottom): *Serged with decorative thread (Decor 6), top seam allowance turned under and stitched, strap—covered by non-frayable fabric (Fabu-Leather here) or strap edges turned under, bias-bound edges.*

Bird Ross, mentioned previously, doesn't bother to finish the edges of her straps, in keeping with her style.

• *Strap.* Cover the seam allowances with a finished strip of fabric, such as Ultrasuede, Fabu-Leather, or a tube of fabric. Edgestitch on either side of the strip. Seam allowances can be stitched to the outside or inside.

• *Bias-bound edges.* Cut excess batting out of seam allowances. Stretch tricot strips like Seams Great over each edge and straight stitch or zigzag. Alternately, cut 1" bias strips of interesting lightweight fabric. Rightsides together, stitch to each edge of seam allowance with a 1/4" seam allowance. Press over edge and stitch in the ditch. If the bias doesn't go beyond the first stitching, trim the seam allowance slightly. *Optional:* Trim close to stitching on underside. The binding at the neck, armscye, and hem will keep the shoulder, center back, and side seams open, so you can't see the raw edge of the bias trim underneath.

6. Bind the edges as described on page 121. Don't forget to trim away the seam allowances on edges to be bound.

Order for jackets and coats:

1. Cut out garment and lining with generous seam allowances, except at the shoulder seams. Remember to flip the front piece. Join the shoulder seams on the garment and press open. Repeat for the lining. Sew a label on the lining. Make a squilt. Quilt, trying to stay out of the side seam allowances. Lay the pattern pieces on the quilted garment and recut.

2. Cut out the sleeve, batting, and lining. Remember to flip the pattern piece for one sleeve. Quilt, staying out of the seam allowances. You do not have to quilt the entire sleeve. You could quilt only the lower part, removing the batting above the quilting to cut down on bulk. Lay the pattern piece on the sleeves and recut. Staystitch the armscye edge inside the seam allowance so it won't show.

3. Set the sleeve into the bodice from notch to notch, leaving the underarm free. Then sew the sleeve and side seam in one long seam. Finish the seam allowances as desired (see choices above). Then finish sewing the armscye circle and finish the seam allowances. Finish hem, neckline, and front opening edges (choices above).

Lined Garments

Easy Vest Lining

1. Remove any extra hem allowance from bottom of vest pattern, leaving a 5/8" seam allowance. Either quilt outer fabric to batting, then cut out pattern pieces; or cut out pattern pieces and batting and quilt. If the latter, leave an extra 1" all around and trim to size after quilting. Do not quilt in the dart area, if possible. Make the dart; then trim out batting from dart area. Sew shoulder seams. Remove excess batting from seam allowances and press seams open.

2. Cut out lining 1/8" smaller all around than pattern. This will help it turn to the inside better. Sew shoulder seams and press open. Sew in label.

3. Rightsides together, sew lining to outside at armscye and around entire front bottom edge, center front, neckline, other center front, and remaining front bottom edge. Sew back bottom edge. Remove batting from seam allowances. Press seams open. Clip and notch curves. Trim seam, grading outside edge slightly longer than lining edge.

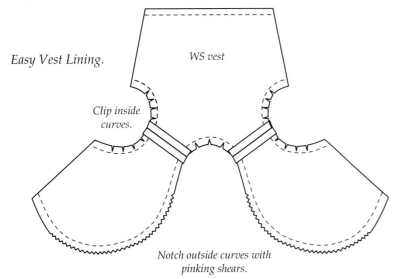

Easy Vest Lining.

WS vest

Clip inside curves.

Notch outside curves with pinking shears.

4. Turn rightsides out through one side seam opening, reaching through the shoulder to pull fronts out.

5. This step sounds impossible, but the minute you do it, you understand the brilliance of this method. I learned it from Ann Boyce, author of *Appliqué the Ann Boyce Way*, but it is widely used. Match rightsides of outside vest together without catching the lining. At the armscye edge, continue pinning rightsides of the lining together for about 1". At the hem edge, continue pinning rightsides of the lining together for about 1". Stitch this line from first pin to last, backstitching. Press the seam open as well as you can.

6. Either handstitch the opening in the lining closed or pinch the lining together and edgestitch the opening closed. Your mother will notice but no one else will.

7. *Optional:* Edgestitch around all openings.

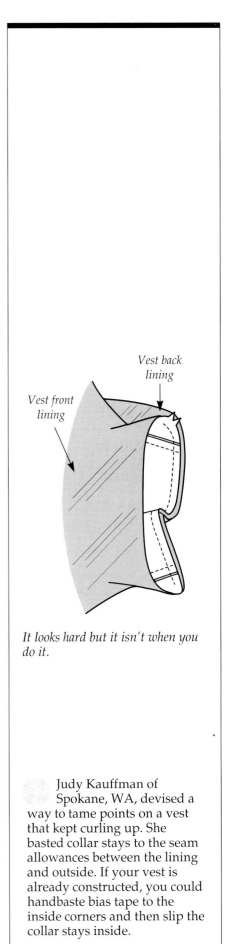

Vest back lining

Vest front lining

It looks hard but it isn't when you do it.

Judy Kauffman of Spokane, WA, devised a way to tame points on a vest that kept curling up. She basted collar stays to the seam allowances between the lining and outside. If your vest is already constructed, you could handbaste bias tape to the inside corners and then slip the collar stays inside.

Gaye Kriegel, Assistant Editor of *The Creative Machine Newsletter,* taught me to stitch on and off at the opening with tiny stitches. This makes a much neater closed edge later.

This book cannot teach you the nitty-gritty of constructing garments. If you would like to learn to sew better, check with your local sewing-machine or fabric store and with adult education, vocational, and junior colleges. So much has changed to make sewing easier that even if you are experienced, it's worth taking classes. Besides, you meet the best people in sewing classes.

I also find it educational to watch videos and the various sewing and quilting TV shows. You can rent a wide variety of videos from the Nancy's Notions catalog.

Jacket Lining

While you can construct the jacket all by machine, called "bagging" by Claire Shaeffer in *The Complete Book of Sewing Shortcuts*, it takes a lot of space to explain and is not easy like the lined vest, so I won't include it.

1. See the instructions above for setting in the sleeve on quilted-to-the-lining garments. Use this method separately for the lining and quilted outside. Join the lining to the outside, rightsides together, around the necklines and bottom edges, leaving a 5" opening for turning. Trim batting from all seam allowances and press seams open as much as possible. Clip curves and trim corners. Turn rightsides out. Turn in opened edges and edgestitch closed.

2. Turn up the jacket hem and slipstitch the lining under (unless your design allows you to get away with extra lines of machine quilting to hold the lining in place).

Nancy Zieman, hostess of TV's Sewing With Nancy *and president of Nancy's Notions, models a reversible, machine-quilted jacket. Photo courtesy of Nancy Zieman.*

Machine Quilting

*F*A.S.T.* Vest

Use an interesting fabric as the backing and a matching plain fabric for the outside. Quilt yardage underside up. The bobbin thread will show on the outside. Follow the shapes and lines of the fabric design and try thicker threads in the bobbin. Then cut out vest shapes and finish edges with binding. People will think you're a genius.

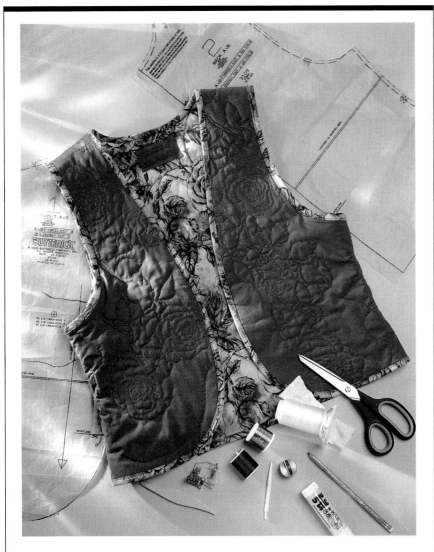

Techniques: *Free-machine quilting with heavy threads in bobbin (page 52)*

* F.A.S.T. Quilting is used throughout this book in sympathy for working people with lots of ambition but little time. The acronym means Fabric-Aided to Save Time.

F.A.S.T. Vest: *P&B fabric, Cotton Classic batting, Coats & Clark Transparent Nylon on top, Madeira Metallic and Coats & Clark Dual Duty Plus Extra-Fine thread in bobbin, Mundial scissors, General's Multi-Pastel Chalk marker, Uhu gluestick, pencil sharpener, Perfect Sew needle threader, generic binding foot from Treadleart, Puts-It from Clotilde. Quilted on a Bernina 1230. Photo by Lee Lindeman.*

See page 228 in the Mini-Encyclopedia for how to make bias binding.

Materials

- vest pattern with no darts, if possible (I used a Butterick pattern)
- printed backing fabric yardage as called for on pattern—buy extra if the motif repeat is large (I used P & B Textile's *Baltimore Beauties* by Elly Sienkiewicz)
- matching solid or print fabric for outside of vest
- 5/8 yd. self-made bias binding (test width on test squilt before cutting yardage into strips)—yields about 5 yards of 2-1/2"-wide bias binding)
- low-loft batting (I used Cotton Classic)
- decorative threads for bobbin (I used Madeira Astro metallic and Coats & Clark's Dual Duty Plus Extra-Fine) and monofilament or another strong thread for the top (I used Coats & Clark's Transparent Nylon Monofilament Thread)
- 12/80 H-J or 14/90 H-J needle
- darning foot
- starch
- Sewing Notebook
- *Optional:* Screw hoop, tool to push extra bias binding under presser foot (chopstick, awl, or Puts-It, which I call the Banana Tool because it's bright yellow)

Directions

1. Make a test squilt about 8" square. Test all stitch tensions first.

2. Preshrink fabrics (and batting, if necessary). Cut off selvages. Starch fabrics heavily.

3. Test pattern fit and eliminate side seams, if desired (see page 112). Cut off armscye and outside edge seam allowances.

4. Layer squilt, printed side up, and baste with safety pins, avoiding the motifs to be quilted. Decide whether to quilt yardage and then cut out pattern pieces or cut large silhouettes around pattern pieces and then quilt. I did the latter. Remember to flip front pattern piece. Put temporary pins to mark the motifs to be quilted so you don't do more work than is necessary.

5. Printed fabric up, free-machine quilt around the design with decorative thread in the bobbin. *Optional:* Use a hoop. Stay away from side seams and shoulder seams for now. Decide how much quilting to put on the back. I free-machine quilted meandering lines, using a blindhem stitch. It resembles the thorny stalks of roses.

6. Cut out vest, remembering to flip front pattern piece.

Machine Quilting

7. Sew label on vest back. Sew shoulder seams (see page 123). Safety-pin baste side seams to check fit. It's your last chance to make improvements. Sew side seams. Add additional quilting over seams if desired.

8. Zigzag vest edges to be bound. Bind as desired—see page 121. As you round outside curves, push extra fabric under the presser foot. As you round inside curves, stretch the binding slightly. Join ends of bias following the instructions on page 230.

9. Make notes in Sewing Notebook about batting used, thread, needle, tension settings, decorative stitches, what you wish you'd done better.

10. Return tension settings to normal. Throw away needle. Clean out lint and oil machine if necessary. Then hug it.

Optional: Make a small fabric pin from the print to wear with vest (see page 152).

Linda Fry Kenzle, Fox River Grove, IL, Starlight jacket. *Hand-painted, stencilled, machine-quilted with metallic thread. Reprinted from* Embellishments *by Linda Fry Kenzle (Chilton, 1993), with permission. Photo by Robert Fogt.*

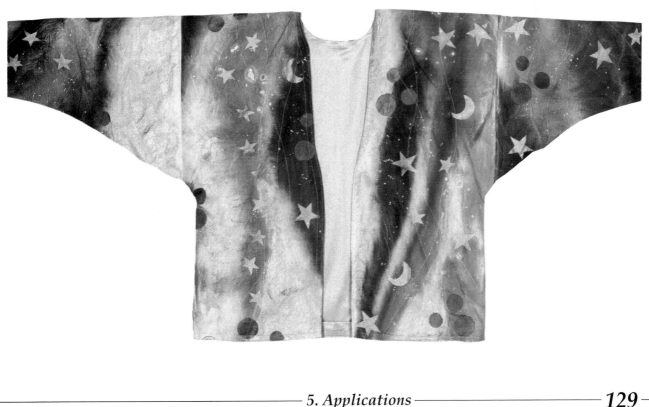

 Wigwarm

Reading in bed or watching TV on icy winter nights is something to look forward to in this easy-to-make project made of warm velour. A snap on either side makes armholes or you can use it flat as a lap quilt. The size is perfect for any other blown-up traditional quilt block you want to try.

We still use the first Wigwarm we made in 1978. One snap has pulled out, but it's become our adult blankie.

Wigwarm: *Velour from stash, Mountain Mist ComfortLoft, Metrosene Plus thread in top and bobbin, Singer Featherweight, 12/ 80 H needle. Quilted on an Elna Super. Photo by Lee Lindeman.*

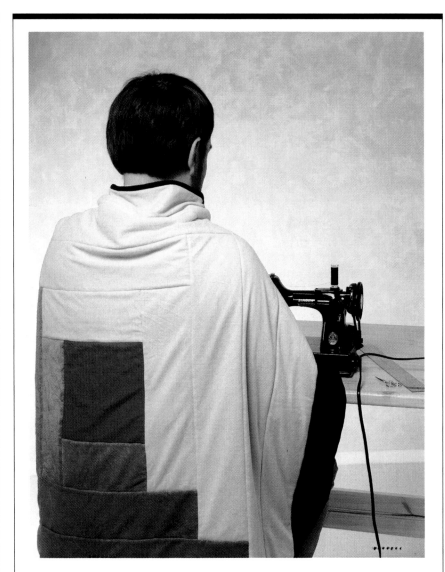

Wigwarm Size: *72" x 40"*
Technique: *One-step quilting (page 40)*
Pattern: *Log Cabin*

Materials

- 3/4 yd. 45"-wide white velour
- 2-1/8 yd. tangerine velour
- 3/4 yd. gray velour
- 1-1/8 yd. black velour
- regular-loft batting 40-1/2" square and 2 pieces, each 16-1/2" x 40-1/2" (I used Mountain Mist's ComfortLoft)
- ordinary sewing (polyester or cotton-covered polyester) thread—tangerine on bobbin, black on top
- 12/80 H
- zipper or roller foot, walking foot
- graph paper, masking tape, cornstarch
- 1" x 10" strip of fusible interfacing
- press cloth
- 5 gripper snaps (or use Velcro buttons)
- Sewing Notebook

Directions

1. Set up a test square of velour, batting, and velour. Test stitch length, tension settings, and needle size.

2. Preshrink velours. If you must iron out wrinkles in the yardage, do so from the underside with a press cloth or the iron will leave marks. Cut an 8-1/2" square out of graph paper. Cut one square of tangerine velour 40-1/2" square and one, 8-1/2" square (use the graph paper for a pattern for the latter). The larger piece is the backing. Find its center point by folding it, wrongsides together, into quarters. Mark center. Then unfold and pin the center of the graph paper square to the rightside center of the velour. Make the edges of the paper and fabric parallel. Pin.

3. On the underside of the tangerine velour, fuse 1" circles or squares of fusible interfacing where snaps will be applied (see cartoon).

Be careful when you're buying velour. To get the colors you want, you may have to buy different widths of fabric. You will then need more or less fabric—see Yardage Conversion Chart on page 254.)

4. Turn the large velour square over. Place the 40-1/2" batting on the wrong side of the velour. Pin around the edges. Zigzag or straight stitch around the edges, using a zipper or roller foot to keep from catching in the batting.

5. Tape the velour to a large window, batting side up. You can now see the outline of the graph paper square. Pin the 8-1/2" tangerine velour square in place, wrongside against the batting. Remove the graph paper.

6. Cut the white and gray velour into 4-1/2"-wide strips. For 45"-wide velour you will need five strips of white and five, gray. Cut the strips so that you have one gray and one white each this long: 12-1/2", 16-1/2", 20-1/2", 24-1/2", 28-1/2", 32-1/2", 36-1/2". In addition, cut one gray strip 8-1/2" long and one white strip 40-1/2" long.

7. Designate one long side of the large tangerine square "bottom." Sew the 8-1/2" gray strip to the bottom side of the smaller tangerine square, rightsides together, in a 1/4" seam, stopping and starting the seam 1/4" from each end so it will look good on the back. Flip out the gray piece rightside up and pin liberally.

8. The next gray 12-1/2" piece is sewn across the end of the previous piece. (Don't get confused or you will have to rip out.) Repeat what you did in Step 5 for each strip around the central square, following the cartoon for color placement and always starting and stopping each seam 1/4" from the ends.

9. Cut two tangerine and two black rectangles 16-1/2" x 40-1/2" each for the ends. Pin the rightside long edge of one black rectangle to the topside of the worked Log Cabin and the rightside long edge of one tangerine to its underside. Sew a 1/4" seam. Repeat for the other end. Flip the ends out so the wrong sides touch.

10. Trim the graph paper square you used in Step 2 to 5" on one side. With an unthreaded needle, sew along the graph paper square 4" in from one side. Place the graph paper on one black end along the seamline. Work cornstarch through the holes of the paper to mark the quilting line, moving the paper along the seamline as needed. Mark two more quilting lines 4" from each other. Repeat for the other end.

11. Cut two rectangles of batting 16-1/4" x 40-1/2". Slide one between each end. Pin liberally and zigzag or straight stitch around the edges of the ends. Machine quilt the three long lines on each black end, pinning liberally along each line. A walking foot also keeps the layers from shifting. If necessary, vacuum the cornstarch off the velour.

12. Put black thread in the bobbin. For the binding, cut 1-1/4"-wide strips of black velour until you have a total of about 226". Sew the strips together on the short ends and press open seams, using a press cloth. Rightsides together, lay the binding along one end of the Wigwarm. Starting about 3" from one end of the binding, sew all around the Wigwarm in a 1/4" seam, joining ends as shown on page 230. At the corners, miter the binding as shown on page 237. Flip the binding over the edge to the underside and pin in place from the topside. Stitch in the ditch of the first seam. There is no need to turn under the raw edge of the velour. Trim the extra velour close to the stitching.

13. Use a heavy-duty snap attacher to apply five snaps as shown on the cartoon.

14. Make notes in your Sewing Notebook about batting used, thread, needle, tension settings, what you wish you'd done better.

15. Return tension settings to normal. Throw away needle. Clean out lint and oil machine if necessary. Then hug it.

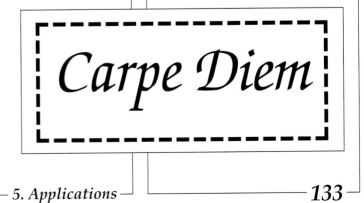

Spartex Baby Bear quilt. The design is sold screened onto the fabric and can be hand- or machine-quilted. Photo courtesy of Spartex.

Interiors

Below: *Lynn Graves, Albuquerque, NM,* Stars at Sea *and* Christmas Cruise at Sea. *Two-sided wallhanging made of Benartex fabrics, pieced to Lynn's Little Foot foundation papers. Photo by Lee Lindeman.*

Quilts quickly moved beyond the bed to the body and the wall. Now they have taken over all parts of the home, office, camper, and hide-away. This section explores helpful hints using less well-known materials for wallhangings, pillows, potholders, and tool covers; but the information can be adapted for anything you wish to quilt for your environment—rugs, window coverings, table toppers, furniture, room dividers.

In all cases, we are concentrating on quilting, not piecing.

Wallhangings

The minute you hang up a quilt, it becomes a wallhanging. If you never intend to use it as a quilt, throw out all the old rules about fiber content, seam allowances, and flatness. This is the time to use strange fibers, any seam allowance you want, and tacked-on goodies like charms, bows, buttons, beads, and more.

Marjorie Ward of Marjorie's in Essexville, MI, convinced me that denim-weight fabric is ideal as a backing on wallhangings. It allows you to machine quilt heavily without the backing puckering and the piece hangs straighter. I used it on *Color, Wheels I* on page 58 and am a convert.

Then Nansi Bainard of Richland, WA, told me she uses craft felt as a backing for the same reasons, but also because she can pull threads to the back, leave them hanging without tying off, and then line the piece to hide any ugliness on the back. I tried this on a second version of *Color, Wheels* and am a convert. Do these beliefs conflict? No. It all depends on the look you want and how the back of your piece looks. If no one will see the back of your wallhanging, use denim. If you're selling or giving the piece, line it.

You will need a sturdy rod pocket at the top of a wallhanging. Marinda Stewart of Walnut Creek, CA, who has hung many quilt shows, suggests that you make a pocket that completely encases the rod. The rod should not touch the back of the wallhanging. If you are entering the piece in shows, she also suggests that you make the pocket 4" wide, which will accommodate most methods of hanging (usually pipes).

If your hanging is large, asymmetric, or doesn't hang as straight as you'd like, Marinda reminded me that many artists put another rod pocket at the middle or bottom and weight the piece with a second rod. You could also use cloth-covered drapery weights or weighted chain, available in decorating sections of fabric stores.

Are you the next Kandinsky? (See page 85.) What if you hung your quilt crooked?

Easy Rod Pocket I

When you plan ahead, you can encase part of the pocket in the top seam before the wallhanging is bound.

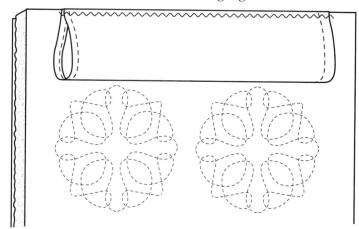

1. Cut sturdy fabric such as closely woven muslin 9" wide by the width of your quilt. If you have a large wallhanging, you may need to piece this strip. I prefer to cut parallel to the crossgrain so the stronger warp threads are supporting the wallhanging.

2. Fold strip in half, wrong sides together, and press. Open up.

3. Turn in the short ends 1/2" on each end and press. Then turn them again and topstitch to hold. The sleeve will now be 2" shorter than the hanging top.

4. Align one long end with the top of the piece, rightsides together. Zigzag it to the top edge.

5. By hand, stitch the pocket to the backing along the pressed fold. Make sure your stitches do not show on the front of the hanging. Use a running stitch and strong thread, like polyester, silk, or hand-quilting thread.

6. Fold the remaining half of the pocket to the top and straight stitch it at the edge of the previous zigzag stitches. The raw edges will eventually be covered by the binding.

Easy Rod Pocket II

If the piece is already finished and needs a pocket, use this method.

1. Repeat Step 1 above.

2. Repeat Step 3 above.

3. Wrong sides together, sew a 1/2" seam. Center the seam on the tube you just made and press open.

4. *By machine:* Align the tube so it barely overlaps the top binding seam. Pin. Turn the piece over and stitch in the ditch with monofilament nylon. *By hand:* Align the tube just below the binding seam and handwhip in place with strong thread.

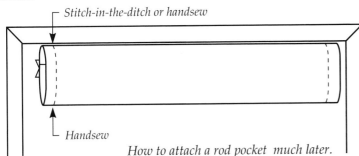

— Stitch-in-the-ditch or handsew

— Handsew

How to attach a rod pocket much later.

5. Sew inside the short end; then handsew across the bottom of the tube and up the remaining short side. This prevents the rod from being inserted erroneously against the quilt.

In either case, you can put a screw through the sleeve into a wooden rod to hang the piece, especially if you are concerned with security. This method is used in galleries to protect quilts from too-envious people.

Temporary Hang-up

Here's an easy solution to those times when we want a fast-and-dirty hang-up and don't want to take any time for handwork—a funny wallhanging you finish just before the birthday party or a seasonal banner or Aunt Mary's quilt before photographing it.

1. Cut 8" lengths of wide ribbon or blanket binding. Loop them with the fold against the top binding seam on the back of the hanging. Safety-pin the bottom edges.

2. With the piece face down, insert the hanging device. Safety-pin again, close to the rod.

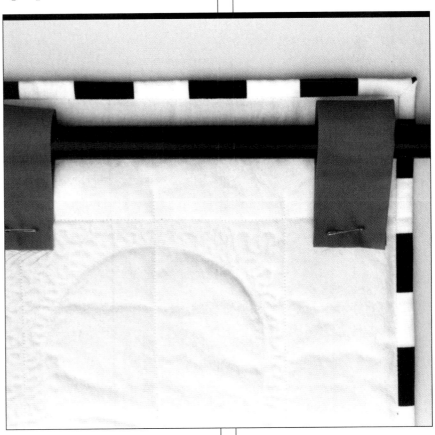

Use ribbon or blanket binding to make temporary hang-up loops.

John Flynn of the Flynn Quilt Frame Company calculated the thickness of pine or fir needed for various weights of quilts. If your hanging weighs more than 10 pounds, use a 1x3 or 1x4 wood support. Otherwise the support may bow.

Heavy Items

If your wallhanging or quilt is made of heavy fabric, you will need a strong hanging device. Tony Jacobson, author of *Quilting Around Your Home*, suggests two:

1. Make a muslin strip 2" – 3" wide and as long as the quilt width, with edges pressed under 1/2". Sew the loop side of heavy-duty Velcro to the length of muslin. Handstitch the strip to the quilt back. Glue the hook side of the strip to a thin strip of board as long as the quilt. Secure the board to the wall; then press the quilt Velcro to the board Velcro.

2. Use a quilt clamp, available in quilt stores and mail-order catalogs (see Resource list). Two finished boards separate and clamp over the top edge of the quilt.

Pillows

Have you seen the price of decorator pillows? Soon, I expect your choice will be to buy five pillows or send your child to college.

You can save a lot of money by making machine-quilted pillows to match your decor. Use either shiny fabrics like silk, sateen, or chintz that catch the light or use heavier thread, so your handiwork will star and not be lost. I like to make removable pillow covers, so I can clean them (see project on page 147).

Marjorie Ward of Marjorie's in Essexville, MI, made a pillow from the Machine-Quilting Sampler *on page 78 for her Creative Machine Cruise roommate, Vicki Redfield of Corpus Christi, TX.*

Patterns for Pillow Covers

Gail Brown's All-New Instant Interiors is my constant companion in constructing anything for the home. She taught me (and Marjorie Ward reminded me) that putting a zipper on the diagonal on the back cover makes inserting the form a breeze. If you can't find a long enough zipper, follow Jackie Dodson's tip: buy them by the yard and cut off what you need.

First you must plan the size of your pillow form. You can either buy ready-made (my choice—faster) or make your own.

Square pillow forms usually come ready-made in these standard sizes:

10", 12", 14" 16", 18", 20", 26", and 30"

Homemade Pillow Form—Three Ways

A. *Batting layers.* Use thick batting and leftover pieces for this form. This makes a soft form.

1. Cut two pieces of fleece the size of the finished pillow. Then cut a series of two pieces of any batting, each 2" smaller than the previous cut—e.g., if your pillow is 14" square, cut two pieces 14" square, two pieces 12" square, two pieces 10" square, etc., until you reach about 4" square. Then cut only one 4" piece.

2. Assemble the middle of the pillow form by building a sandwich of the batting strata, with the smallest piece in the middle. You can also put leftover pieces in there.

3. Zigzag or serge around 2-1/2 edges of the fleece. Put the batting strata inside and finish sewing.

4. Cover the form with muslin or stuff in pillow cover as is. You can always fill out the corners of a pillow with wads of batting (everybody does it).

B. *Stuffed form.* This works better when you are closing the pillow cover by hand along one edge.

1. Cut two pieces of fleece the size of the finished pillow. Sew or serge close to the edge around three sides.

2. Put the pillow form inside the pillow cover. Fill the form with polyfill in tiny handfuls and stuff it firmly, but don't overstuff the middle. Pin edge closed.

3. Remove the pillow form and sew the last edge. Reinsert into pillow cover and sew or serge cover closed.

C. *Your way.* Undoubtedly, you have invented a better way.

Now make a paper pattern for the pillow cover.

1. Add 1/2" seam allowances to the pillow size, unless your pillow form is extremely soft, in which case don't add extra. Write the dimensions on the upper left corner of the paper.

2. Cut the pattern on the diagonal and add 3/4" seam allowances to the upper diagonal edge. Make sure the pillow cover dimensions are on this half. Throw away the other half. You will use a lapped zipper technique.

Making the Pillow Cover

1. Decorate the front.

2. Use the paper pattern to cut out two pillow backs.

3. Rightsides together, baste the back cover halves together, using a 3/4" seam allowance, loosening top tension. Be gentle—this is a bias edge. Return tension to normal. Lay the zipper on the stitched line and center it. Mark its two ends with pins. Stitch over the basting with a regular stitch length from the pins to the outer edges, backstitching at the pins. Press the seam open.

Yvonne Perez-Collins, author of Soft Gardens, uses hemostat scissors to insert stuffing in small shapes.

Gail Brown taught me to stuff the pillow form while it's inside the pillow cover.

Marilyn Highley of Oklahoma City, OK, makes a small pillow form to take on trips. She packs the form in her suitcase, then uses it as an extra reading pillow—but if she finds fabric to buy and she needs the space in her suitcase, she leaves the pillow behind.

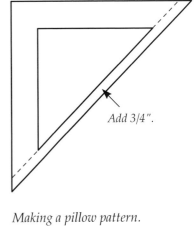

Making a pillow pattern.

Add 3/4".

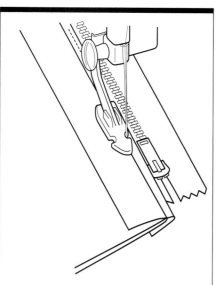

Put in a pillow cover zipper on the diagonal, for easier insertion of the pillow form.

If you're really in a hurry and can't put any time into construction, browse garage sales and Goodwill. Buy any used decorator pillow that has a decent edge (piped, ruffled, etc.) and a color you like. It helps if it has an opening on the back. Remove the pillow form. Quilt shapes separately. Then fuse them to the cover. I call these bandit pillows.

4. Extend one seam allowance. Put the rightside of the zipper against the extended seam allowance, matching outside edges. The zipper stops should fall between the pins. Using a zipper foot, stitch on the zipper tape guideline.

5. Fold the pillow cover away from the zipper and edgestitch the fold through all thicknesses. This will be the underlap.

6. Gluestick the edge of the opposite side of the zipper tape. Flip the zipper face down on the opened seam allowance. Sew across the end, up the other zipper guideline, and across the remaining end.

7. Remove basting stitches. Open zipper. You could use Velcro or snap tape instead of a zipper. You could also install the zipper without basting first, but this way is more accurate.

8. Match front and back covers, rightsides together. Before you sew them together, learn how to avoid dog ears at the corners.

Avoiding Dog Ears Two Ways

The corners of pillows can be too pointy. Gail Brown and Jan Saunders taught me how to avoid this.

1. *Rounded corners.* At the corners, measure in an additional 1/2" from the seam allowances and put a dot. Divide each side of the pillow cover in quarters and put dots where the quarter mark closest to the corner falls. Connect the dots (the sharpest angle on a pocket former template helps). After sewing, trim curved seam with pinking shears or serge the edges.

2. *Wrapped corners.* Finish the edges by serging or zigzagging. Sew two opposite sides in straight lines. Fold the seam allowance under. Then sew the remaining two sides, catching the first seam allowances in the stitching.

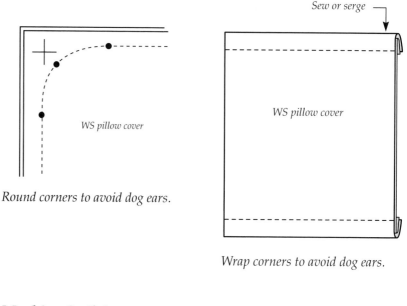

Round corners to avoid dog ears.

Wrap corners to avoid dog ears.

Potholders

Doris Hoover, author of Too Hot to Handle? Potholders and How to Make Them, *made these simple potholders. They make wonderful quick gifts.*

Purchased potholders are never big enough, they get dirty in minutes, and they don't hold up to washing. That's why I like to make my own. These mini-textiles make great gifts, yet they can be finished in an evening.

I'm concerned with the insides of potholders, not the outsides. How to keep from burning your hands? A new material makes the question obsolete: Iron Quick is Teflon-covered yardage that looks like some ironing-board covers (see Resource list). Use it doubled inside a potholder with the silver side out, surrounded by batting. I like to quilt one or both sides of the potholder to the batting, then assemble the squilt, so that I'm not quilting through the Iron Quick.

Since polyester batting melts when hot, it is not a good choice for batting in potholders.

You can use potholders lots of other ways, too. Doris Hoover's charming *Too Hot to Handle? Potholders and How to Make Them* suggests eyeglass holders (good place to store your rotary cutter, too), room dividers, pockets, and as a cushion around a shoulder belt in the car. Gail Brown sent a photo of a row of potholders used as a curtain valance.

Nancy Ward, author of *Stamping Made Easy,* uses sweatshirt fleece inside potholders.

Kathleen Kelley of Redwood City, CA, likes to buy large (16") used napkins from garage sales and flea markets. She watches for motifs that will delight friends, then uses the napkin as a potholder. Inside, she often uses old cotton mattress pads.

*F*A.S.T.* Placemats

Use some of the gorgeous coordinated fabrics now available to make fast, easy, quilted placemats—or as here, use an apron panel. Why not make a different set for every month of the year?

This is actually a smaller version of the Easy Miter technique shown on page 235.

* F.A.S.T. Quilting is used throughout this book in sympathy for working people with lots of ambition but little time. The acronym means Fabric-Aided to Save Time.

F.A.S.T. Placemats: *Springs Amish Quilt apron panel, Timtex batting, DMC Size 50 and YLI Wonder Invisible Thread, 12/80 H-J needle, rose from Tony's garden. Quilted on a Pfaff 1475. Photo by Lee Lindeman.*

Placemat Size: *16" x 11"*
Techniques: *Mock handquilting (page 28)*

Materials

- For four: 1/2 yd. 45"-wide fabric for center of placemat (unless design runs parallel to selvage—then increase yardage as needed); 1 yd. 45"-wide fabric for border (unless design runs parallel to selvage—then increase yardage as needed) (I used a Springs *Amish Quilt* apron) *Optional:* For matching 21" napkins, buy 1-1/8 yds. extra.
- 4 pieces of low-loft craft fleece, each 16" x 11" (I used Timtex, a thin, stiff, washable batting that won't tip over a glass when set on it, unlike soft battings).
- polyester or cotton thread, monofilament nylon (I used DMC Size 50 and YLI Wonder Invisible Thread in a smoke color)
- 12/80 H-J or 14/90 H-J needle
- walking foot or open-toed foot
- 1 roll paper-backed fusible web, 3/4" wide (I used Wonder-Under)
- marking pencil, ruler (preferably 2" wide)
- Sewing Notebook

Directions

1. Set up a test square of center fabric and fleece. Test stitch length and width, tension settings, and needle size.

2. Cut the border fabric as shown.

3. Press strips of paper-backed fusible web to the underside edges of the border. Remove paper. Press the border hems 3/4" to the underside.

4. On the underside of the border fabric, draw the hemline 1-3/4" from each edge. At each corner, use the Easy Miter shown on page 235. Trim corners and press mitered seams open. Turn border rightsides out.

5. Measure the finished size of the border silhouette. Cut the centers and fleece for the placemats as shown.

6. Back centers with fleece. Use your ruler to mark a 2"-wide diamond grid.

7. Review the direction for mock handquilting. Set up the machine with monofilament nylon on top, regular thread in the bobbin. The bobbin thread will show. Tighten top tension. Quilt.

8. Slip quilted center into border. Edgestitch, topstitch, or stitch with a decorative stitch around the center opening.

9. *Optional:* Make napkins to match.

10. Make notes in Sewing Notebook about batting used, thread, needle, tension settings, decorative stitches, what you wish you'd done better.

11. Return tension settings to normal. Throw away needle. Clean out lint and oil machine if necessary. Then hug it.

Quick Napkin Creations by Gail Brown has wonderful ideas for no-sew, sewn, and serged napkins. Napkins are the perfect gift.

Don't cut the fleece until you make the frame, in case your measurements are not accurate.

Border fabric
16"
21"

11"
16"

Above: *Agnes Mercik, Enfield, CT, piles of pillows, quilted on Berninas with the scallop stitch, stuffed with fiberfill. Photo by Lee Lindeman.*

Below: *Gabriella Verstaaten, Melbourne, Australia, machine-embroidered and -quilted pillows. Layered fabrics, free-hand embroidery and quilting, machine beading, worked on a Bernina 1630. Photo courtesy of the artist.*

Simple Sashiko
Pillow Covers

Save money and spruce up a room by making simple pillow covers. I made these to remind myself to Keep It Simple, Silly (K.I.S.S.)—in life. Try combining straight stitches with the decorative stitches. If your machine has memory, store five to ten straight stitches, then a decorative stitch like the closed ball. On alternate lines, stitch a message or names. You can also use sashiko stencils for the quilting design (see Resource list) or design something to echo motifs in your upholstery, curtains, or rugs.

Simple Sashiko Pillow Covers: *Denim from stash, Metrosene Cordonnet on top and Coats & Clark Dual Duty Plus in bobbin, Lammertz 16/100 needle, Dritz Press-on Fleece, small pillow form made from Putnam's Special Edition SoftShapes and Craft & Quilting Fleece, large pillow is a Morning Glory Decorator Pillow form, pocket former from Clotilde, scissors from Gingher, CloChalk from Clotilde. Quilted on a Bernina 1230. Photo by Lee Lindeman.*

Pillow Cover Size: *10" square*
Technique: *Straight/decorative stitch, sashiko grid (see page 69)*

If you want a F.A.S.T.* grid, use a pre-printed plaid or gingham fabric, either on the top or the underside of the quilting. In the latter case, the pre-printed fabric will not show in the finished pillow.

* F.A.S.T. Quilting is used throughout this book in sympathy for working people with lots of ambition but little time. The acronym means Fabric-Aided to Save Time.

Materials

- fabric for the front and back of pillow cover (I used denim)
- muslin or old sheeting for backing of pillow top
- batting to match size of fabric top (I used Dritz Press-on Fleece)
- cordonnet or buttonhole twist, or two strands of thread through the needle (I used Metrosene Cordonnet); polyester for bobbin (I used Coats & Clark Dual Duty Plus)
- 16/100 H-J or topstitching needle
- walking foot
- zipper as long as the longest finished side
- pillow form (purchased or homemade) (I made one with Putnam's Special Edition SoftShapes on the inside and their Craft & Quilting Fleece on the outside)
- pattern for front and back to fit your pillow form (see page 141)
- marking device (I used CloChalk), 2"-wide ruler
- Sewing Notebook
- *Optional:* sashiko stencil (see Resource list), gluestick

Directions

1. Set up a test square of denim, fleece, and muslin backing. Test stitch length and width, tension settings, and needle size.

2. Make a pattern for your pillow, following the directions on page 141.

3. Cut the pillow front cover, batting, and muslin to match. Draw diagonal lines 2" apart. Quilt a simple design, using a long straight stitch (about 8 – 10 stitches per inch or 4mm).

4. Install a diagonal zipper as explained on page 142.

5. Place the pillow front and back rightsides together. Sew 1/2" seams. See page 142 for how to avoid pointy corners. If you wrap the corners, finish the edges with zigzag or serging before seaming.

6. Turn the pillow cover rightside out.

7. Insert the pillow form. If the space seems too large for the form, wrap it in additional batting or take out the form and put in a line or two of topstitching.

8. Make notes in your Sewing Notebook about batting used, thread, needle, tension settings, decorative stitches, what you wish you'd done better.

9. Return tension settings to normal. Throw away needle. Clean out lint and oil machine if necessary. Then hug it.

Anne Cottenden, Bridgetown, NS, Canada, Elizabethan Crazy. Appliquilted autobiographical fabrics, badges, labels, and crests. Photo courtesy of the artist.

Bonnie Lyn McCaffery, Hawley, PA, Garden Kaleidoscope, 39" square, 1993. Flowers dance together in the center, while others form a circle around the outside. Photo courtesy of the artist.

Crafts

This category covers everything else that you might want to machine quilt: seasonal items like ornaments and stockings; small quick gifts like tooth fairy bags and awards; dolls; jewelry; totes; and whatever else you dream up.

These small projects can usually be finished in an evening and use up leftover batting and threads. They are the perfect place to test new threads, color schemes, and techniques, because if they don't work, you haven't invested a lot of time. Here's a review of your choices.

Fabric: Anything. You generally don't need to preshrink it because the item will never be washed—good time to play with Ultrasuede, Fabu-Leather, and other synthetic trims.

Thread: Any, especially the metallics

Batting: Any, but this is the time to play with unusual batting—foam, high-loft, wool, etc.

Techniques: The small scale of the projects makes them especially ripe for decorative stitches and free-machine straight stitch. For appliquilts, this is the time to abandon clean edges.

Notions: Buttons, bows, small bits of trims, beads

Additional tools: Fabric glue or hot glue gun

Care: Plan ahead. If the piece must ever be washed (rare, with craft items), preshrink fabric and don't use non-washable trims.

We will practice on a fabric pin and on holiday yardage from which you can make many other items. But first, let's learn how to apply a bead by machine.

For more in-depth information on thread and batting, see the Mini-Encyclopedia on pages 250 and 220.

See page 183 for a discussion of glues.

Beading by Machine

I learned how from Ann Boyce, co-author of *Putting on the Glitz*. The bead must be big enough to slide onto the machine needle, but not so big that it doesn't fit under the needle screw when the needle is at its lowest position.

1. Remove the presser foot and put the fabric in a hoop, if possible.

2. Lock threads on the fabric (watch your fingers!). Stitch to where you want a bead and stop with the needle in the up position.

3. Take your foot completely off the foot pedal. Hold the bead with two fingers of one hand and brace it with one finger of the other. Slide the bead up the needle.

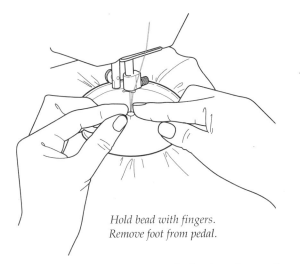

*Hold bead with fingers.
Remove foot from pedal.*

Take your foot off the pedal when you put the bead on the needle.

4. Turn the handwheel toward you one revolution.

5. Move the hoop over the distance of one bead and turn the handwheel another revolution. The bead is now secure and you can stitch away from it.

This is admittedly a slow process, but faster than putting the beads on by hand. You can use the same process with single sequins.

I learned this safety tip from Pat Rodgers' video, *Free Motion Embroidery and Beading by Machine*—see Bibliography.

FA.S.T.* Fabric Pin

Flower pins are especially pretty to make. You can design your own flower forms or, as here, take advantage of a fabric designer's skill by machine-quilting ready-made designs, displayed either topside- or underside-up.

* F.A.S.T. Quilting is used throughout this book in sympathy for working people with lots of ambition but little time. The acronym means Fabric-Aided to Save Time.

Pin Size: *Depends on fabric design*

Techniques: *Free-machine quilting (page 47), beading (page 151)*

F.A.S.T. Fabric Pin: *Robert Kaufman Kona Gold fabric, Spring Ultrasuede, Hobbs Poly-down DK batting, Sew Art Invisible Thread and DMC Size 50 on top, Gütermann Sew-All in bobbin, 12/80 H-J needle, charms by Stylex, scissors from New Home, Creative Feet Satinedge Foot, Fiskars wavy-edge blade. Quilted on a Brother Pacesetter PC-7000. Photo by Lee Lindeman.*

Materials

- scraps of fabric for top (I used *Kona Gold* prints from Robert Kaufman Co)
- denim-weight backing or Ultrasuede
- tearaway or water-soluble stabilizer
- scraps of regular-loft batting (I used Hobbs Poly-down DK because it's dark)
- monofilament nylon, extra-fine machine-embroidery for satin-stitch edge (I used Sew Art's Invisible Thread and Size 50 DMC)
- sharp-pointed needle, 12/80 or 14/90 H-J
- darning foot, appliqué foot
- *Optional:* Creative Feet's Satinedge Foot
- spring or screw hoop
- beads, charms (I used sewing charms from Stylex—see Resource list)
- pinback (available in fabric and craft stores)
- Sewing Notebook
- *Optional:* jewelry glue or hot glue gun (I used Goop)

Directions

1. Set up a test square of backing, batting, and top. Test stitch length and width, tension settings, and needle size.

2. Put the backing in a hoop and put two layers of batting on top wider than the fabric to be decorated. Pin the top fabric over all.

3. Set up your machine for free-machine quilting with monofilament on top. Quilt the main shapes. Add beads, if you wish, making sure they are an appliqué presser-foot distance away from the outside edge.

4. Stitch around the outside of the shape. Remove the hoop from under the needle but don't remove the backing fabric from the hoop yet.

5. Holding the top fabric out of the way, trim the batting close to the outside stitching.

6. Set up the machine for satin stitch, using the extra-fine machine-embroidery thread. Return the hoop under the needle. Run one row of loosely spaced satin stitch on the row of straight stitching.

7. Take the hoop away from the machine. Remove the fabric from the hoop. Trim close to the satin stitching.

8. Put the pin on two layers of water-soluble stabilizer. Satin stitch around the edge, this time with a wider, closer stitch. Tear away the stabilizer.

I backed one of the pins with Ultrasuede and cut it later with Fiskars' wavy-edged rotary cutter blade.

Creative Feet's Satinedge Foot helps make a beautiful 3-D edge—no buckling of the fabric.

9. *Optional:* To add charms at bottom of pin, before tearing away the water-soluble stabilizer, lay one charm at a time on the stabilizer and attach as for beads. Tear away excess stabilizer.

10. Handstitch or glue a pinback to the underside.

11. Make notes in Sewing Notebook about batting used, thread, needle, tension settings, what you wish you'd done better.

12. Return tension settings to normal. Throw away needle. Clean out lint and oil machine if necessary. Then hug it.

Variations

• Satin stitch the pin to Ultrasuede. Cut the edges beyond the satin stitch in a decorative way.

• Instead of satin stitching the outside edge, serge it with decorative thread.

• Instead of satin stitching the outside edge, line the pin the way you did the Message Board (page 18).

• Load decorative threads in the bobbin and stitch underside up, following the pattern on the fabric.

Shirley Adams, hostess of TV's The Sewing Connection, *models a silk jacket machine-quilted on her* Viking #1 *with decorative stitches that suggest the Taj Mahal. Photo courtesy of Shirley Adams.*

Holiday Yardage

The fusing technique used here eliminates seaming fabrics together before decorating the edges. On craft items, you don't have to worry as much about finished edges because the pieces won't receive the same kind of stress that quilts or clothing do. This technique is a great way to explore the decorative stitches on your machine and to play with your fabric stash. Gather fabrics, trims, buttons, and thread that make you think of a specific holiday and the people who will be there. Make a large amount of crazy-quilted yardage; then cut it up for many projects. Here the theme is Christmas, but you could also celebrate Valentine's Day, Mother's Day, Fourth of July, special family events, or any other day.

Holiday Yardage: *White-on-White Medley from Keepsake Quilting, Fairfield Extra-Loft batting, Sulky rayon and Stream Lamé Tinsel thread, 14/90 H-J and 4,0/100 H-J twin needles, Cutting Edge circle wedge ruler, Pigma Micron pen, Japanese hera from Keepsake Quilting. Quilted on a Viking #1. Photo by Lee Lindeman.*

Yardage Size: *8-1/2" x 11"*

Materials

- 3 – 6 holiday fabrics at least 9" square (I used Keepsake Quilting's *White-on-White Medley* and have lots of fabric left)
- 8-1/2" x 11" piece of muslin for squilt backing plus enough extra for test square
- 12" square scrap for stocking lining and back of heart ornament
- 8-1/2" x 11" regular-loft batting (I used Fairfield's Extra-Loft)
- decorative threads (I used Sulky rayon and Stream Lamé Tinsel Thread)
- 14/90 H-J needle, 4,0/100 H-J twin needle
- walking foot
- *Optional:* Creative Feet's Sequin 'n Ribbon foot and Satinedge Foot
- paper-backed fusible web (I used HeatnBond Lite)
- 3-1/2 yds. 1/4"-wide satin ribbon (I used Offray, 100% polyester)
- thumbtack, eraser, tape
- 2 sheets 8-1/2" x 11" paper of cardstock weight
- ruler and rotary cutter (I used Marilyn Doheny's wedge ruler by Cutting Edge Quilt Designs), pinking shears
- pencil
- butter knife or hera (see page 190)
- white artist's tape or removable Scotch tape
- press cloth
- Sewing Notebook

Below: *Charlotte Warr Andersen, Salt Lake City, UT,* Burning Bush. *Moses, the burning bush, and the mountain. Photo courtesy of the artist.*

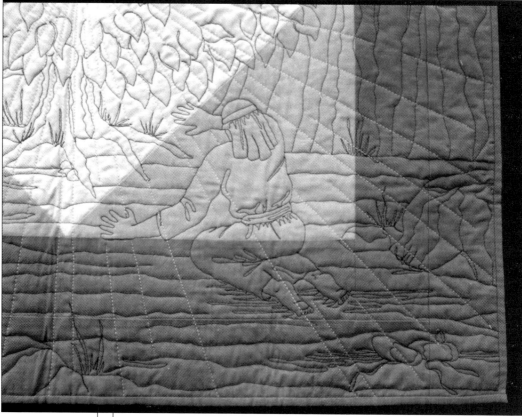

Directions

First we will construct the yardage. Then we'll construct the Crazy-Quilt Stocking, Heart Ornament, and Heart Card.

Yardage

1. Set up two test squares, one of fused fabric and one of backing and batting. Test stitch length and width, decorative stitches, tension settings, and needle size.

2. Set one holiday fabric aside for the back of the stocking. Back all the other holiday fabrics with paper-backed fusible web. When cool, remove the paper.

3. On one piece of fabric, measure the width of the shortest side and divide by 2. That's the widest radius you can use for a full circle. To make a circle, set up the tack slightly less far from the needle than that measurement (see page 30).

4. Fold the piece of fabric in half both ways and finger-press to find the center. Do the same on the test fabric. Press the marked center over the tack. Practice stitches on the test square. Then stitch concentric circles of decorative stitches on the actual fabric, moving the tack closer to the needle with each row. *Optional:* Stitch messages, names, dates, and so forth on this fabric square instead of circles.

5. Stack all the fabrics, including the stitched one. With a ruler, cut wedges in the fabrics with one end about 1" wide and the other about 2-1/2".

6. Layer the batting on the muslin rectangle. At the ironing board, arrange a row of wedges across the bottom third of the rectangle, flipping the wedges so short ends are next to larger ends. The wedges will hang off the squilt. Cover the arrangement with a press cloth and press lightly.

7. Set up the machine with a straight stitch and the twin needles. Lay satin ribbon over the joins of the fabric and stitch in place. I used one spool of Sulky rayon and one spool of Tinsel lamé. The Creative Feet Sequin 'n Ribbon foot makes it easy to be accurate. Trim all thread ends without worrying about tying off. They will be covered. Trim off the excess fabric.

8. Lay the trimmed ends from Step 7 along the right edge of the rectangle and hide joins with the ribbon as before.

9. Continue to build the crazy quilt on the squilt. Don't worry if you back yourself into a corner and find an unfinished edge. You can always avoid that spot when cutting out the objects or cover it with a free-form shape zigzagged into place. Now you are ready to make the objects.

I like Lois Smith's idea of a Time Capsule Crazy Patch in *Fun & Fancy Machine Quilting*. Write messages in thread about the major events of the year or show them through stitched pictures.

Crazy-Quilt Mini-Stocking

Stocking Size: 7" high

The stocking has a crazy-quilted front, a plain back, and a lining.

1. Blow up the cartoon so that the stocking is 7" high (enlarge the cartoon about 250%).

2. Trace the blown-up cartoon on a corner of one sheet of cardstock. With the machine unthreaded, set the straight stitch to just above 0 ("fine" or about .5). Stitch the outlines of the stocking. (Remember seventh grade home-ec sewing class where your first task was to follow lines on paper?) The stocking should fall out of the background with little help.

3. Decide which way you want the stocking to face. Move the cardstock around the fabric until you find a crazy-quilt arrangement you like. (But remember that you need to get two hearts out of the yardage, too.) Trace the shape with a pencil on the topside. Thread the machine and stitch around the penciled shape with a short straight stitch. Trim 1/4" away from the stitched line.

4. Lay the front of the stocking on the fabric saved for the stocking back, rightsides together. Trace around the stocking. Cut out the backside of the stocking.

5. Use the backside of the stocking as a template to cut out two lining stockings, rightsides together.

6. Cut a 5" piece of ribbon. Fold it in half and pin to top back corner of front side, raw edges of ribbon matching raw edges of stocking.

7. This step shows you an easy way to line the stocking; you can use the same principle to line anything. Rightsides together, stitch about 3" down the heel side of the stocking at the top. Open out flat and press seam open lightly. Repeat for lining.

8. Place rightside of lining against rightside of stocking. Stitch across top in 1/4" seam. Open out and press lightly. (*Optional:* Topstitch on lining side.)

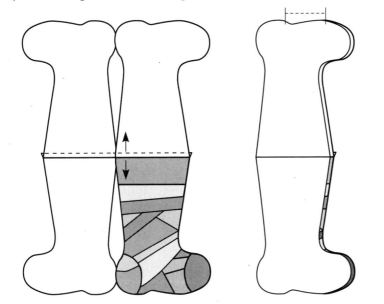

A clever lining technique worth knowing about for other objects like bags.

9. Fold stockings in half the long way, so that rightsides of stocking and back match and rightsides of lining match. Pin. Stitch one long seam from toe of lining down all around stocking to heel of lining, leaving an opening as shown. Clip inside curves and notch outside curves with pinking shears. Press seam open as best you can.

10. Reach through opening in lining and pull stocking rightside out. Turn under raw edges of lining and zigzag closed. Push lining inside stocking.

The gods send thread for the web begun.
Leif Smith

Heart Ornament

1. Trace the heart cartoon on page 81 on another corner of the sheet of cardstock you used for the stocking. With the machine unthreaded, set the straight stitch to just above 0 ("fine" or about .5). Stitch the outlines of the heart. It should come away from the paper with little help.

2. Move the cardstock around the fabric until you find a crazy-quilt arrangement showing through that you like. Trace the shape with a pencil on the topside. Thread the machine and stitch around the penciled shape with a short straight stitch. Trim 1/4" away from the stitched line.

3. Lay the heart on leftover fabric from the back of the stocking. Cut a 5" length of satin ribbon. Fold in half and insert between the layers at the top point of the heart. Satin stitch around the perimeter with a narrow, slightly loose stitch. Cut close to the stitches, avoiding the ribbon loop. Satin stitch again with a wider, closer satin stitch. (Creative Feet's Satinedge Foot makes a gorgeous satin stitch for 3-D edges like this.)

Heart Card

1. On the remaining cardstock, measure halfway down the 11" side. Score with a butter knife or hera and fold in half. Open flat. This is the inside.

2. Center the heart template on the inside bottom half of the cardstock and trace with pencil. With the machine unthreaded, set the straight stitch to just above 0 ("fine" or about .5). Stitch the outlines of the heart. It should come away from the paper with little help.

3. Move the heart over the crazy-quilt yardage until you like the look. Pinch the yardage to the card with your fingers and turn everything over. Trim the yardage to fit the lower half of the card and tape it in place temporarily.

4. Set up the machine for a zigzag and attach the yardage to the card on the perimeter of the heart shape. Remove the tape and trim 1/4" away from the stitching.

5. Close the card. Trim the bottom evenly, if necessary. Zigzag around the three open edges. Write a message.

6. Make notes in Sewing Notebook about batting used, thread, needle, tension settings, decorative stitches, what you wish you'd done better.

7. Return tension settings to normal. Throw away needle. Clean out lint and oil machine if necessary. Then hug it.

Left: *Shirley Botsford*
Middle: *Miriam Gourley*
Bottom: *Gina Butler*
See captions on facing page.

Joan Bechtel, Midland, TX, On the Oregon Trail at Chimney Rock, 42-1/4" x 47-1/2", 1993. Extensively textured with free-machine quilting, including meander or stipple quilting, irregular clamshell or cobblestone pattern, could lines, and cracks in the mud. Made as a birthplace memory quilt for the baby daughter of friends. Photo courtesy of the artist.

Elizabeth Gurrier, Yarmouth Port, MA, Pattern II, 58" x 78", 1989. Photo courtesy of the artist.

*S*pecifics

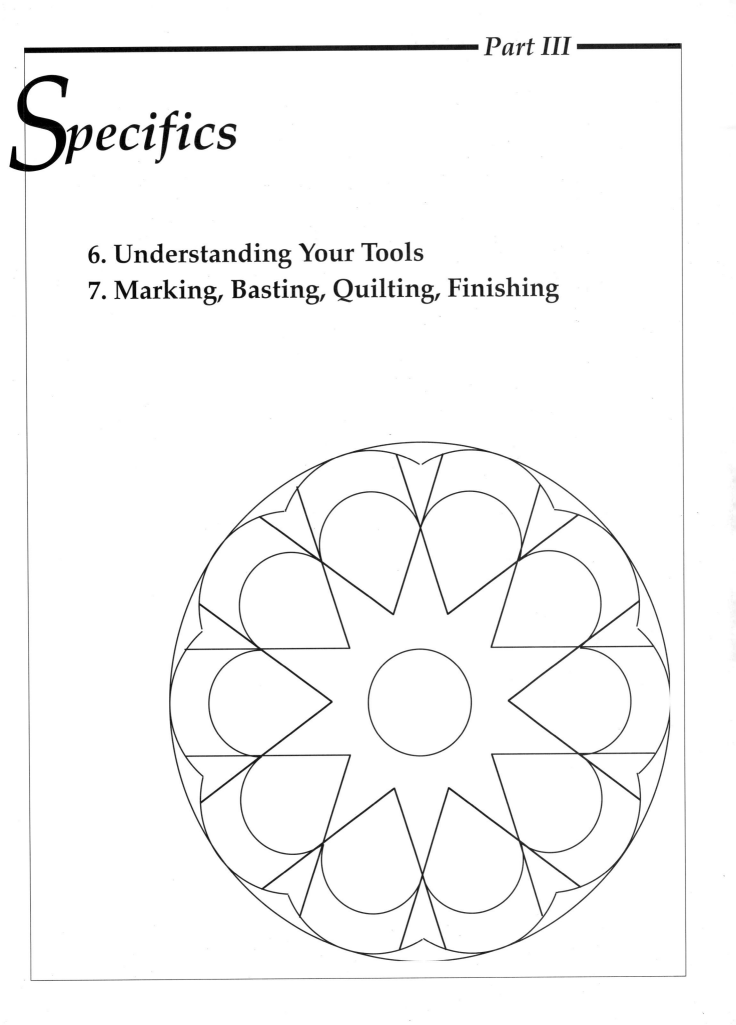

Left: *Iris Gowen, Kathmandu, Nepal,* Menagerie, *71" x 74", 1990. Used over 3,000 yards of orange thread, decorative stitches on the Bernina 1130, fabrics from over 12 countries. Photo by Karen Bell.*

Below: *Sonya Barrington, San Francisco, CA,* Bed Quilt, *86" x 93", 1993. Fabrics hand-dyed and marbled from Sonya's company, quilted by Dorie Whipple, with monofilament on a Bernina. Photo courtesy of the artist.*

Chapter 6

Understanding Your Tools

Get the right tool for the job. Your work will be easier and more pleasurable if you take the time to assemble the tools you need and to organize them in a usable way.

The more you machine quilt, the more you appreciate the value of using good tools. Here's an introduction to your choices, biased by what I use and like. For more in-depth information, see the Mini-Encyclopedia on page 220.

Machines

Is there one best sewing machine for machine quilting? Ask 100 quilters and you'll get 100 heated answers. I've sewn on all the top-of-the-line machines and can truthfully say that there is no one machine that has everything—and I love each one for something different, as if they were my children.

It is, however, worth owning a computer machine for these five features:

1. *Needle up/down.* By pushing a button, you tell the machine to end each stitch with the needle either up or down. How did we live without this feature? It makes quilting large items like quilts so much easier.

2. *Auto-lock.* Being able to push a button and have the machine stitch in one place several times simplifies machine quilting.

3. *Low-bobbin warning.* No more running out of thread and quilting miles before you realize it.

4. *Memory.* Playing with decorative stitches and quilting is addictive. Combining and storing stitches in memory means you can recall them at any time.

5. *Unlimited stitch patterns of great intricacy.* You say you won't use them? You probably would have said the same thing about a zigzag. I believe we rise to the level of our tools. I especially love the alphabets on computer machines. It delights everybody to receive quilted messages.

More important than the brand of machine you buy is the dealer you buy it from. A good dealer not only teaches how to use your magic machine, she or he keeps you inspired, informed, and enthusiastic.

Also important is to keep your machine clean and well oiled, especially in the bobbin area where a lot of lint collects. If as you quilt you notice one of the threads emerging from the bobbin area slightly dirty, stop quilting. Remove the squilt, presser foot, top and bobbin threads. Remove the needle plate. What you see may make you ashamed—clean out that disgusting lint. Even the best machine cannot make good stitches when lint collects.

For more in-depth information on machines and how to buy one, see page 256.

AN IMPROVED QUILTING MACHINE.

The accompanying cut represents a new and valuable attachment for all family sewing machines, as by its use one lady can quilt comforts, quilts, coat linings, dress skirts, and any other article which it is desired to have filled with cotton or wool. The construction is simple, and any one who can run a sewing machine can operate one provided with this attachment. The top of the work to be quilted is rolled up on the inside roller, and the lining of the goods is rolled up on the outside roller, the cotton or wool is laid on the lining,

DAVIS' NEW FAMILY QUILTING MACHINE.

Taking a machine to class? See the list of favorite portables on page 256. In the market for a new machine? See How to Buy a Sewing Machine on page 256 and Sewing Machine Wish List on page 257.

I like to clean out lint with a mini-vacuum set from Clotilde.

Sharman Neel of Muncie, IN, writes the kind and color number of her bobbin thread on peel-and-stick dots and puts one on the bobbin when it's not in use.

Machine Quilting

In addition to the open-toed, appliqué, walking, and darning feet, discussed in Chapter 1, I love these feet.

Patchwork foot: machined to be exactly 1/4" from the needle to the edge of the foot (generic versions fit any machine—see Resource list)

Blindhem foot: Not all brands are movable, but if yours is, you can get a perfect 1/4" seam allowance; also makes a wonderful edgestitch

Straight-stitch (or topstitch) needle plate: the round hole (rather than the wide slot of the zigzag plate) prevents the needle from letting the squilt dip into the hole just enough to cause puckers—standard equipment on some machines, extra on others (see chart on page 255). One reason the old treadles made such a beautiful stitch is that they had a small-hole needle plate and a narrow presser foot. Don't forget to change back to a wide needleplate for zigzag.

Left-sided presser foot: a less-expensive alternate to buying the straight-stitch needle plate for machines which can decenter the needle—decenter to the left and use this foot to hold the fabric securely as the needle enters the fabric

Buttonhole foot: has two parallel grooves on the underside to permit both rows of satin stitch to pass easily under the foot—can substitute for open-toed appliqué foot

Zipper foot: useful for quilt-as-you-go (see page 40) so the toe of the foot doesn't catch in batting; also for applying piping to edges

Roller foot: if you don't have an even-feed foot, you can pinch-hit with a roller foot. It helps to loosen presser-foot pressure, if your machine has this feature.

Quilting guide: movable gauge that attaches to the needle shaft and is guided along the previous line of quilting—not accurate enough for numerous straight parallel lines on a whole quilt, but fine for outline quilting, clothing, placemats, and other small items

Piping foot: has a groove underneath that allows you to make piping and attach it at the same time; also useful for corded quilting and appliquilting (see Chapter 3)

Binding foot: folds fabric over the edge perfectly but may be limited in width of finished edge and can be extraordinarily expensive on some brands ($100 and up)

Be sure you know the shank size of your machines (see page 10) because you can sometimes buy generic feet to fit. See the Resource list for companies that sell generic feet.

Presser Feet

Karen Johnson of Ishpeming, MI, took the metal straight-stitch foot for her Viking to her dealer. He ground it down to an exact 1/4", for which he charged her $3. What a deal!

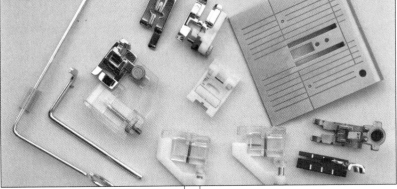

Helpful presser feet (clockwise from top): *Bernina straight-stitch plate, Bernina patchwork foot, Lynn Graves Little Foot, Creative Feet Satinedge Foot, Creative Feet Sequins 'N Ribbon Foot, New Home quilting guide, walking foot guide from Clotilde, generic binding foot from Treadleart, Viking buttonhole foot upside-down, Pfaff blindhem foot, Elna roller foot.*

Try to find the movable kind of zipper foot to fit your machine. It holds better and you can do more with decentering the needle.

There is now a quilting guide that will attach to a walking foot. Ask your favorite dealer or buy through mail order.

I am especially fond of Creative Feet's Satin-Edge Foot. It makes a beautiful satin stitch over a pin behind the bar.

Use Post-its to warn yourself you've changed needleplates or you will break as many needles as I have.

Machine Accessories

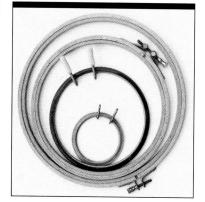

Screw-type hoops and spring hoops keep the squilt taut.

• Extra bobbins
They don't cost that much. Why not give yourself a present of ten extra bobbins? If you have wound a special thread onto a bobbin and don't want to forget which spool you used, poke a vegetable tie or pipe cleaner up through the center of the spool and the bobbin and twist the ends together. You can also buy bobbin holders which fit into the spool hole or over the top of the spool.

• Oil and brush
Follow the instructions for oiling your machine, making sure to use nothing but sewing machine oil. Because you are sewing three or more layers and because batting throws off an enormous amount of lint, you may need to oil more than once during a large project. Machines differ, but generally yours should run smoothly and quietly. If it clatters and sticks when you press the foot pedal, oil it.

If it still sticks, take it in to a good sewing machine store for cleaning and possible repair. It may require more than oil. The brushes inside my machine once wore out, which made it delay and stick when I pressed the foot pedal. No amount of oil could fix this, but a simple replacement of the brushes worked miracles.

• Machine-embroidery hoops
Keeps the squilt, top, and/or backing fabric taut, depending on what technique you're using. There are many types of embroidery hoops to choose from. While the spring type are easier to move around the fabric, you may not be able to fasten them on regular-loft batting.

New attachments, feet, and accessories are constantly being developed for use on your machine. Keep in touch with your local sewing machine store for new developments.

Needles, Machine

For more complete information on needles, see page 239.

I keep track of what needle is in the machine by writing on Post-it Notes.

Keep a full range of sizes from 8/60 to 16/100, universal and sharp (H-J), as well as the novelty needles like twin and triple, leather, wing. Since machine quilting calls for sizes 10/70 – 14/90 most often, buy an extra package of those sizes. If you have trouble reading the sizes on the needle, paint the base (non-sharp end) of the needle with fingernail polish or model airplane paint and put a corresponding dot of polish or paint on the needle package or case. Then religiously return color-coded needles to their correct package. (Roberta Losey Patterson's idea is good enough that the companies which produce machine needles should follow it and save us the trouble.)

Be sure to use the needles recommended for your machine. Some needles have a deeper scarf than others (significance of scarf explained on page 239). If stitches are being skipped on an expensive machine, it's a good bet that inexpensive needles are being used.

Return a used needle to the package turned over so the flat side faces out. Then you'll know that's not a new needle. (Throw used needles away after every major project.)

It is the handling of thread that sets machine quilting apart from hand quilting. (Once it was realized that the secrets were in using two threads, not one as for hand sewing, and putting the eye in the pointed end of the needle, the lockstitch sewing machine was invented in the 1830's.) We can use different colors and types of threads in top and bobbin, more than doubling the design possibilities.

This is not a new idea. In the delightful and scholarly *Quilts in America* (see Bibliography), the Orlofskys report "To emphasize the fact that she was using a sewing machine, the [late 1800's] quilter used threads of different color to quilt and to give prominence to the quilting stitch as well as for decorative purposes. Quilts of the period frequently show white thread quilting on red, green, or brown material."

The choice of thread for machine quilting depends on what technique you're using, how large the quilted item is, whether it is whole-cloth (such as a sheet) or constructed in blocks, how close together the quilting lines are, and what fabrics you've chosen. For example, when stitching with the presser foot on, any thread you use for regular sewing or hand quilting may be used. On the other hand, for free-machine quilting, I prefer to use extra-fine machine-embroidery thread on top (see Resource list).

Years from now, after your machine-quilting has been through the washer/dryer several dozen times, you will appreciate the subtleties of thread/fabric selection. It's better if you prepare for it now, while you are constructing the project.

If you're making a wallhanging or special clothing that won't be washed, you can use almost any thread. For washable home-dec projects like placemats and for quilts, use almost any thread. Since it's easier to repair stitches than shredded fabric at seamlines, try to choose thread less strong than your top fabric. For example, use cotton-covered polyester thread for piecing and quilting if both the backing and quilt-top fabrics are polyester blends. Otherwise use sewing-weight (not extra-fine machine-embroidery) 100% cotton thread.

Some rayon threads have a nasty habit of slipping down off the spool and tangling themselves on the thread holder of your machine. You don't notice this until the thread mysteriously breaks. Some machines have a special gadget to prevent this or have horizontal thread holders, but Jane Warnick of Houston, TX, suggests circumventing the problem by taping a tapestry needle, eye-up, between the spool and the first thread guide on your machine.

Another way that helps is to cut a 1" tube of Surgitube, a knit material sold in pharmacies meant for finger splints. Slip it on the spool. It doesn't impede the flow of the thread.

If that doesn't work, try a thread stand behind the machine, both for larger cones of thread and for slippery threads.

Threads for Machine Quilting

You can never have enough threads.

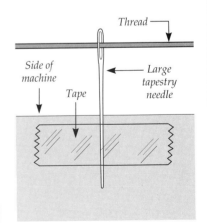

Tape a tapestry needle to the machine to the left of the spool and run the thread through it before the first thread guide. This keeps the thread from slipping off the spool.

You can rig a thread stand by punching a hole in each end of a strip of template plastic cut 1" x 4". Hang it off the back of the vertical thread holder, tape the end to the machine with artist's tape, put the thread in a cup or small jar, and thread it up through the hole and the regular tension guides.

I would not use monofilament in a baby quilt. I've heard too many scare stories about dogs requiring surgery after swallowing monofilament thread and babies getting caught in leftover loops.

Sometimes when you're free-machine quilting with monofilament and turn a corner or curve, the strength of the nylon pulls the bobbin thread to the surface. Kaye Wood taught me a simple trick: lock the thread two or three times in the corner before continuing to stitch. I wish I'd known this before I made Nicky's Quilt (see page xiv). (Fortunately, he and his parents know nothing about thread burbles. They love the quilt and the accompanying book.)

Stephanie Cornet of Tempe, AZ, who has a machine-quilting business called Quilt Works, loves metallics but would only use them in wallhangings or in quilts that will be rolled, not folded. She has noticed that the metallic thread in a five-year-old quilt are breaking on the fold lines.

See page 238 for the Fabric/Thread/Needle Chart and page 250 for a more in-depth discussion of threads.

Extra-fine monofilament nylon thread (size .004) in the top and/or bobbin gives a machine-quilted item almost a hand-quilted look. However, it is extremely strong and doesn't give. If stress is put on your quilt, such as hanging over an edge, the fabric will rip before the invisible thread breaks. Also if you goof and have to rip out stitches, it leaves holes and may shred fabric. On smaller-than-bed quilts, there's no problem.

Because my eyes are getting worse, I often cannot see the end of the monofilament thread to thread it through the needle. I keep a permanent black Sharpie pen next to the machine and dot the end of the thread with it. Then I can aim the dot at the eye of the needle.

Be careful about using monofilament nylon in plastic bobbins. Sometimes they explode when you're winding them. Some people compensate by winding only half-full bobbins. Wind the bobbins slowly so the thread won't stretch and don't put it through the winding tension guides. Use your fingers as a tension guide.

Metallics have gotten finer in recent years and now come in a dazzling array of colors. Use a needle expressly designed for metallics, like the Lammertz, or a topstitching needle. Putting a line of silicone lubricant like Sewer's Aid or Sew Slick directly on the spool can also help keep the thread from fraying.

Keep your eye open for new threads. Some are not directly related to quilting, but will make other parts of the process easier. For example, loading ThreadFuse, a fusible thread, into the bobbin when making double-fold binding (see page 229) means you can fuse the binding into place for a temporary bond before the final stitching.

Deb Wagner taught me to use Wash-away Thread in the top and ThreadFuse in the bobbin on appliqués. Straight stitch around the shape. Cut away excess and fuse appliqué in place. Satin stitch with a narrow width. This makes a beautiful edge.

If you see thread you like, buy a lot. Remember that a king-size quilt can take 1300 yards of thread—or more!

Two matters cannot be stressed enough: 1) test threads and needle sizes on a test squilt before quilting; and 2) buy the best quality thread you can afford. The cheaper thread frays, breaks, and shreds over the years. It's not worth saving pennies if it later causes hours of work.

One of the many joys of machine quilting is that, unlike hand quilting, any washable fabric is fair game, from the traditional 100% cotton to closely woven polyester-blend sheets to double knits to corduroy to velour to denim. You can use non-washable fabrics, too, if you're willing to handwash or dry-clean the project (I have seen a breathtaking leather, Ultrasuede, and fur quilt). Keep in mind that a quilt top pieced of wools, corduroys, or denims is extremely heavy when it is quilted. So if you use one of the heavier top materials, choose a lightweight batting like interfacing fleece, light flannel, or thin polyester batting. Alternately, leave out the filler and quilt directly to a backing (say, flannel sheets).

Be sure to play with the many hand-dyed fabrics today. (See Resource list.) They give a special look to quilted projects.

Fabric Selection

Four characteristics of fabrics play important roles in machine quilting:

1. Weight and texture
2. Scale of pattern (large or small)
3. Washability
4. Color and value

Weight and Texture

The light- to medium-weight fabrics (especially 100% cotton) have traditionally been used in quiltmaking because it is easy to push a short sharp needle through them by hand. We machine quilters do not have to so limit ourselves, as long as we realize that the heavier the material used, the more the overall weight of the project increases. Thus you should choose correspondingly lighter battings and backings as the top increases in weight. Also be sure the mixture of fabrics in the quilt top is compatible in weight; heavy corduroy used in one area and light-weight cotton in another will not hang, feel, or wear right unless you carefully balance the areas. With a little care in planning, you can exploit the machine's ability to handle different textures and weights. You can then use all kinds of fabrics in your quilts—furry, ribbed, satiny, bumpy.

A loose way to gauge fabric weight for quilting is by how you'd use it in general sewing:

- *Lightweight fabrics* are those you'd make a blouse or shirt from—calicoes, ginghams, most sheets, and similar weight fabrics.
- *Medium-weight fabrics* are those suitable for skirts and pants—poplin, Kettlecloth, double knits, and such.
- *Heavy-weight fabrics* are those for jackets and duffel bags—denim, duck, canvas, and the like.

Fabrics for Machine Quilting

Fabrics with metallic highlights should not be dry-cleaned because the process dulls the highlights and makes them fade. Instead, machine wash in warm water in the gentle cycle and tumble dry on low.

Appropriate fabrics for backings are discussed in *Chapter 5. Applications* for each category: quilts, clothing, interiors, crafts.

Large, medium, small: what is the scale of your fabric?

Also see the Fabric Care Chart in the Mini-Encyclopedia on page 238x.

Beware of fabrics that are so lightweight and light-colored that seams show through the top. This is especially important in one-step quilting (see Chapter 3), where you cannot choose which way to press the seams. When you are buying fabric, make sure that you're not fooled about its weight by feeling the doubled fabric. Slip your hand over one thickness and crush it lightly. Does it wrinkle easily? Then it won't look right tied or if the quilting lines are far apart. Turn the edge under with your fingers. Can you see the "seam" through the top of the fabric? Be wary. But if such a lightweight fabric has a special color or texture that you simply must use, back the fabric with another piece of lightweight light-colored fabric, treating the two as one.

Scale of Pattern

Since this book does not discuss piecing of quilt tops (except directly to batting), I'll ignore the ramifications of large vs. small prints. See the Bibliography on page 266 for good books on this subject. If, however, you plan to quilt a preprinted design, carefully match the scale (large, medium, small) of the print to your experience with machine quilting. On a large quilt, for example, an inexperienced quilter may feel more confident using a hoop. This is easier than wrestling the bulk of a whole quilt unaided. Can the motif you've chosen fit into a hoop? If not, you could build the quilt around large prints cut into smaller pieces, machine quilting the designs and inserting borders.

Washability

Once you discover that you can use almost any material for machine quilting, you may forget in your enthusiasm that one of the beauties of machine-quilted projects is their easy care in washing machines. Think twice about using scraps of non-washable fabrics like wool, silk, felt, or leather, if you will need to clean your projects often. Of course, if you are machine-quilting a wall-hanging, then you needn't worry about washability very much, and you can let your imagination go wild.

For clothing, you can have them dry-cleaned (although a dry-cleaner ruined the gorgeous quilted wedding dress by Marina Brown shown in our *The Complete Book of Machine Embroidery*).

For very large quilts (double-bed and up), you may find it easier on you and the quilts to wash and dry them in the large machines at a laundromat. Pulling a large wet quilt out of a small home washer puts tremendous strain on the quilting thread, which may break.

Make life easier on yourself: when you buy fabric, jot down the fiber content and the care information on your sales slip, with an identifying phrase ("green polka dot"). When you get home, cut off the selvage and staple an inch of it next to the fabric description, date bought, yardage, and price in one of your Sewing Notebooks (see page 15).

Color (and Value)

Color is the one quality of fabric that makes people gasp with pleasure. However color, like love, does not exist alone in the world; it is defined and changed by everything around it. Put an all-red quilt in a bedroom with black walls and it won't look at all like the same quilt in a white-walled bedroom. Similarly, each color you choose to put in a project is affected by the colors around it.

Organize the fabrics you're considering first into piles of darks, mediums, and lights, and then by color. If you're not sure which of these three values (light, medium, or dark) a color has, stand back from it and squint. Usually, this reduces what you see to light, medium, or dark grays.

If you own an instant camera, take black-and-white pictures of your fabrics to check the values. Another trick is to cut off 2"-wide strips of the fabrics you're considering; paste, tape, or staple to paper; and make a photocopy of the fabrics (the copy-machine operator may look at you as if you're insane, but just give instructions to lay the fabric side face-down on the glass plate, and smile).

Several devices help judge value. I use a small gray scale, available in art stores. It has holes cut into gray bands. When you hold the scale over fabric, it quickly becomes apparent where a color falls on the gray scale.

You can also buy a Fabric Value Filter and a Ruby Beholder tool for colorwash quilts (see That Patchwork Place in the Resource list). A former student uses the red acetate on report covers for the same task.

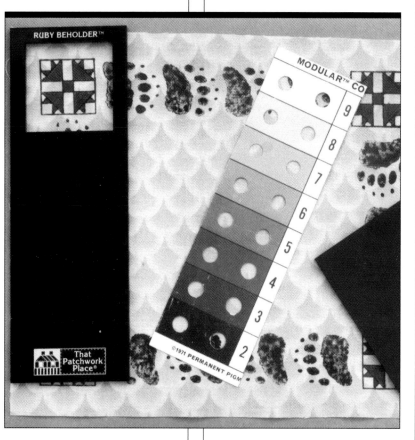

Be sure to examine any fabric you're considering buying in natural light. The fluorescent lighting in many fabric stores changes the true color of a fabric. Also look at the underside of the fabric—sometimes it looks better than the top.

If you work full-time and have time to sew only at night, think twice about working on dark fabrics—browns, navys, purples. Tired eyes have trouble following the quilting line.

Tools to help judge value: *Value Viewer bought long ago, Modular viewer from acrylic paint set, Ruby Beholder from That Patchwork Place, all on top of stamped fabric from Pelle.*

To preshrink fabric, wet it thoroughly (it's already clean, so you don't have to wash it with detergent), spin out the excess water, and put the fabric in the dryer. Clip across the corners or serge the raw edges to prevent a tangle of threads.

For intense colors like red, wash separately. Then wash again, safety-pinning a square of clean white fabric to it. If the white fabric is pink after washing, wash again, testing a new white square of fabric.

Research seems to show that putting salt or vinegar in the water to set dyes does not work, but some of us do it anyway.

Preventing shrinkage is not the only reason to preshrink: it removes the resinous finish on new fabrics which can deflect the needle on cantakerous machines and cause skipped stitches.

Fabric Preparation

To Preshrink or Not To Preshrink: The Great Batting/Wheel Cover Test

I come out of a garment-construction background and have always preshrunk fabric without thinking. The minute I get fabric home from the store, I throw it into the next wash, then dry it.

When our daughter, Kali, was a teenager, she was inspired by Anita Hallock's *Fast Patch* to make a small quilt. She picked out the fabric and design, we cut and strip-pieced it together, and she disappeared. I was having fun, however, so I finished the piece and quilted it with a zigzag in a few Saturday morning hours, listening to Eric Ambler's *Light of Day* on tape. The finished quilt was beautifully starched and pressed, but I needed to wash out the marking lines. When it emerged from the dryer, it was all wrinkled. I was dismayed.

Kali said, "Oh, Mom! It's beautiful—it looks like a *real* quilt!"

This prompted me to wonder what would happen if I didn't preshrink the fabric or batting.

Meanwhile, new battings were appearing all the time. I wondered how they would hold up in machine-quilted quilts. Would they beard on dark fabrics? Would they pull away from lines of stitching?

At the same time, as a person who doodles endless circles, I became aware of the beauty of wheel covers on cars. (Hubcaps are not the same thing as wheel covers.) Look around at the next parking lot. See all the magnificent machine-quilting patterns on wheel covers? I bought a Polaroid, put a towel in my car, and began jumping out and flinging myself on the ground next to tires, hoping I'd live through the photography session before an incoming car flattened me.

I put everything together in The Great Batting/Wheel Cover Test. Read through what I did not only for the batting information, but for the various construction tips. You are making a quilt in miniature and the principles apply to bigger objects.

Kali's real *quilt.*

I bought three yards of off-white muslin and three yards of navy blue cotton. Using my Bias Square from That Patch-

Machine Quilting

work Place, I cut nine 8" squares of each fabric and of nine low-loft battings, including polyester, cotton, and cotton blend.

On each navy square, I free-machine embroidered the name of the batting with white DMC size 50 cotton, using a hoop. On each white square I ironed a laser print of the wheel covers Tony designed on the computer. (The lines do not completely wash out, so you have to cover each line well.)

I decided to make finished pillows that could be tied together for display, so I included 12" lengths of polyester twill tape at the centers of all sides. These I first basted to the edge of the white muslin, then pinned them out of the way in the center.

Rightsides together with the batting underneath, I stitched around the 8" squilt, leaving a small opening for turning and taking two tiny stitches across corners. Gaye Kriegel, Assistant Editor of *The Creative Machine Newsletter*, taught me to stitch on and off at openings, as it makes a better edge for closing.

I trimmed the batting close to the stitching and pressed the top seam allowance back on itself to get a better turned edge. Then I trimmed the corners and turned the squilt rightside out. At opposite corners, I tied the tape in a loose overhand knot so it wouldn't get caught in the stitching. Finally, I edge-stitched the squilt, closing the opening at the same time.

Many of the machines have circle-making devices, but the Elna 9000 makes it easy by putting holes in the flat-bed extension. I skewered the center of the wheel cover design with the pin Elna provides and stitched the circle with the roller foot (because at the time I didn't have a walking foot).

Then I used my Bernina 1230 to free-machine quilt the inside of the wheel cover. The knee lift on the Bernina that raises and lowers the darning foot allows you to leave your hands on the work at all times—a joy.

I used Mettler 02 extra-fine cotton thread in the top and a 12/80 H-J needle. I tried a universal point first, but it

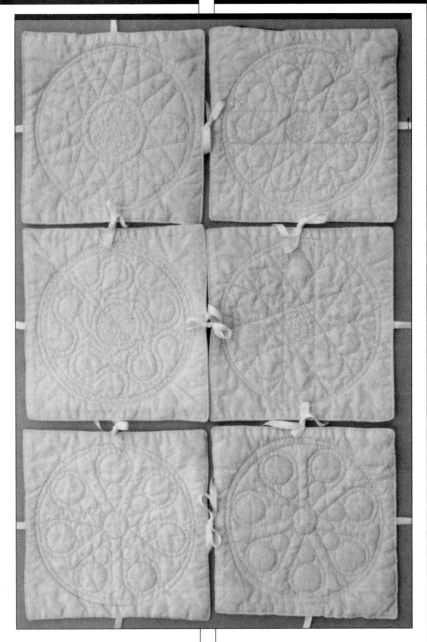

Unshrunk fabric and batting measurements after washing, right to left, top to bottom:

Glory Bee I, 6-5/8" square; Cotton Choice, 6-1/2" x 6-5/8"

Old Fashion Cotton, 6-3/4" square; Thermore, 6-5/8" x 6-3/4"

Cotton Classic, 6-1/2" x 6-3/4"; Poly-down, 6-5/8" square

Left shows previously unshrunk fabric and batting after washing, right shows preshrunk fabric and batting after washing and using identical designs. Measurements are (starting top):

Warm & Natural
6-1/2" x 6-3/4"; 6-5/8" square

Heirloom Cotton
6-5/8" x 6-3/4"; 6-5/8" square

Quilt-Light
6-5/8" x 6-3/4"; 6-3/4" square

seemed to catch slightly. The sharp HJ point punched easily through all layers.

When you are working with a light thread on top, a dark thread underneath, low-loft batting, and free-machine quilting, little dots of one color or the other are going to show here and there. If it bothers you on the dark side, you can cheat a bit by coloring the thread with a permanent fine-point pen. On the light side, hope that your friends will think the salt-and-pepper effect is what you intended.

When I was done stitching, I threw the mini-quilt into the wash. Then I measured it. Each squilt measured 7-1/8" before quilting. Each washed mini-quilt shrank at a different rate. Also, sometimes the quilt shrank more in one direction than another.

To make the experiment even more valuable, I repeated the same designs and battings on preshrunk fabric and preshrunk batting (when called for) for three battings I use often. The photo shows what they looked like after washing.

What did I learn?

1. *Quilts:* For quilts that will be washed, I don't like surprises. I would preshrink the fabric and batting. It may not puff up as much after washing, but it will be the size I planned. (If you were to preshrink the fabric but not the batting, the batting might pull away from the stitches as it shrank the first time you washed it.)

2. *Clothing:* For clothing that will be washed and where I want an antique-puffy look, I would not preshrink the fabric or batting. I would quilt yardage, serge the edges, wash the yardage so that the quilting would puff up, and then cut out the garment.

3. *Interiors:* For wallhangings that will never be washed: It is harder to achieve a noticeable quilted look when the piece will not be washed. I often don't preshrink fabrics for wallhangings, and I use regular-loft polyester battings.

4. *Crafts:* Why bother to preshrink?

Preparation of Fabric: Five Steps

1. Decide whether or not to preshrink your fabric (see discussion above). If you are of the Always Preshrink School, as I am, preshrink fabric as soon as you get home from the store, even if you won't use it immediately. (Directions are on page 174.)

2. Cut off the selvage, which may shrink at a different rate than the rest of the fabric and should not be used in quiltmaking. This means the usable width of your fabric is 1" – 2" less than the given width. Keep this fact in mind when estimating yardage.

If you can't cut off the selvage, as with the F.A.S.T. Baby Quilt on page 105, clip it on the diagonal.

3. Straighten the crosswise edges. Do this either by tearing across an end, cutting perpendicular to the fold, or pulling one thread across an end.

To tear or not to tear, that is the question. The answer is yet another question: can you make accurate seams if you tear? The edges of torn fabric vary from perfectly behaved to dreadfully rippled and stretched. The only way to find out is to tear a sample from your fabric, both cross-wise and along the selvage. Press it lightly and examine the results—can you sew 1/4" from the torn edge accurately, or are the edge fibers puckered and unhappy?

If the latter, you must cut your fabric. Straighten the grain at both ends of the fabric by pulling one thread all the way across; then use the space where the thread was as a cutting guide. Sometimes the thread breaks partway. Pull it out, cut as far as you can, pick out the broken thread end with a pin, and pull again until you're all the way across the fabric.

4. Decide whether to straighten the grain. Fold the fabric in half lengthwise. Pin lengthwise edge and straightened ends. If fabric doesn't lie flat, take out pins and gently pull on the bias. Some permanent press fabrics have the grain permanently locked in and you can't straighten it.

In the years since the first edition of this book, fabric seems to be less and less on-grain. Since it wastes a lot of fabric to straighten the grain, a lot of people don't bother, figuring the machine quilting will stabilize the fabric.

Think about the size of cut fabric you're using for the project. If it's a large expanse of fabric to be quilted and you leave it off-grain, on a wall your quilt may hang unevenly. On a bed it usually doesn't matter. If you're cutting the fabric into many strips and pieces, the seamlines and quilting will stabilize the fabric.

If you're following the design on the fabric in cutting, ignore grain and go for straight lines of design.

5. Iron and spray-starch your fabric. The starch makes lightweight fabric in top and/or backing firmer and less likely to pucker as you cut and sew it. Once the project is quilted, it's not easy to iron. I spray-starch the back in case

I understand that the sizing in 100% cotton resists mildew. If you live in damp areas, maybe you shouldn't prewash until you're ready to use the fabric.

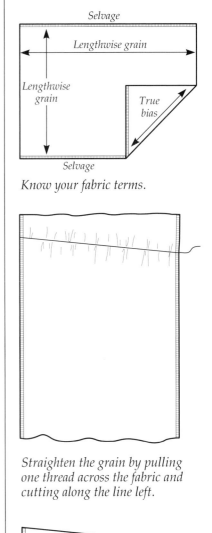

Know your fabric terms.

Straighten the grain by pulling one thread across the fabric and cutting along the line left.

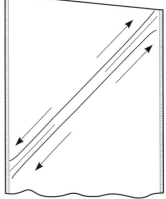

If after straightening the angle is not 90°, pull gently on the bias of the fabric until the grain is straightened.

the iron leaves flakes. Then I can still use the fabric in wallhangings, which will never be washed, and the starch flakes won't show. Barbara Zagnoni of Rowenta tells me that if I were more patient and let the starch be absorbed by the fabric before ironing, I wouldn't have flakes.

Deb Wagner says that when you mark a spray-starched fabric with temporary marking pens, they disappear in the first wash, as if sliding off with the starch.

Collecting Fabric

Official truth: The reason we work is to make enough money to buy more fabric—and sewing machines and sergers and notions and….

However, some people have less money available for fabric. For my student daughter's first king-size quilt, for example, paying $8 – $9/yard times many yards was more than her grocery budget for the month. Therefore, it helps to have other fabric sources in addition to fabric stores. Here are a few suggestions. In each of these cases, you will not be shopping for specific colors for a specific quilt, but stockpiling for the future.

Garage and tag sales are good places to find interesting, cheap fabric. I restrict myself and buy only if there are at least three yards of a fabric available. Otherwise I'd be knee-deep in small scraps of pretty but unused fabric.

Thrift shops also often sell yardage or used sheets, which are easily dyed. Don't forget to look at the old ties there. Many are part or all silk and can be combined with other fabrics for crazy-quilt and string-quilt projects.

The want ads in local and "shopper" newspapers sometimes list yardage for sale. You can also advertise in free neighborhood papers for "cotton yardage or used sheets" with some success. (As I said, white sheets are easy to dye. Snap them up whenever you see them.)

If you live near an industrial area, call clothing, shirt, and bridal factories to see if and when they sell off bolt ends. Check in a good bookstore or your public library for local guides to bargain hunting (also do this during your travels to metropolitan areas while on vacation).

And finally, if you belong to a quilting guild, arrange a periodic fabric swap/sale. It's surprising how often someone else's discards will fill in your fabric collection.

In writing this section, I mistyped fabric hoard as "horde." The image of a large moving throng of yardage appeared: "Let's all move under the guest bed!" "No, let's take over the linen closet! the extra bedroom! under the table in the living room!"

Unlike our ancestors, who had only wool or cotton batting (or the less satisfactory newspaper, pine needles, or horsehair), we have a wide choice of fillers for our quilted projects today. Machine quilting gives even more latitude than hand quilting because the machine can handle such difficult materials as foam, down, and blankets. I prefer to choose batting first by loft, then by final effect wanted, then by fiber. For quilts, once I've made these decisions, I look at size, then choose a brand.

In choosing batting for machine quilting, first choose loft:

- *Low loft:* up to 1/4" thick
- *Regular loft:* 1/4" to 1/2" thick
- *High loft:* thicker than 1/2"

Choose the loft according to your experience and the technique. The thicker the loft, the more experience needed.

If you are making clothing or large heavily quilted quilts, work with low or regular loft. The more loft, the more difficult it is to get the squilt under the head of the machine. Also, the higher the loft, the porkier you feel in quilted clothing.

Why would you choose high loft? For machine-tied comforters or wall hangings with little quilting.

Next choose the final effect you want.

A lot depends on: 1) how you will care for the final piece—wash it? dryclean it? hang it?; 2) the look you want from machine quilting—the puckered look of antique quilting? puffy areas next to areas matted by stitching?; and 3) what materials you use in it—lamé? suede? fur?

The results of the Great Batting/Wheel Cover Test on page 175 can help you decide, but tests you do for yourself are better. When you plan a project that is washable, use the instructions on page 174 to construct tests with fabric and batting that is both preshrunk and not preshrunk (of course, polyester batting does not need to be preshrunk).

The chart on the next page should help you ask some questions about the effects you want from machine quilting.

Finally, choose fiber.

If you are allergic to man-made fibers, your choice is simple: cotton, wool, or silk.

Cotton batting is still available to quilters. It is a thin batt which makes it easy to handle (and which is why old-time hand quilters were able to get so many stitches per inch). It must be quilted no less than 2" apart to hold the batting securely. It is better used as one large piece than cut up for modules or quilt-as-you-go, as it tends to tear away from machine seams.

Wool and silk batting are new on the scene. The newest wool battings are machine-washable. Silk must be encased

Batting

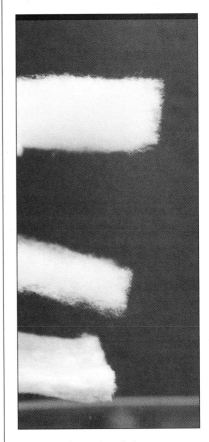

High, medium, low loft.

See the batting charts on page 224 for specific brand information.

Look desired	Washed	Worn and drycleaned	Displayed
Antique puckered	Work design on yardage. Then wash fabrics and batt (if part cotton). Plan for at least 5% shrinkage. Use low- or regular-loft batting.	What you see is what you get. If it isn't readable as antique machine quilting when worked, it never will be. Will it be hot? What will happen to closures in drycleaning? Use any fabric except those with metallic highlights (see note in Chapter 6).	Must use washable fabrics to achieve this look. Wash after quilting and before constructing final hanging.
Flat pressed	Preshrink fabrics and battings. Starch heavily. Consider using polycottons to maintain flat-pressed look if quilting will not be close together.	Design is more important than fiber content of fabric. Use colored or metallic thread and elaborate quilting.	One-step quilting (Chapter 3) good technique. Starch heavily on underside of fabric. Use regular- to high-loft batting.
Three-dimensional	Use poly batting in regular to high loft. Plan for quilting to shrink in item. Preshrink fabrics.	Must use regular- to high-loft batting. Quilt first on pieces cut at least 2" larger than final shape.	No need to stick to 100% cottons—use anything that works (wools, velvets, lamés). Plan to vacuum piece and display out of sunlight. Use high-loft batting.

G Street Fabrics and Keepsake Quilting both sell a sampler of battings.

between layers of china silk before adding the top and bottom layers, to prevent bearding of fibers through the outside layers.

For the rest of us, the choices are mind-boggling: cotton/poly blends and polyester with various finishes.

The only way to choose is to try them all. Buy 1/4 yard of everything you can find. Be sure to label brand, name, and loft immediately, because you will forget. (I store them with labels in large Ziploc bags.) Test them as I did on page 174. Then keep track of the results in your Sewing Notebook (see page 15).

The G Street batting sampler.

One note: Polyester battings are often sold by weight, instead of loft. The two are unrelated. Two battings can have different weights but have the same loft.

Packaged batts are sold in pound weights. Obviously a quilt made with 2-1/2 pound batting will be warmer than 1-1/4 pound batting. Batting on the bolt is sold in ounce weights, meaning how many ounces a yard weighs. For comparison, a 3-1/2 oz. 45"-wide batting is roughly equivalent in weight to a 1-1/4 pound 81" x 96" packaged batt. But you still won't know the loft of the batting. The charts on page 15 will help with brand-name battings and their loft.

If you are making quilts for warmth as much as for decoration, choose a heavier weight batting. Also useful as batting are interfacing fleece, old blankets and quilts, flannel (yardage or sheets), mattress pads, down, pre-quilted remnants, and old clean nylons.

If not secured immediately by seaming or a machine-quilted line, batts from a bolt should be pieced together with either a large herringbone stitch or a three-step zigzag on the machine (loosen top tension). Otherwise, they will pull apart from each other over the years of washing.

For a more complete discussion of batting, see page 220.

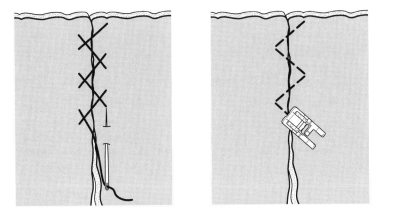

Piece batts with a hand herringbone stitch or a machine multiple zigzag or serpentine stitch.

Before using packaged batting, take it out and let it rest, preferably overnight. If you're in a hurry, you can steam it by holding an iron over it. (Don't let the iron touch the batting.)

Stabilizers

HTC's Easy Stitch, Sulky's Totally Stable, Palmer/Pletsch's Perfect Sew, Clotilde's No-Whiskers, Sulky's Water Soluble Stabilizer, HTC's RinsAway.

Anything that puts stress on the fibers of your quilt may need additional stabilizing. Satin-stitch quilting (see page 35), for example, pulls in the fibers. You have at least six choices for stabilizers:

1. *Wet stabilizers.* My first choice is to starch the daylights out of any fabric. For appliqué, you may want to stiffen the fabric in a non-permanent way, unlike fusing something to the back. Two products help:
A. Dissolve water-soluble stabilizer in water until it is a gooey mess. Soak your fabric in it and let it dry. After quilting, the stabilizer will wash out.
B. Spread Perfect Sew, a product invented by George Bodnar of Australia, on the fabric. I use an old credit card to spread it, but Nancy Ward, author of *Fabric Painting Made Easy*, also recommends a collar stay. You can hurry the drying process by using a hair dryer.

2. *Tear-away stabilizers.* These can be paper or fabric. If the former, use typing-weight paper. I like doctor's examining paper (see Resource list); Sharee Dawn Roberts, author of *Creative Machine Art*, likes deli sandwich paper, which you can sometimes buy in discount warehouses like the Price Club or Costco.
   Other tear-aways are Stitch 'N Tear, Tear-Away, HTC's Easy Stitch and RinsAway and Clotilde's No-Whiskers.
   The difficulty with all of the tear-aways comes with straight-stitch quilting, free or presser foot on. When you tear, you may distort the stitches. Be sure to experiment on your test squilt.

3. *Press-on stabilizers.* Specifically made for machine work, Totally Stable by Sulky can be used and reused. You can also use waxed freezer paper, ironing the shiny side onto the underside of the squilt. To remove either of these, press gently and pull away the excess.

4. *Rinse-away stabilizers.* Water-soluble stabilizer can be used on top or underneath a squilt. If it doesn't seem to be doing the job, use two or more layers. Be sure to save all the scraps you tear off. Keep them in a see-through bag. Then you can later use them as a wet stabilizer (see #1 above).
   A new product is GlissenGloss Melt-A-Way by Madeira, which dissolves in near-boiling water. This is obviously only appropriate for small projects that can be immersed.

5. *Fabric stabilizers.* If your project allows, use a heavier weight fabric in the backing, such as denim. (See page 137.) It also helps puff the quilting on the front more.

6. *Your stabilizer.* What have you discovered?

As manufacturers pay attention to our needs, they are producing new fusibles and glues that are exciting. The paper-backed fusible webs for appliqué become stronger yet more lightweight; repositionable glues are available to help "baste" batting and make templates movable.

Here are some good brands. Ask your favorite store to order them for you. See the Resource list for other sources.

- *Fusible webs.* Solar-Kist's Fine Fuse and Tuf-Fuse; HTC's Stitch Witchery; Dritz's Stitch Witchery; and Pellon's Wonder-Web require the use of a Teflon pressing sheet because they are not paper-backed.

- *Paper-backed fusible webs.* Aleene's Hot Stitch Fusible Web; Dritz's Magic Fuse, Stitch Witchery Plus With Grid; HTC's TransWeb, Stitch Witchery Plus, and TransBond; Pellon's Wonder-Under; Sew Art's AppliHesive; and Therm O Web's HeatnBond Original and HeatnBond Lite

- *Liquid fusible glue.* Beacon's Liqui Fuse

- *Repositionable spray glues.* Gunold + Stickma's KK100, Sprayway 22, Plaid's Stikit Again and Again

- *Permanent spray glues.* Osage County Factory's Good Glue, Sprayway 66

- *Repositionable glues.* Dritz's Insta-Tack, Kuretake's Zig 2Way Glue (can also be permanent), Clotilde's Sticky Stuff, EZ International's Stick 'n Stitch

- Wash-out glues: Clotilde's No-Pin Basting, any gluestick

- *Permanent glues.* Aleene's White Glue, Stop Fraying, OK-to-Wash-It; Slomons' Stitchless Fabric Glue; Dritz's Liquid Stitch; Kuretake's Zig 2Way Glue (can also be temporary); Velcro Adhesive; Plexi 400 Stretch Adhesive; No-Sew Adhesive; EZ Fabric Glue; Fabric Mender; Brohman's Glu-N-Wash; Unique Stitch; Eclectic Products' E6000, Goop; Beacon's Gem Tac, Fabri Tac

If you are spray-gluing, be sure to protect your surface with paper and to work in a well-ventilated area.

Fusibles and Glues

Stan Rising Co. manufactures a bag called Needle Release. If your needle gets gummed up with fusibles, stitch directly through the bag several times to clean the needle. See the Resource list.

If your fusibles get wrinkled, press them lightly between a Teflon sheet folded over the fusible. When the Teflon cools, you can pull the fusible off it.

As I went to press, Tammy Young was writing a comprehensive book on glue for crafters. Ask your retailer for the exact title.

Irons, Presses, and Boards

A good steam iron is a must. If you're buying one, read *Consumer Reports* magazine (available in your public library) to find out what's the best buy for the money. Then look for a thick soleplate that stays hot while producing a lot of steam.

Be sure to use whatever kind of water the manufacturer recommends—not necessarily distilled water, as in the old days.

One iron is not enough if you do a lot of sewing and quilting. I have different irons for different reasons.

I am so totally spoiled by my Sussman gravity-fed iron (an iron used by professional tailors) that I have considered stealing an IV-unit from the doctor so that I can take my iron to class with me.

Sometimes you only need finger pressure to press a seam, as in one-step quilting or tubes. Ardco Templates sells a wooden "iron"—an angled piece that presses seams nicely. (See Resource list.) Another nice, small iron is Tower Hobbies' Custom Sealing Iron, recommended to me by Nancy Ward. It is available in craft stores.

Anita Hallock uses a curling iron to press seams before turning fabric tubes.

Having a press is also useful for fusing fabric, for drying spray-starched fabric quickly, and for ironing lengths of preshrunk fabric.

An adjustable ironing board with sturdy legs is convenient for setting up right next to your machine chair so you don't have to get up to press seams. I have the June Tailor Quilter's Cut 'n Press behind my machine on a table. I can easily swivel around and press small pieces.

You can also rig a temporary ironing board by using a cardtable, board on chair arms, table top, or stool, using a towel or blanket as an ironing pad (or make the Machine-Quilting Sampler on page 78).

If you have a Teflon cover on your board, replace it with a heavy 100% cotton cover. The Teflon heats up too much and reflects back too much heat. Save used Teflon board covers; they are perfect for the insides of machine-quilted oven mitts. Pad the board with a layer or two of old wool blankets.

Use a press cloth, available in fabric stores, to protect delicate fabrics or to keep polyester batting from scratching

Love in the bowling alley (my sewing room is 8' x 39'): I love my gravity-fed Sussman iron so much I want to take it to class. On the bulletin board to the left is the beginning of a two-sided 25th wedding anniversary hanging, designed on computer using the Half-Square Element Key from Barbara Johannah's Crystal Piecing. *The shapes come from our anniversary date. On top of my ironing board is the Spaceboard with a small sample being blocked after washing, and my starch sprayer. I like this portable Spaceboard. You can keep it next to your cutting board for pressing small pieces, put it on a table for pressing larger pieces, and prop it up for a black design wall when you're not using it for pressing.*

the iron. You can also use an old sheet or the backing from paper-backed fusible web.

Always press gently, preferably from the underside, with respect for the fabric; ironing—i.e., sliding the iron along the fabric and possibly stretching the seam—is not pressing.

I also use my June Tailor tailor board a lot, especially for pressing open seam allowances, and I like Belva Barrick's Seam Stick, a half-dowel, for pressing seam allowances flat, then open. See Resource list.

Accidents happen, of course, and you can clean up many by setting the hot iron on an unscented softener sheet (used in the dryer) for 15 seconds. Then run the iron over an old towel or cotton scrap. I learned this trick from Nancy Ward, author of *Fabric Painting Made Easy*, who learned it from the people at HeatnBond.

Nancy also learned from the people at Aleene's that you can set a cold iron for 30 minutes on paper towels saturated with rubbing alcohol. After the alcohol has evaporated, wipe off the iron with a damp cloth and all the accumulated gunk will disappear.

If your iron or press can tolerate it, use something like Dritz's Iron-On, but work with the windows open. The fumes are strong.

Barbara Zagnoni of Rowenta tells me that a common maneuver of impatient quilters is to press the burst-of-steam button repeatedly. This floods the soleplate with water, cools the soleplate so that it can't produce steam, and causes the iron to drip. The lesson? One burst of steam every 3 – 5 seconds is plenty.

Kaye Wood, hostess of the Quilting in the 90s *TV show, is standing in front of a Lone Star wallhanging which has been stipple-quilted and has a stencilled wreath design. Photo courtesy of Kaye Wood.*

Scissors, Rotary Cutters, and Mats

You can never have enough scissors.

For more complete information on scissors, see page 249.

Blades can be sent away for sharpening for about $2/blade. See Resource list.

• Scissors

The prudent quilter keeps many kinds of scissors, all closely guarded (from the family)—for cutting paper, for fabric, a short sharp-to-the-point pair, and duckbilled for appliqué and embroidery. I am prone to hide these scissors and to growl at intruders because I have suffered the pain of trying to cut fabric accurately with fabric scissors nicked by cutting paper, string, strapping tape on packages, and toenails. As an attempt at prevention, I also keep scissors bought by the peck at discount warehouses for the family readily available in the living room, kitchen, bedrooms, and bathrooms.

Scissors can and should be kept sharpened. Either learn how to do it yourself, which isn't difficult (ask someone experienced in sharpening hand tools to show you how), or send them out for sharpening. Most fabric stores will sharpen scissors, but if yours doesn't, look in the Yellow Pages of the phone book under "Sharpening Services." People who sharpen saws, knives, or lawn mowers will usually sharpen scissors.

• Rotary cutters and mats

How did we get along before these pizza cutters took over sewing and quilting? They make the job of cutting anything a breeze. But not all cutters and mats are created equal.

Blades from one cutter do not necessarily fit another, so be sure you can find replacement blades.

I am fond of the curved cutters because they put less stress on my wrist.

Several of the cutter manufacturers have put out wavy or scallop blades. These give an interesting edge to nonfray fabrics like Ultrasuede (see the fabric pin on page 152).

Above all, teach yourself to close the cutter after every cut. A friend accidentally knocked an open cutter onto her toe and required stitches at the emergency room.

A good place to store your cutter is in a soft eyeglass case.

Mats are made of one of three materials: laminates, polyethylene, or styrene. The laminates are stiffer and are limited in size, although they can be butted together to make a larger surface. Olfa, Fiskars, Kai, Omnigrid, and Dritz make laminated mats.

Polyethylene and styrene mats are softer and can be rolled; therefore, you can buy enough to fit a whole cutting table. If you intend to use the grid printed on the mat, measure it with an accurate ruler (see below) before buying to be sure it's precise in *both* directions. Sew/Fit makes both these mats.

Mats are best stored flat. If yours is warped, try putting it in a bathtub filled with hot water for 20 minutes. Then weight it on a flat surface. Don't dry it with a hair dryer and don't ever set an iron on it (personal experience: disaster!). Intense heat, as in a closed car or in the back of trucks, and mats are enemies.

Before we added a sewing room to our home, I used to store my cutting mat under the bed. Gil Murray of The Sewing Emporium warned me not to store it without covering the mat well. Dirt and dust get pushed into the cuts on the mat, which quickly dulls a blade. He suggested that I hang up the mat in a closet.

Speaking of which, if you are getting skips in your cutting—small bridges of fabric that the blade missed—it could be a dirty blade (take it apart and wipe it clean), a dull blade (don't be cheap here—blades, like sewing machine needles, do not last forever), a nicked blade, or scars in the cutting mat from repeatedly working in the same area. Rotate your cutting mat from time to time and invest in another one when yours looks like a battlefield.

Over time, your mat will develop burrs, nicks, and cuts. You can sand it with a small block of wood wrapped with fine-grit sandpaper or steel wool, but you'll lose the printing. Better yet, buy another one. Mats don't last forever.

Clean mats with liquid dishwashing detergent and warm water. Don't ever use alcohol.

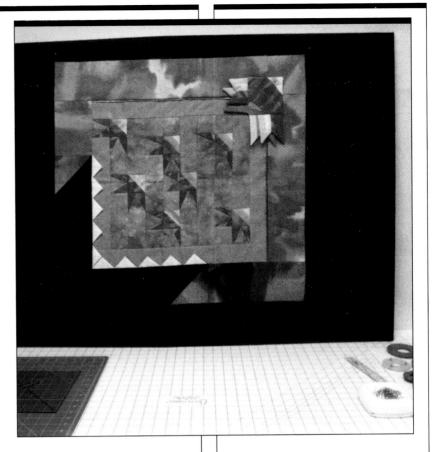

Above: *I use many mats and cutters. My cutting table is from Sew/Fit, as is the long mat. The short mat is from Omnigrid. I use weights from Nancy's Notions, as well as tile samples. In the background is the black felt side of the Spaceboard. I've pinned up the piece I did on Doreen Speckmann's Mexican quilting cruise. I still haven't decided how to quilt it. It's called* The Meek Shall Inherit the Earth—Not!

Gil Murray of The Sewing Emporium says you can spray a Q-tip with silicone lubricant, then wipe the cutter blade with it, to keep it rolling well.

Consider buying an entire system—cutter, ruler, mat—from the same manufacturer. They have made tools that complement each other. When you start crossing brands, you may be shortening the life of each tool.

Measuring Devices

John Flynn, author of Braided Borders, *developed a handy tool called The Cutting Edge. Lay the fabric horizontally, with the bulk to the left. Measure with a ruler from the right edge toward the left. Lay The Cutting Edge against the ruler, remove the ruler, and cut against The Cutting Edge. No more flipping the fabric around to cut.*

• Rulers

Rotary cutters require a stable edge to cut against. You will be amazed at the variety of rulers you can buy: large rectangular, square, triangular, specific shapes as for Double Wedding Band. Examine any ruler you want to buy closely. If it has 45° angles on it, do they intersect the corner of the ruler exactly? I was amazed to discover how inaccurate many rulers are.

One of the most accurate, reliable brands is Omnigrid. John Flynn taught me that the yellow outlines around the black marks on an Omnigrid ruler are 1/32" from the center black line. This occasionally is important to know, as with John's Braided Border that I used in the Anniversary Wallhanging on page 184.

I most often use a 6" x 24" Omnigrid, 1" x 12" Omnigrid, 2" x 12" C-Thru, 8" Bias Square from That Patchwork Place, and 12" square Omnigrid (although I have many other rulers).

Be careful when you start cutting. It's easy to slice the corner of the ruler. Randy Schafer of Omnigrid suggests that you set the cutter 1/2" in from the ruler edge and draw it back toward you. Then reset the cutter and continue the cut away from you.

Rulers do not last forever. They can be chipped, cracked, and scratched. The ink wears off eventually (the printing must be on the bottom of the ruler in order for your cuts to be accurate). If you put sandpaper strips on your ruler to keep it from moving on the fabric, be careful that you do not store that ruler against other rulers. It will scratch the next surface.

• Right angle

To check that the corners of quilting frames are at 90° angles, to construct perfect rectangles and squares, to help miter corners.

• Flexible ruler

Bendable, reinforced with metal, useful for wavy lines and rounded edges (see section on marking fabrics).

• 120" tape measure

Traditionally, a soft #2 lead pencil was used to draw directly on the quilt top—soft, so that quilters didn't have to press hard, which would distort the fabric. Then we discovered that pencil marks do not always wash out of all modern fabrics. People began using #3 and #4 hard pencils, but they are hard to see on prints and medium- to dark-colored fabrics. While this can be an advantage after the quilt is finished, it can be distinctly frustrating while you are sewing.

An alternative is to use colored pencils on light fabrics and a white charcoal pencil (available in quilt and art stores or see Resource list) on dark. But beware: white charcoal rubs off with the continued rolling and unrolling of machine quilting. If you will not finish quilting in one or two sessions, use something else for marking quilting lines—or mark only as much as you can quilt in one session. Many people recommend the Berol Verithin Silver 753 pencil because it can be seen on both light and dark.

I tested some pencils by drawing lines on an 8" square of preshrunk 100% cotton. Then I cut it in half and washed one half in detergent with the family wash. The only marks that completely washed out were General's Fabric Chalk, Dixon's Washout Cloth Marker, Clotilde's Fine Tip Water Erasable pen, and Mark-B-Gone blue washout pen.

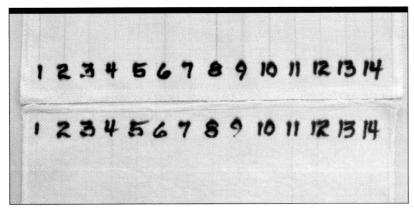

1. Dixon Ticonderoga #2 soft pencil
2. #2-5/10 medium
3. #3 hard
4. #4 extra-hard
5. Smocks and Kisses #4
6. Berol Turquoise #4B
7. Berol Verithin #753 silver
8. General's Multi Pastel Chalk Dark Grey
9. General's Fabric Chalk
10. Dixon Washout Cloth Marker Blue
11. Ultimate Marking Pencil for Quilters (.5mm)
12. Pentel Quicker Clicker
13. Clotilde's Fine Tip Water Erasable pen
14. Mark-B-Gone blue washout

Marking Devices

You can never have enough marking devices.

The National Quilting Association warns against using lead pencils because the oil base makes it hard to remove marks from fabrics. They have successfully tested the washable Karisma Graphite Aquarelle by Berol, available at art supply and some quilting stores.

Nancy Ward, author of *Fabric Painting Made Easy*, uses chalkboard chalk with a holder to mark fabric. She says the marks brush off easily without the chalk getting all over you.

This may not be a fair test. The makers of the Ultimate Marking Pencil warn you that their pencil marks will not wash out in the washing machine. They suggest dissolving a small amount of Ivory Liquid in a jar of warm water. Use a toothbrush like an eraser on the pencil marks. If the lines are still visible, add rubbing alcohol to the mixture. They say it is not necessary to rinse. I tried this procedure on one of the batting/wheel cover pillows and it worked well.

Water-erasable pens have blue ink that flows on like a felt-tipped pen, but disappears when touched with a Q-tip dipped in cold water. Be sure to test (by marking on fabric scraps) that the pen marks disappear on both the top fabric(s) *and* the backing fabric, because the marks sometimes bleed into the batting and come up in other places on the top and backing. If you forget to wash the marks out when you finish the quilt, it is possible that the first time your quilt hits the washer, the blue lines may become set in the fabric.

I don't use air-erasable pens because my projects always take months and the marks disappear in 48 hours.

If I'll be washing the piece before displaying it, I mark straight and broad curving lines with a sliver of soap.

Most quilters shy away from using ballpoint pens to mark fabric. Even if the ballpoint line is outside a seam line and theoretically won't show, the ink may run onto the quilt top in washing.

Also available in fabric and quilt stores are transfer pens, in which the pattern is first drawn on paper and then ironed onto the fabric. The dyes in the pen are heat-activated and sometimes bleed when wet. Be certain to practice on a test cloth before you use such a pen.

Dressmaker's carbon paper, available in fabric stores, is used with a marking wheel or a dried-up ballpoint pen to transfer design lines to quilt tops.

For the prick-and-pounce method described on page 205 in Marking Methods, use light-colored pounce powder (a powdered charcoal) or any imaginative substitute—cornstarch, talcum or foot powder, cream of tartar, etc.—on dark fabrics and on light fabrics, use cinnamon.

You can transfer designs by photocopying them, then ironing them on fabric with a hot dry iron. The lines are permanent, though, so be sure they will be covered by quilting lines. Also, Jane Hall and Dixie Haywood, co-authors of *Precision Pieced Quilts Using the Foundation Method*, tell me that some copiers distort in one or both directions. Test carefully.

Binding-Making Tools

Tools to make binding (clockwise from top right): *Fastube from the Crowning Touch, WH Collins Bias Press Bars (nylon), Clover binding tape maker, Miniturn from the Crowning Touch, Bias Bars from Celtic Design Company (metal), Bias Press Bars from Heirloom Stitches (nylon).*

Georgia Bonesteel, Hendersonville, NC, Portrait of Georgia Bonesteel, *hostess of TV's* Lap Quilting With Georgia Bonesteel, *machine-quilted by Sue Alvarez. Photo courtesy of Georgia Bonesteel.*

Eye Enhancers for Tired Eyes

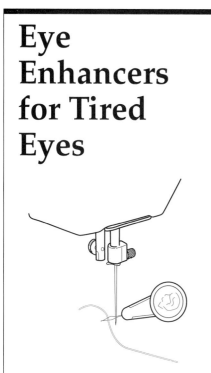

Insert needle threader from back to front of machine needle.

• *Needle threader.*

Those of us over 40 seem to go through these at an incredible rate. Use them both for hand and machine sewing. In the latter case insert the threader from the back of the needle.

Variations are long wire serger threaders, available from your sewing machine dealer and by mail order (see Resource list); dental floss threaders, available in drugstores; and a handy device invented by George Bodnar of Australia called Perfect Sew Universal Needle Threader and Needle Inserter.

Sometimes, instead of using a needle threader, I remove the needle from the machine, thread it separately, and reinsert it.

Top of the line machines have built-in needle threaders—some work; some don't. The Pfaff and New Home threaders are particularly reliable.

• *Magnifying glass or linen tester.*

Useful for reading the needle size, helping to thread the machine needle, and counting the number of machine stitches per inch or centimeter so you know precisely how to set the machine stitch length. (Linen testers are available from photography stores, as well as from fabric stores. It's worth owning one. Linen testers are also useful for designing from photographs or magazines, for examining fabric grain, for enlarging details of quilts and quilt photographs, and for examining all kinds of insects, leaves, cat hairs, and fingerprint whorls.)

I have several magnifiers around the machine, some from office supply stores, some from scientific supply stores. The kind that gets a higher magnification by stacking lenses doesn't work. The layers distort except in a small central area.

Magnifiers and tweezers help tired eyes.

Don't be afraid of the tools of precision. They are indispensable in machine quilting.

Many of us have had no art training and we are not aware of the wealth of art tools that make the design of machine quilting both exciting and easier. If you do not normally use art supply stores, I recommend that you spend a lunch hour or Saturday morning browsing in a well-stocked one for such useful supplies as those listed below.

• *Translucent graph paper.* Large pads of so you can make slopers (see page 87), try out different color schemes, copy shapes for easy enlargement. I use 1/8", 1/4", and 10-to-the-inch most often.

• *Tracing paper.* A roll of inexpensive paper (about $1.25 for 18" wide, eight-yard roll) so you can copy parts of designs, letters, shapes that can be moved around, rearranged, manipulated—then overlaid with more tracing paper to copy the final design.

• *White artist's tape.* As much as you can afford in various widths from 1/4" to 2" or wider. A 60-yard roll of 1"-wide tape costs about $13. Use it in designing to tape down paper; use it in cutting to mark widths or strips; use it in marking for straight quilting lines; use it in basting to hold down the edges of the backing; lay it on the needle plate of your machine to elongate the inscribed sewing lines for more precision in sewing seams.

You can use masking tape, but it may leave residue. My favorite product for removing gunk is Goo Gone, available in hardware stores.

• *Paper cutter.* Expensive, but worth it. I sometimes fold and cut four layers of fabric on mine, starching them heavily first. The higher the polyester content, the less my cutter can cut through the layers sharply. And I don't try to cut widths less than 3". When you use a paper cutter on cloth, it's important to be sure that you're always cutting on-grain. Fiskars has a new paper cutter that works with a rotary blade, which can be changed easily, unlike a traditional paper cutter. The Fiskars cutter easily slices starched fabric.

• *Spray glue.* To mount graph-paper designs onto sandpaper or acetate for templates. I've also experimented on wallhangings with spray-gluing the top fabric to the batting and the backing fabric to the batting. Use in a well-ventilated area. Don't use spray glue on functional items—glue is extremely flammable and might burst into flames in the dryer. KK100 is a brand developed expressly for fabrics (see Fusibles and Glues on page 183 and Resource list).

• *X-ACTO knife.* For cutting precise templates—used with a straight-edge or plastic ruler. If you don't have a self-healing mat, put newspaper or an old telephone book underneath so you don't mar your work surface.

Art Tools For Machine Quilting

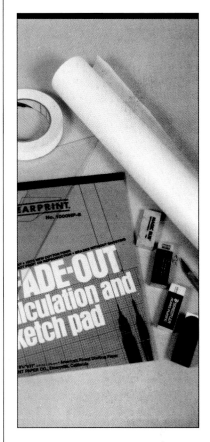

Some art tools to make your job easier: *tracing paper, X-ACTO knife, erasers, translucent graph paper, right angle, artist's white tape.*

If you live in a metropolitan area, check the Yellow Pages for Medical Supplies. Physician's examining table paper also works well. (See Resource list for a mail-order source.) I like it for a stabilizer, too.

What was the biggest change between the first edition of this book in 1980 and today? Not rotary cutters, not Wonder-Under, not needle stop up/down—but the personal computer. In 1978 we actually wrote the first edition of this book on a computer (not personal) and suggested to Chilton that we submit the book on magnetic tape. This was beyond their comprehension at the time. Now it is standard to submit a book on diskette.

If you have a personal computer, you do not need press-on letters. You can design letters with the computer.

Perhaps the third edition of this book will come to you on CD-ROM.

Sue Hausmann of Viking White recommends using the see-through Lexan flat-bed extension available for their machines as a makeshift light table.

• *Art gum eraser.* Erases pencil marks on some fabrics.

• *Press-on letters.* Art stores carry sheets of letters in any style you like, such as formal, italic, or lower-case. By putting the sheet over paper and rubbing the letters, you transfer the letters from the sheet to the paper. If you rub them off onto graph paper, you can blow the message up to the size you need (see enlarging methods on page 200). Copy this onto tracing paper and use as full-size patterns for cutting out of fabric.

• *Light table.* See page 202 for ways to rig a light table. It's worth the investment, however, to buy a permanent one. A clever portable light table is offered by Me Sew Inc. (See Resource list.)

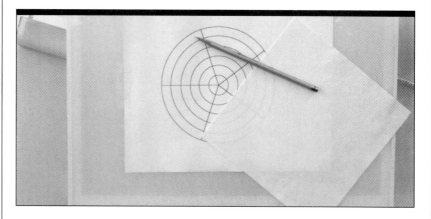

I like the Me Sew portable light table, lit by an inexpensive under-the-counter fluorescent light.

Donna Wilder, hostess of the Sew Creative *TV show, stands in front of a machine-quilted quilt. We also have Donna to thank for the yearly Fairfield Fashion Show. Photo courtesy of Fairfield Processing Co.*

- *Needle-nose tweezers.* The uses for this handy tool are so numerous—bringing up the loop of the bobbin thread, helping to thread the needle, extracting pins at the last moment before you sew over them, cleaning out lint from the bobbin case—that undoubtedly a gremlin will walk off with them. Buy two and hide one near your sewing machine.

- *Pins, cushions, safety pins, paper clips, bulldog clips.* Use several pincushions to keep pins separate—regular sewing pins in one, long (1-3/4") glass-headed pins in one, and silk pins in another.

    If you are making your own pincushions, don't fill them with foam rubber. The pins resist going in. Use loose polyester batting or sawdust instead (fill the toe of an old clean nylon stocking; then cover it with something nice).

    Magnetic pincushions are useful, but keep them away from needles and scissors, which will also become magnetized. Esther Cheal, of *Scattered Patchers Newsletter,* nicked her scissors because they attracted pins and she cut over them. (Also keep them away from computer diskettes.)

    Keep boxes of #1 nickel or brass safety pins available for basting squilts.

    Large paper clips with the ends bent open slightly so they won't snag on fabric are useful for handling bulk on small projects (like the Machine-Quilted Sampler on page 78).

    For basting (see page 206) and for securing small amounts of bulk, use bulldog clips (available from stationery stores).

- *Bicycle clips.* Before Harriet Hargrave introduced bicycle clips for handling the bulk of large quilts, we suffered. But beware: Harriet warns that the clips must be oval, not round, or they will fly off the quilt. See page 94.

Holding Devices

Closing safety pins can wreck your fingers. It's handy to have a tool for closing safety pins. I use a Kwik Klip—see Resource list—but some people use a grapefruit spoon.

- *Cutting tables.* Make sure yours is high enough so you don't get a backache and not so high your shoulders are scrunched up as you rotary cut. If you get a large enough cutting table, you can clear away a corner among the bills, fabrics, patterns, magazines, and tools, and actually use it to cut.

- *Sewing tables.* It's pleasant to have an extended flat sewing surface when working on large projects. If you have a cabinet, make sure you can sit in front of the needle, not the opening. Otherwise you'll get terrible aches from leaning left.

    I bought three Sirco tables, which have an extension to the left that is customized to fit around the various brands I sew on. (Tony took one for the Elna press—hmpf!)

Furniture

I like the portable table by Sew/Fit because it is trimmable to your height.

Useful Miscellany

Decimal Conversion Chart

Decimal	Fraction	Inches in Fraction of yard
.125	1/8	4-1/2"
.250	1/4	9"
.333	1/3	12"
.375	3/8	13-1/2"
.500	1/2	18"
.625	5/8	22-1/2"
.666	2/3	24"
.750	3/4	27"
.875	7/8	31-1/2"

Deb Wagner taught me to do industrial-strength spray-starching. I use this herbicide sprayer from a garden shop.

- *Calculator.*
I use mine constantly—to figure yardage, to help lay out a picture of how to cut for piecing, to calculate length of bias strips, and much more.

When you use the calculator, all the numbers will be decimal. If you calculate that you need to buy 2.30 yds of material, round up to the next fraction (in this case, .333) and buy 2-1/3 yds.

If your memory is rusty about fractions, here's a Decimal Conversion Chart. You may want to type these on a pre-gummed address label, cut it to fit any empty space on the top of your calculator, and stick it there for ready reference. Alternately, photocopy and cut out the table; then laminate it with clear shelf paper (or have the copy shop laminate it for you).

- *Needlecases for needles, hand.*
I love to sew by hand and I'm attached to certain needles, so I keep two needlecases (both machine-made, of course), one for tapestry, embroidery, and regular sewing needles; and one for my beloved short sharp betweens for hand quilting, the slightly curved one that I use for appliqué, and the curved needle I sometimes use for basting.

- *Turning bodkin.* For coaxing pointed corners out

- *Post-it Notes.* To remind yourself about needles, threads, settings

- *Good pencil sharpener.* To keep marking pencils sharp—At home I use an electric sharpener. In class I use a heavy brass one.

- *Spray starch.* Deb Wagner, author of *Teach Yourself Machine Piecing and Quilting*, taught me to starch fabric heavily even before cutting it. It keeps it from creeping under the rotary cutter.

- *Surge protector.* Avoid a power spike frying your $3000 computer sewing machine. Invest $20 in this insurance.

- *Seam ripper.* I also like to use an awl. (See page 213 for a fast ripping technique.)

Visit your fabric, sewing machine, and quilt stores often. New tools and gadgets are constantly being introduced, many of which will save you time and fuss in machine quilting.

Right: *Arnold Savage, Avon, OH,*
The Star Shall Lead Them. *An*
exercise in blending colors.
Photo courtesy of the artist.

Below: *Carol Goddu, Mississauga,*
ON, Canada, Tapping in the
Attic, *68" x 80". Machine-*
appliquéd and -quilted, hand-
embroidered faces, hand beadwork.
Photo courtesy of the artist.

Dottie Moore, Rock Hill, SC, Suspended, 23" x 27", 1992. Coat's & Clark Dual Duty and a Bernina 1530 help Dottie work directly with the fabric. She rarely sketches first. Some hand stitching. Photo courtesy of the artist.

Gail Hunt, North Vancouver, BC, Canada, A Piece on Canada, 52" x 56". Blueprinted images of Canadian scenes. Photo courtesy of the artist.

Chapter 7

Marking, Basting, Quilting, Finishing

Now you have made choices about project, fabric, batting, and technique. You're reading to mark the top, baste, quilt, and finish edges.

Enlarging Designs: Five Ways

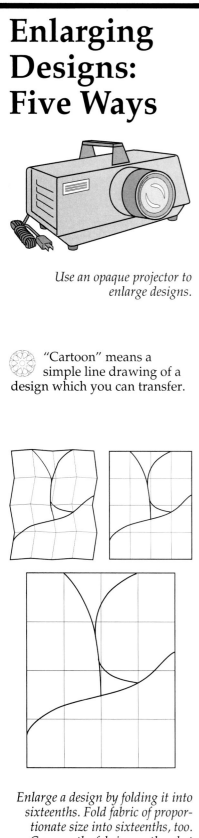

Use an opaque projector to enlarge designs.

"Cartoon" means a simple line drawing of a design which you can transfer.

Enlarge a design by folding it into sixteenths. Fold fabric of proportionate size into sixteenths, too. Copy on the fabric exactly what you see in each square of the original design.

Since most books and magazines are smaller than your projects, you will often be faced with the need to enlarge a design to fit the quilted project you have in mind. There are four ways appropriate to machine quilting:

1. The simplest, fastest way to enlarge a design is to use an opaque projector. You can buy a variety of models, ranging from $8 to $100 to $1000 in art supply stores (or see Resource list). The disadvantage of the smaller ones is that your design to be enlarged is often bigger than the area the projector can cover, and it is awkward to keep moving the design (or the projector) until you finish copying the cartoon.

If you belong to a guild, members can chip in to buy a large opaque projector (and a light table, if you're really enthusiastic). This equipment is as useful in quilting as a sewing machine. Otherwise, try to talk a quilt shop owner into buying one for customer use.

To buy a used opaque projector, call elementary or secondary schools (private and public), colleges and art schools, printers, or advertising agencies. Also try advertising in the wanted pages of local or shopper newspapers.

An *overhead* projector is not the same as an *opaque* projector. The former requires a see-through image to project. This means you must trace or photocopy your design source onto acetate transparencies before projecting them.

2. If you know the fabric area into which the design must fit, divide the fabric into 16 rectangles by folding it in half vertically, pressing lightly with a hot iron. Fold in half vertically again and press. Open up the fabric and fold in half horizontally—press carefully without destroying your previous pressed lines. Fold again horizontally and press. You have made your fabric into a 16-block grid.

Either copy the design (including the outside edges of the square or rectangle frame) onto tracing paper or photocopy the design. It is important that the paper on which your design resides be of the same proportions as the fabric you've already gridded out. For example, if your fabric is 16" by 20", you'll get strange results if your paper is 6" by 12", but everything works fine if your paper is 8" by 10". Fold your paper into 16 blocks as you did the fabric. Crease well with your fingers or a butter knife to get sharp folds.

Now copy onto the larger fabric grid what you see in each smaller paper grid. If a line crosses at the halfway point on one, make it cross halfway on the other. Duplicate one block at a time and before long, your design will be perfectly blown up to the exact size you need. If you have trouble with this, turn the original design upside down while you're working. Somehow it's easier; you get less confused.

3. The graph paper method is the same as #2, but more detailed. Lay graph paper over your design and trace it, using a light table, if necessary. (Or draw a grid of 1/2" or 1" blocks over your design.) Decide how much bigger (or smaller) you want the design—let's say twice as big. On the same scale graph paper (you may have to tape several sheets together), rule off every second line in each direction. You now have squares twice as big as the original. As in #2 above, copy into each larger square what you see in the smaller. If the design is complicated, number and letter each piece of graph paper as shown in the illustration to keep from becoming confused.

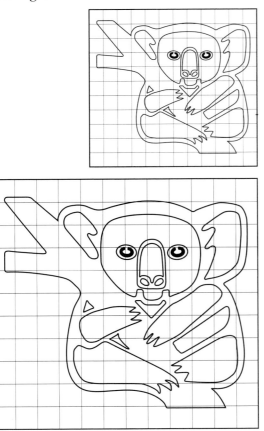

To trace a pattern, lay graph paper over the design and trace. Decide how much bigger you want the design and make a grid that large. Copy on the larger grid what you see in the smaller.

4. Use a photocopier to enlarge a design. Some photocopiers can blow up to any size; others have built-in settings. Study the final image. Is it distorted in any way? If you're happy, photocopy extra images, checking to be certain that photocopying from the original enlarged image does not vary on subsequent copies. (See note on page 190.)

5. Your way. Who will invent the next best way to enlarge designs?

Transferring Designs

Trace designs by taping cartoon to window and placing fabric over it.

Rig a makeshift light table by putting a bare light bulb in a cardboard box, placing an old window or a glass picture frame over the open top of the box, and covering the glass with plain white paper to diffuse the light. Now you can easily trace your design onto fabric.

In general (but not always) the top is marked before basting the three layers of the squilt together. The term "cartoon," which is used freely below, means a simple line drawing of a design which you can transfer.

To transfer design lines to fabric, review marking devices, templates, and measuring devices on in Chapter 6. They are used in two ways, for direct and indirect marking methods.

Direct Marking

Trace directly onto the fabric. If you're brave, trace free-hand or let your child, family, or class draw free-hand on the fabric. A lovely tradition is to have guests at a wedding sign their names, write messages to the couple, and/or trace their hand on pre-cut squares of fabric. These messages are later quilted and assembled into a special quilt for the newlyweds. The same idea is used in celebrity quilts, where the famous sign fabric which is then quilted. It helps to bond freezer paper to the back of the squares; writing is easier.

Otherwise, trace around templates, again respecting the fragile nature of woven fabric.

For large designs, trace the cartoon onto newsprint or tracing paper. During the day, you can tape the paper to a picture window and tape the fabric over it, centering the design carefully (don't center by eye—first fold the fabric into quarters, mark center with X, match centers). This works even for some dark fabrics. At night, use the lit TV screen on a channel you don't receive. Or go outside, and use the window method by looking into a well-lit room.

Or better, use a light table. If you can't afford to buy one (see page 194), rig a make-shift light table. Put a sheet of clear plastic or an old window on a cardboard box (or sawhorses or two chairs or an open drawer or in the space where a table leaf goes—use your ingenuity). Into or under this, set a bare-bulb lamp. Cover the plastic with plain white paper so the light is diffused. Now tape down the cartoon, put the fabric over it, weight or tape it down, and trace the design.

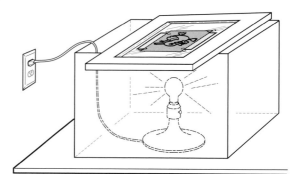

Indirect Marking: Six Ways

1. Iron on the design, either from tracings by a transfer pen or fabric crayons, or from a photocopied image. Follow the ironing directions for the pen; for the photocopied image, use the highest heat your fabric can stand, with no steam. Be sure to test on a scrap; the photocopy line does not wash out of every fabric (see marker test on page 189). Be sure to draw letters and other direction-dependent images in reverse before transferring.

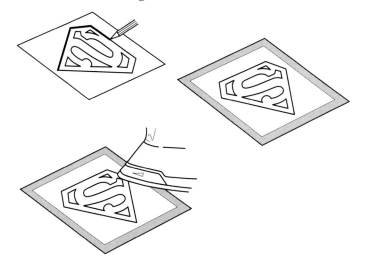

2. Trace the design onto tracing paper (available at art supply stores—it's worth owning several rolls). Pin the tracing paper to the fabric, on either the top or the backing, depending on the technique, and stitch through the paper and the squilt. When you are done, gently tear the paper away. Left-over paper scraps caught in the stitches can be removed with needle-nose tweezers. The remainder will fall out and disappear the first time you wash the project.

When you are quilting with the presser foot on, you can stitch from the topside through the tracing paper, because the even perforations make it easy to remove the paper. However, when you are free-machine quilting, there are often several small close stitches preventing a clean break of paper, so stitch with the underside of the squilt up (mean-

Check in craft stores for Tolin' Station Vellum. You can photocopy onto it; then iron onto fabric.

Iron-on designs: *Trace the design with a transfer pencil (reverse letters and direction-dependent images). Place the transfer on the rightside of the fabric, pencil lines against fabric. Iron at a setting compatible with the fabric.*

I photocopied the fabric, blowing up one butterfly until the image got too fuzzy. Then I traced it onto graph paper and used Method #3 on page 201 to enlarge it. I copied the enlarged design onto tracing paper and now I'm ready to quilt through it. Hanging pieced by Mary Losey of West Lafayette, IN.

Right: I copied one of Hari Walner's designs from her Miniature Collection (Beautiful Publications) onto tulle with an extra-fine point Sharpie, then marked through the tulle onto the fabric with a Multi-Pastel Chalk from The Stencil Company. It's easy to misplace the tulle pattern. Keep colored paper nearby and tape the tulle pattern to it with removable tape. This hanging is one of the color exercises in Roberta Horton's Amish Adventure, which I've been working my way through.

ing that the thread seen on top is the bobbin thread, so select it carefully). When working from the underside, be sure to use the wrong side of the tracing paper for non-reversible images like letters. Otherwise, you'll find that the front stitching ends up in reverse.

A variation of this is to trace the design onto water-soluble stabilizer, lay it on top of the squilt, and quilt. Tear away as much water-soluble stabilizer as possible. The rest will wash away when spritzed with water.

3. Use dressmaker's carbon between the traced design and the fabric. The Artist Delight Transfer System is similar (see Resource list).

4. Trace the design onto bridal tulle or net with a permanent pen like a Pigma or Sharpie. Let it dry. Then put the tulle over the fabric and trace the design again, this time with a washable marking pen. It leaves a trail of little dots that you can follow. This method is particularly good for already-layered squilts.

Above: Ginger Cullins of Just My Imagination (runnin' away with me) copies her design on net with a fine-point Sharpie, paints through the net onto wet fabric, and lets it dry. She lays the net on top of the painted fabric and redraws the design with a disappearing pen. Then she has a line to follow for free-machine quilting. Ginger sells patterns of whimsical cats, floral fantasies, and Doodle Shirts. See the Resource list.

5. The prick-and-pounce method is ideal for machine quilting as it's done with the sewing machine. Use a 10/70 unthreaded needle (so the holes won't be too big) and a piece of typing paper, acetate (available in art stores or as transparency blanks for overhead projectors), or a manila file folder. (I like acetate because you can see what you're doing.) After copying the design, use a regular sewing stitch line, halfway between basting and fine sewing, and a presser foot. Follow the main lines of the design. Roll up a pad of felt and force pounce powder (see Marking Devices on page 189) through the holes of the acetate onto the fabric. Gently lift off the acetate and connect the lines. Blow off excess powder. Save the pounced pattern for future use (many museums have old pounced patterns on file that women used and shared long ago). This method is especially useful for repeated quilting patterns.

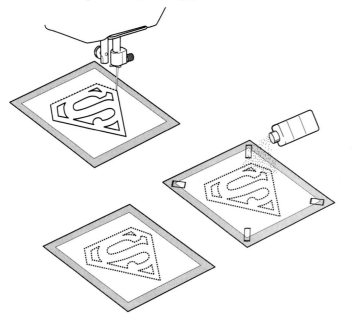

Left: To prick-and-pounce by machine, use a small unthreaded needle to machine stitch around your design. Tape the pricked design to fabric and run pounce powder (talcum powder, cinnamon, anything) through the holes. Remove the paper and connect the dots with a pencil.

6. Your way. Have you come up with something unusual? Tell us all about it.

Below: Elna has come up with a unique way to transfer designs. The Amazing Trace Tracing Embroiderer is like the old-time pantographs. You put the design in a tray to the left of the machine and the squilt in a hoop under the needle. As you move a stylus over the design and run the machine, the hoop moves. The device fits any low-shank machine.

Basting

The Secret of Pucker-Free Machine Quilting

The single greatest problem of machine quilting comes from the very nature of a quilt—it is three layers of material, which can become misaligned. Here's how to overcome it.

Let's assume that you have a finished top, some batting, and a backing, all ready to be quilted together—in other words, a squilt. How do you keep the components of the squilt together while you pass them through the machine? How do you keep them from clumping, lumping, and puckering after you've sewn them together?

Most instructions for machine quilting blithely tell you to baste the squilt in intersecting thread X's from the center out or in a grid of thread lines. Most of those who have tried this are still wondering why they have puckers on the backing.

One secret to pucker-free machine quilting is proper basting, which depends on your **treatment of the backing**, not on the basting itself. If, as usually instructed, you lay the backing on a flat surface, smooth the batting and top in place, and pin- or thread-baste, chances are you will have puckers on the back unless you are extremely experienced. The backing must be treated sternly, and you have five good choices for doing this, each of which will be explained in detail below.

1. Put the backing in a traditional quilting frame while you baste the squilt.
2. Double-baste.
3. Tape all edges of the backing to a firm foundation like a tile floor or pingpong table before basting.
4. Clip the edges to a tabletop in sections.
5. Pay for a professional quilter to machine-baste the quilt for you.

But you can't be so zealous that you overstretch the backing—it will bounce back when you remove it from the frame (or take off the tape) and cause puckers in the top.

For all these methods, try to remember to take the batting out of the package the night before. Unfold it, spread it out, and let the wrinkles pop out with time. If you forget, you can gently steam out most wrinkles, but don't let the iron touch the batting.

1. Frame Basting

Quilting frames have been around a long time, and many hand-quilters do most of their quilting on the frame. But for machine quilting, none of the quilting is done on the frame. Only the basting is. If you don't own a frame, skip ahead for instructions on making one.

To baste in a traditional frame (which can often be borrowed for several hours from a friend or guild), balance the frames on sawhorses or chairs or work on the floor. If you can manage to work over a table, so much the easier—but it's not necessary. The ironed backing should be placed topside down; if you pieced it, you're looking at the seams. Straight-pin one long side of the backing to the tape on the frame, working from the center out. Repeat for the opposite long side.

Using C-clamps, fasten the short sides of the frame to the long sides. If there is canvas tape on your frames to pin into, put the short frames (tape side down) on top of the long frames (tape side up). Check where the two boards meet with a right angle to be sure the boards form a perfect 90° angle. Now straight-pin the short sides of the backing to the short sides of the quilting frame. Remember not to over-stretch the backing. When you are done with this step, the backing is entirely attached at its edges to the quilting frame.

Spread the batting over the backing, smoothing it out. Then spread the marked quilt top over the two layers. Smooth it out by stroking it with a yardstick. Pin all around and perpendicular to the perimeter of the squilt, placing the pin heads out and the pin points in. Pin and repin until you are satisfied with the placement of the top.

Now you are ready to begin the actual basting of the squilt components to each other. Take your choice of three methods of basting:

- straight pins,
- thread, or
- safety pins.

If you use straight pins, use extra-long ones with large glass heads. Always pin in one direction only, so that when you finish machine quilting, you can run your hands over the quilt to check for missed pins and not impale yourself. The extra-long pins, available in quilt or fabric stores (or see Resource list), are less likely to jump out of the squilt as you sew. This method of basting is not recommended for quilts larger than crib-size. Even the long pins will come out as the larger squilt is later rolled and unrolled. If you do use pins, be sure they are stainless steel. They may stay in your quilt for a long time, depending on how fast you work, and you don't want them rusting in the fabric.

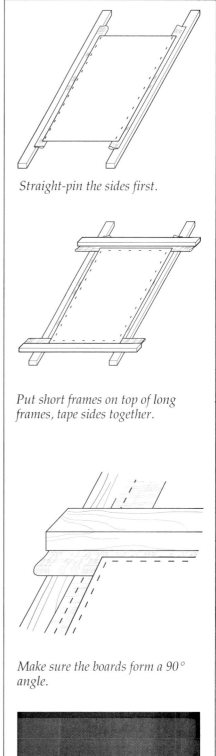

Straight-pin the sides first.

Put short frames on top of long frames, tape sides together.

Make sure the boards form a 90° angle.

While long straight pins can be used for basting, they tend to pop out on big quilts.

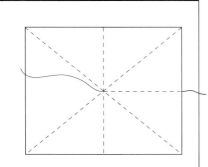

Baste in intersecting Xs. A trick: Cut your thread twice as long as you normally would. Start in the center and pull the thread halfway through, leaving half the thread at the center. Baste out in one direction to the edge. Then thread the needle with the long tail left in the center and baste out in the other direction. Caution: If you don't secure the backing, this kind of basting is not enough to prevent puckers.

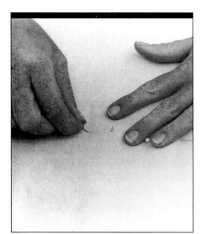

A curved needle makes thread-basting easier.

❀ The first time you drop 200 safety pins, you'll switch to using a magnetic pincushion to hold them.

❀ Ruth McDowell doesn't like safety pins. She pins parallel to the roll of the quilt, inserting each pin with two stitches. She removes the pins after stitching anchoring lines about 4" apart. Then she goes back to add more quilting.

Thread-basting is done by hand with one strand of any sewing thread, taking deliciously long and sloppy stitches. You can even let children help baste—you don't have to worry about the look of their stitches, since the stitches will come out. If you make parallel rows of stitching along the long side of the squilt, spacing the lines 6" – 8" apart, you need only put in three or four rows of thread-basting the other way, across the quilt. Some experienced quilters recommend the tailor basting stitch. Others like to use a curved needle to baste; since both hands work on top, you can reach in farther before needing to roll the squilt. To roll up the squilt as you baste, undo the C-clamps on one long side. Unpin the backing only, and roll the quilt onto the long side. Replace the C-clamps. For large quilts, it's much easier to have someone help you roll the squilt.

Safety pins are the simplest way to baste. Use #1 nickel or brass safety pins, again so they won't rust in the fabric. These safety pins are about 1" long. Ernest B. Haight (see page 65) uses about 200 safety pins for an 80" x 96" quilt, placing them 6" – 7" apart. I would use even more, to be sure the layers don't shift. Look in resale stores, Army-Navy surplus stores, and at garage sales for used safety pins. (But don't buy bigger ones—they make giant holes that may damage the fabric.)

Your fingers can take a beating while you are trying to close these safety pins (and it's worse if you used a cotton/poly sheet as a backing). I use a wonderful tool called a Kwik Klip (see Resource list) to help close the safety pins. You could also use a grapefruit spoon.

Whichever method of basting you use in frame-basting, when you are done, remove the rest of the straight pins that hold the backing to the frames (but don't remove those that hold the squilt together). Take the basted squilt to the machine and using a walking foot, machine-baste 1/4" from the edge all the way around the squilt, removing the perpendicular straight pins holding the top to the backing as you reach them. Sewing over pins dulls the needle; don't do it. This line of stitching stabilizes the edge of the squilt and keeps it from stretching.

You are now ready to machine quilt. See page 212 and Chapters 3 and 4.

Use lots of #1 nickel or brass safety pins to baste.

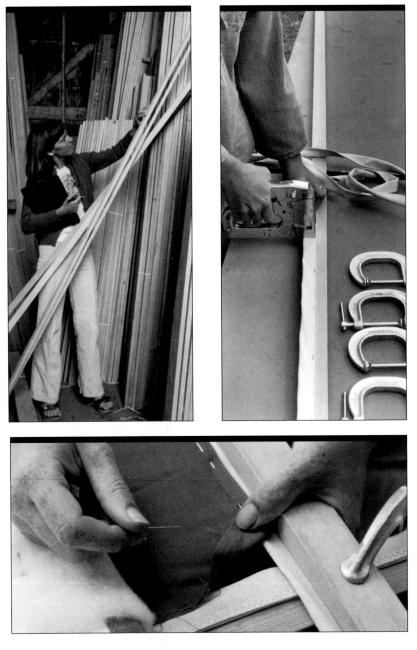

Left: *Use straight pins to attach backing to frame.*

If you don't own a quilting frame, you can make one easily. It's well worth it to take advantage of this satisfying method of basting. Write down the measurements of your quilt. Take this book to a hardware/lumber store and read this to the lumber attendant.

"Please, madam, give me:

- two straight-grained fir 1x2s, each a foot longer than the long side of my quilt (see standard measurements, page 228)
- two more lengths a foot longer than the short side of my quilt
- four 2-1/2" C-clamps. Thank you."

(This would cost about $20 for a king-size quilt.)

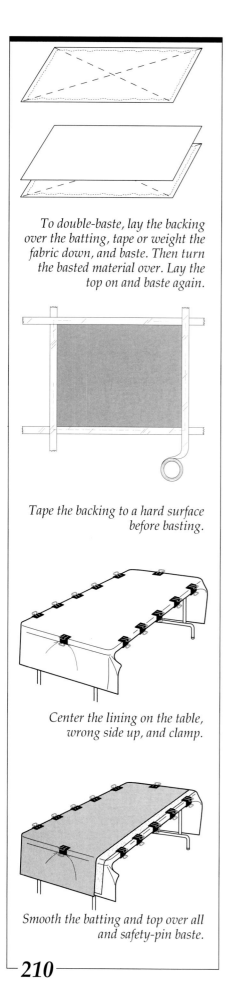

To double-baste, lay the backing over the batting, tape or weight the fabric down, and baste. Then turn the basted material over. Lay the top on and baste again.

Tape the backing to a hard surface before basting.

Center the lining on the table, wrong side up, and clamp.

Smooth the batting and top over all and safety-pin baste.

Staple denim, pillow ticking, or canvas tape to each wide edge of the four frame pieces (see illustration, where I used a doubled layer of canvas material 4" wide, doubled over like belting). If you're really a perfectionist, you will mark the center of each board on the tape. When you clamp the pieces together, always make sure the pinning fabrics face each other.

2. Double-basting

Another method to ensure pucker-free machine-quilting is to double-baste. This means basting the backing to the batting, then the top to this double layer. For this method try to have the backing 2" wider than the batting or top (not always possible if, for example, you're using sheets). Spread the batting on a flat hard surface. Smooth the backing **over** the batting, underside of the backing against the batting. Tape or weight the edges down. Do not over-stretch the backing. Straight-pin or thread-baste the two layers together. Release the edges and turn over so the backing is underneath. Tape the edges again. Smooth the top in place and safety-pin or thread-baste. You have now double-basted. If you pin-basted the backing, remove the pins from the lining side.

3. Taping the Backing For Basting

Tape the backing all the way around, without over-stretching it. Smooth on the batting and top. Pin- or thread-baste the squilt. Since you can't get your fingers underneath to help push pins through and up, thread-basting is easier, especially if you can learn to use a curved needle.

4. Table-top Basting

This method was developed by Harriet Hargrave. It is useful when you do not have enough space to baste large quilts. Safety pins will scrape the work surface, so be sure it isn't something important, like your dining room table. A lunch table about 30" x 5' is ideal. You will need 10 – 15 bulldog clamps (available at an office supply store).

Mark the center of all four sides of the table. Also mark the centers of your top, batting, and backing.

Start by centering the lining over the table, wrong side up. Match center marks. Clamp one long side of the lining to the table. Smooth the fabric across the table to the other side and clamp. Then clamp the ends. (If the table is longer than your quilt, tape two ends.)

Smooth the batting over the lining, centering it. Then smooth the top over all, also centering it. Safety-pin baste the tabletop area, keeping pins out of areas that will be machine-quilted, if possible.

When you have finished the central area, unclamp the lining, slide the pinned area off the top, and clamp another three sides of the lining (you never clamp the batting or top). The weight of the pinned area will keep the backing taut on the fourth side.

5. Use a Professional Quilter

For my daughter's king-size quilt, which she started and I finished, not only did I not have time or space to baste it, but she and her then-fiancé (now hubby) had chosen cotton/poly sheets for the backing, which are murder to safety-pin baste.

I had once interviewed Julie Nodine of Belmont, CA, about her machine-quilting business and remembered that she could also baste a quilt. Since she charges by the square yard, for almost the same price it would have taken to have her machine quilt, I had my quilt basted in a day, for $43. The money was well-spent, because it enabled me to finish the quilt, instead of feeling guilty every time I walked past it because it wasn't basted yet.

Additional Basting

Even though I've safety-pin basted, I will often pin-baste additional areas when I'm free-machine quilting shapes. I like Ruth McDowell's method of running each pin through the squilt twice.

A Method of Basting *Not* Recommended

The only way heartily *not* recommended for machine quilting is to smooth the backing, lay the other two layers on, and baste (the usual advice). When you do it this way, if your fingers can easily get in under the backing to baste, so can Pucker's.

Deb Wagner suggests a clever way to handle high-loft quilts or even large quilts. Stretch the backing as in any of these methods, but cut the batting into thirds. Layer it and baste as usual. Then machine quilt to within 1" of the edge of the batting. Join the second third of batting to the first with a herringbone stitch (see page 181). Baste; then machine quilt. Finally finish the last third.

See Julie's machine on page 258.

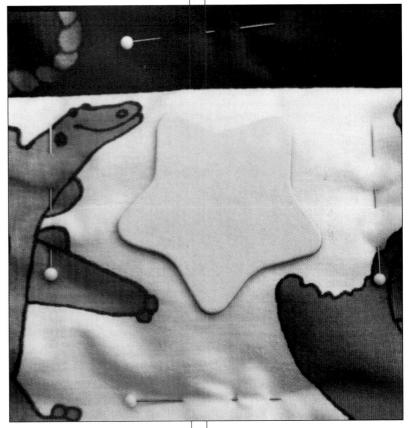

I often do additional pin-basting when free-machine quilting, running the pin through the squilt twice.

Machine Quilting

Glitches and Gremlins

Remember that the most common problems you will encounter are caused by the mismatching of machine settings, thread size and type, and fabric. Most of these annoying glitches fall into four categories: Creep, Pucker, Skip, and Fray. As you recall, there is a gremlin for each glitch, of the same name, and a sure method for foiling each gremlin. Let's review how to foil each one:

Creep: baste well, use a hoop, use a walking foot.
Pucker: match needle size, thread, and fabric better; use fingers as tools; make back taut; baste well.
Skip: hold fabric firmly against needle plate; use fingers or an appropriate presser foot; adjust tension.
Fray: match needle size and thread size to fabric.

Checklist for Machine Quilting

Before each quilting session, check your machine thoroughly:

☐ Clean out the bobbin case (remove the bobbin and vacuum around the case, if possible)—remove dust bunnies, lint, broken threads. Clean feed dogs, if necessary, with a toothbrush.

☐ Oil your machine before each major project as specified in your instruction book (unless your machine does not require oil).

☐ Check the needle size and condition—a bent or snagged needle will fray the top thread. You know how you got that snagged needle, too—from sewing over pins. Some say that sewing into fine sandpaper will smooth burred needles. Others feel that a new needle is the answer.

☐ Check the needle plate—a burr on the metal surrounding the hole will break threads. If you have done a lot of free-machine embroidery, your needle plate may look like a battleground. Sand the burr smooth with fine sandpaper or crocus cloth (available at hardware stores) or ask your friendly sewing machine dealer to help.

☐ When you choose your thread, wind a full bobbin. Better yet, treat yourself to a gift of ten extra bobbins and wind several at the beginning of each sewing session. Remember to check the bobbin before starting each long line of machine quilting. It is especially annoying to run out mid-project, because you usually don't notice until the end of the line. Bless the new machines. They beep or a light comes on to signify a low bobbin.

How to Start, End, and Remove Threads

Your choice of how to start and end threads depends on how much of a stickler you are for craftsmanship. Always remember to hold the threads behind the presser foot as you start stitching, so they won't be drawn into the bobbin case. Here are seven ways:

1. Set your stitch length dial close to 0 (or "fine" on some machines). Take three to four tiny stitches. Then reset the dial for the stitch length you want. Also end with small stitches. Threads are locked; clip ends.

2. Hold back the fabric when you start and finish. It causes the machine to take tiny stitches. Be careful not to bend the needle. (Alternately, take tiny stitches for 1/4".)

3. Holding the threads, machine quilt. Later, pull the threads to the back, tie a square knot (so it won't pull out), and cut off the ends. Some put a spot of glue on the knot for extra insurance.

4. On your stitching line, begin stitching 1/8" in; stitch backwards to the beginning of the line; then stitch forward as usual. Threads are locked; clip ends.

5. Holding threads, machine quilt. Later thread each end through a hand needle, tie a knot near the surface of the fabric, and lead the thread through the top and batting only (or backing and batting only) about 1" away. Gently pop the knot through the fabric, into the batting. Clip end. (If you are using extra-fine thread and a fabric not too closely woven, you can pull ends to the back, knot them together, thread them into one needle, and pull them through the backing fabric and batting together.)

6. Design your quilt so most, if not all, quilting lines end in a seam allowance, to be covered by binding, other blocks, or lattice strips.

7. Your way.

An easy way to remove stitches from an entire seam is to cut threads with a seam ripper every three or four threads. Place a strip of masking tape over the seam. Turn the quilt over and pull the other thread, which will be long and uncut. Separate the fabric. Then pull off the masking tape and all the cut stitches will come off on the tape.

If you have a lock-off feature on your machine, use it to lock stitches.

When clipping threads, I clip the top first, then the back. This pulls the top thread into the batting. Scissors with tipped ends are especially useful for this task.

When you remove the masking tape, all the loose ends pull out with it.

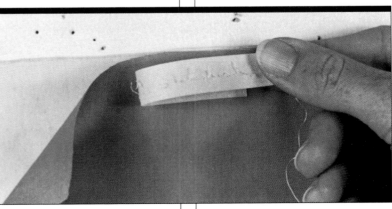

Here's a terrific tip from Sheryl Lentini (whose address I cannot find—sorry, Sherry). When your machine-quilting grid crosses an appliqué, lock threads at the edge of the appliqué, clip the needle thread, and stitch across with an unthreaded needle. Rethread at the appliqué edge, lock threads, and continue stitching. Afterward, clip excess threads.

The Closed Fist Test

You can put in enough anchor lines to stabilize the piece, use it, and add more quilting later.

How Much Quilting?

Before machine quilting, be sure to experiment on a test cloth to see what stitch length you prefer; generally the shorter the stitch, the puffier the effect.

In this book "regular stitch length" means 10 – 12 stitches per inch. If you own a European or Japanese machine with 0 – 5 settings, set your machine at .5 intervals (.5, 1, 1.5, 2, 2.5, etc.) and machine quilt a line on a test cloth. Measure at each of those settings how many stitches per inch and write it directly on the test cloth. Pin that cloth to this page or near your machine.

Stitch length, however, is not absolute. There is no one stitch length that is right for all machine quilting. Stitch length also depends on the type of fabric used. Lighter-weight fabrics may pucker with stitch lengths that are too long. You must experiment on a test squilt for each new situation.

The amount of quilting to put in a quilt depends on the thread, seam allowance, and type of batting used. (For smaller-than-full-quilts, you have much more latitude.)

If the quilt hangs over the side of a bed, tremendous stress is put on the thread every day when you pull up the quilt, fluff it up, and smooth it on the bed. If you use extra-fine thread (as for free-machine quilting), plan to break up the quilt top into modules. The joining strips do relieve some of the stress.

If your quilting lines are more than 3" apart, you should probably use 1/2" or wider seam allowances, again to relieve stress and pulling on the fabric.

A cotton batting needs lines of quilting no farther apart than 2-1/2" (2" is better). But a bonded polyester batting needs quilting only every 4" – 6" and here's where standards of craftsmanship start to slip.

The current trend in both hand and machine quilting is to put in fewer and fewer lines of quilting. This is not always pleasing, depending on the quilt-top design.

My own standard for large pieces (but not necessarily for smaller items), which I am flexible in meeting, is the Closed Fist Test. I put my closed fist on the quilt and if there are not quilting lines nearby and all around my fist, I add them. Sometimes I do this from the back. It's easier to see the gaps. One of the joys of machine quilting is that we can put in the extensive quilting so attractive in the quilts of our forbears.

Edges

There are at least seven ways to finish the edges of quilted pieces, described in detail in the Mini-Encyclopedia under *Binding* and under *Edges, Inserted*. The Mini-Encyclopedia also shows how to join piping and binding attractively.

1. *Continuous binding:* Sew one long piece of binding around the edges of the work.

2. *Lapped binding (for rectangles):* Sew a strip of binding on each edge, and lap the bindings at the corners.

3. *Double-mitered corners:* Sew strips of binding on each edge and miter the corners by machine.

4. *Machine blindhem:* Use the machine's capabilities to create a hidden stitch.

5. *Inserted edge:* Place edge material like ruffles or rickrack between the batting and the top and sew into place.

6. *Back to front:* Bring the backing to the front and miter it by machine (called *Easy Miter* under *Edge Finishes* on page 235).

7. *Your way:* What have you discovered?

Many of these ways call for binding. It is faster, initially, to use purchased bias tape, but there are several reasons why you should think twice about it. For one, the colors do not always match your fabrics exactly. Secondly, the turn-under is usually only 1/4", which makes for a weak edge. You could always buy wider bias tape, iron it flat, and use a wider seam allowance. And finally, on light-colored binding often the fabric of your quilt shows through, which looks awful.

The binding is usually the first part of your quilt to show wear. If you have to replace a purchased bias-tape edge with homemade bias binding sooner than normal, how much time have you really saved? If you persist in using purchased binding, be sure to pre-shrink it.

Your quilts will look better if you make the long strips from material which matches the rest of the quilt. This edging can be made from either the bias or the straight-grain of the fabric. (Ernest B. Haight preferred the latter.)

How much binding will you need to make? Add the width of your quilt to its length, multiply this sum by two, and add 10" for safety. Divide the number by 36 to get the number of yards needed. Easier, consult Standard Bed Size Chart on page 228.

Finishing

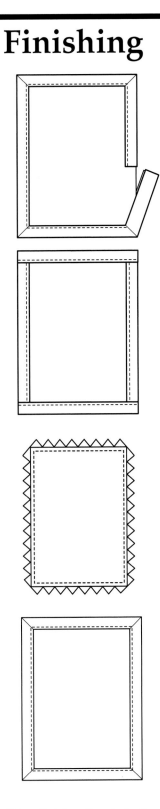

Edge finishes (top to bottom): *Continuous binding, lapped binding, inserted edge, backing brought to front in Easy Miter.*

🌸 See these entries in the Mini-Encyclopedia for in-depth how-to information: *Binding* (many entries) and *Edge Finishes*.

Remember, in order to put the binding on all by machine, plan to **work from the back of the quilt to the front**.

With the wide range of materials and techniques available to machine quilters, you can expect to see an increasing number of non-traditional finishes to machine-quilting—fringes, loops, scallops, tucks, Ultrasuede binding, and more. (For example, the side drops on quilts do not necessarily have to be quilted, as long as they are balanced in weight against the quilted part. Why not take giant tucks or stitch overlapping rows of 3-D clamshells, instead of quilting that part?)

Labels

Always sign and date your work, for your own pleasure and for that of your descendants. The easiest way is to free-machine quilt directly on the work. You can also stitch separately on ribbons or other fabric labels and appliqué them.

Final Inspection

Let the quilted piece rest for a day or two, if possible. You need some distance from it. Then look at both the front and back from an oblique angle. You can sometimes see leftover threads easier that way. Run your hand over the surfaces to be sure there are no pins left. Make a circle of masking or duct tape and sweep the surfaces to remove stray batting, threads, and other sewing detritus.

Hug Your Sewing Machine

When you finish a project, clean out and oil the bobbin area, throw away the needle, return the tension settings to normal—and hug your beloved machine.

The label for Kali and Jonathan's wedding quilt. Central lettering stitched on a Brother Pacesetter PC-7000; free-machining worked on a Bernina 1230.

A Short Treatise on Workmanship and Personal Standards...

How much of a perfectionist should you be? If there's one pucker on the back of your work, should you lose sleep over it?

Only you can set your own personal standards. Mine are modified according to the purpose of the quilted item. If it's for a show, I'm strict with myself: no puckers, no overlapping stitches, thread ends must be hidden, no thread burbles on the back where I've locked stitches, quilting must pass Closed Fist test and hang well.

But if it's a present or a piece for ourselves, merely to enjoy looking at or sleeping under, not to examine minutely, I do the best I can at the time and don't worry about the mistakes.

If standards of excellence are preventing you from producing, don't be a perfectionist. Instead bring to each new quilt the knowledge you've learned from mistakes.

...And a Final Word

We've covered many techniques in this book and I hope you're filled with enthusiasm and ideas. However, if you've learned only these two things, I'll be happy:

1. the proper way to baste for pucker-free machine-quilting;

2. to savor your machine as *the* tool to mold fiber and fabric.

And now there's only one thing left to say:

Machine quilt the world!

A Final Word

Done is better than perfect.

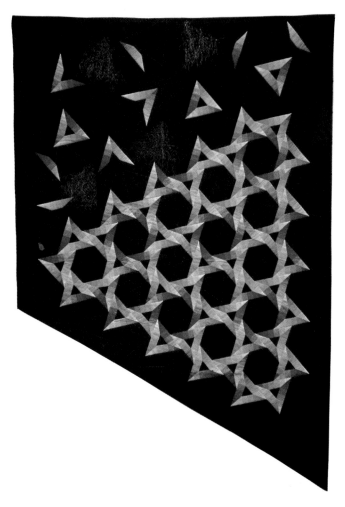

Left: *Anita Krug, West Lafayette, IN,* Falling Into Place. *Photo courtesy of the artist.*

Nancy Taylor, Pleasanton, CA, Victorian Woman. *Wallhanging for P&B Textiles using Victorian Wheeling fabrics. Photo courtesy of P&B Textiles.*

*A*ppendices

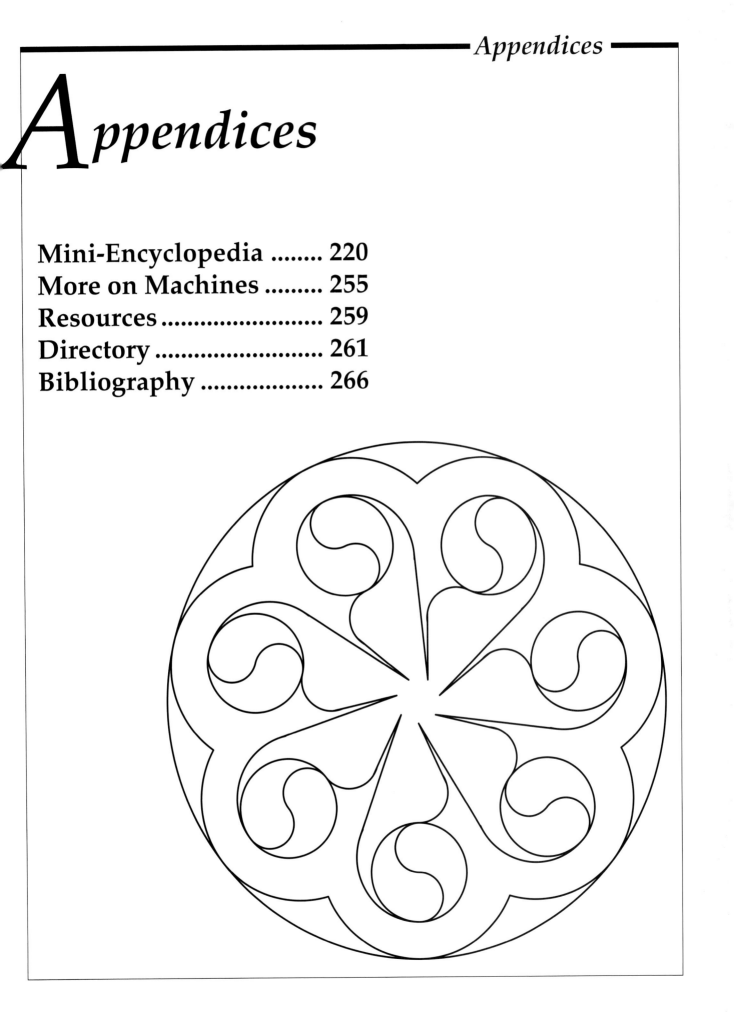

All companies mentioned in the Mini-Encyclopedia can be found in the Directory on page 261.

Battings. If you define batting as the material between two layers of fabric in a three-layer quilt sandwich, then "batting" can be anything from interlock knit to house insulation. While most discussions of batting focus only on quilts, we are concerned with batting in four areas: quilts, garments, crafts, and home decorating (abbreviated to home dec).

First, let's honor an unsung hero: Wallace Hume Carothers. In 1941, working at Dupont, he put together the first polyester chemical string. By 1951 Dupont was selling Dacron. Most people trace the current quilt explosion to an exhibit at the Whitney Museum in the 1960s. I think it couldn't have happened without the invention of polyester batting. No longer did people have to quilt 1/2" apart. No longer did we have to worry about kids and peanut butter on precious quilts. We could make those quilts easily and quickly by machine and wash them safely in the washing machine.

Today we have five choices in batting materials: cotton, blends, polyester, silk, and wool.

Cotton

The handquilters often prefer cotton because the needle glides easily through the thin quilt sandwich. Because cotton will shift and tear, however, quilting stitches must be close together. Cotton will shrink when washed, which is why some quilters do not prewash their piecing or backing fabrics: they want the fabrics and batting to pucker around the quilting stitches, giving the quilt an antique look.

Quilts: Two companies produce all-cotton batting for quilts. 1) Mountain Mist (Stearns Technical Textiles Company) makes both *100% Natural* and *Blue Ribbon*. The former must be quilted no further apart than 1"; the latter, 1-1/2" to 2". Because of a finish treatment, Blue Ribbon won't shrink when washed. It's also slightly easier to needle by hand. 2) Morning Glory's *Clearly Cotton Batting* comes in both natural and unbleached and can be quilted up to 6" apart. Why would you want one over the other? On light-colored top fabric, the flecks in the unbleached batting might show through. On the other hand, some people object to the harsh chemicals used in the bleaching process. Both of these products are needlepunched (explained on page 221).

Garments: If your garment features piecing over quilting, you may want to use *100% cotton flannel* as a batting. You can piece directly to it, with no backing needed, and later line it. Buy flannel either in narrow widths (diaper flannel), in wider widths, or as sheets. In hot climates, you may want to try even lighter materials; Naomi Baker suggests *100% cotton interlock knits*. Obviously, you won't get a puffy look, but if your emphasis is on piecing, not quilting, it doesn't matter.

Cheryl Trostrud-White has seen "wonderful jackets made with a cotton batt and unwashed fabric. The large quilted piece is washed several times before cutting out the pattern. It then resembles an old quilt."

Crafts: Morning Glory is the only company offering *All Cotton Stuffing Fiber*, especially useful if you're making gifts for babies or people with sensitive skins who cannot tolerate man-made fibers.

Make batting for potholders out of many layers of cotton batting. To ensure against burns, either cut up an old *Teflon ironing-board cover* and put inside or use a layer of *Iron Quick*, sold by Nancy's Notions.

Home dec: Upholstery supply places have *cotton batting* at cheap prices. Look in your Yellow Pages. It's not something you'd want to use for quilts, because it's lumpy and full of cotton junk.

Some people hang wide widths of *cotton flannel* on walls to serve as a design wall while making quilts and wallhangings.

Blends

Because quilting has become big business, the market has responded to quilters' needs. One of those needs is a batting that is thin and cool like cotton without the hassle of close quilting and that lasts like polyester without its bearding. The answer is a batting blended of the two. The polyester part of the blend comes from a thin scrim that helps hold the cotton together and retards shrinkage.

Quilts: Several companies make blended batting. 1) The grandmother of blended batting is *Cotton Classic* by Fairfield Processing, which has been available for over 12 years. It is 80% cotton/20% polyester, about 1/8" thick, and can be quilted up to 3" apart. This batting is bonded with a light resin to hold it together. The batting hardly shrinks, but some people prefer to soak it before use to soften it. Deb Wagner is particularly fond of Cotton Classic, using it in her award-winning quilt (see page 16). She reminds us that "machine quilting looks hideous until you wash it and it puffs up." 2) Warm Products, Inc., makes *Warm & Natural*, a needlepunched cotton batting "bonded" only by the needles punching through a scrim inside. This gives it tensile strength so that copious quilting is not required to hold it together. You can quilt up to 10" apart. The batting is not bleached; therefore, you should wash it before construction to remove flecks and oils. If you don't prewash it and you allow it to sit wet the first time you do wash it, oils could stain light fabrics. To prewash, put it in the bathtub or washing machine, but don't let the machine agitate. Drain the water and throw the batting into the dryer. Warm & Natural is available in packages or by the bolt. New for them is a 124"-wide bolt—this should be carried by Keepsake Quilting if your local store doesn't. 3) Harriet Hargrave, author of *Heirloom Machine Quilting*, has designed an 80/20 blended batting for Hobbs Bonded Fibers, called *Heirloom Cotton Batting*. It is long-staple cotton, lightly needlepunched and bonded, but it will shrink about 5%. This means you must plan ahead. Are your fabrics preshrunk? Then you might want to preshrink the batting by soaking it in tepid water in a washer. Be sure not to agitate it, or the batting will disintegrate. Spin out the water and dry in the dryer set on air or fluff. You can quilt up to 3" apart. 4) Newer on the blend scene is Mountain Mist's needlepunched *Cotton Choice*, a 90/10 blend. You can quilt as much as 8" apart and do not need to presoak. This batt was designed specifically for machine quilting and is harder to hand-needle. Hari Walner, who has been using pre-washed Warm & Natural for her continuous machine-quilting designs, loves the feel of Cotton Choice. "It's heavier than Cotton Classic." 5) Morning Glory's *Old Fashion Cotton Batting* is needlepunched through a thin polyester scrim and can be quilted up to 12" apart.

Garments: Cotton Classic is a favorite of garment makers. Ann Boyce splits the layers to make an even thinner batting. For her Fairfield Fashion show garments, Cheryl Trostrud-White, former head of the Wearable Art Connection of Southern California, quilts Cotton Classic with no backing. She lines the garments and doesn't wash them. (If she were planning to wash them, she'd back the batting to enclose it.) "I prefer to pre-soak Cotton Classic, although it is not necessary for machine quilting. I like the feel and smell better afterwards. I have destroyed three batts by forgetting to skip the agitating cycle. I tried putting Downy Softener in the soak water once. Because it didn't agitate, I ended up with areas of blue on the batt. I buy the largest

batt available and use it for several garments. I save all the leftovers for smaller projects."

We don't think of outerwear insulation as blends, but they are. The RainShed's *Thinsulate*, developed by 3M, is 65% olefin/35% polyester. They also have *Thinsulate Lite Loft*, 77.5% polyester/22.5% polyolefin. They say "the feel is the closest thing to down."

Polyester

Most of us are ignorant about the grades of polyester batting. If we're price-conscious, we go to the local chain store and buy the cheapest polyester on the bolt for our quilts. It is only later, when the polyester begins to beard through the top fabric or the quilt has lost its loft or the dark fabric on the back affects the color of light fabrics on the front that we wonder what happened.

The higher the percentage of virgin polyester strands in a mixture, the better the polyester batting and the whiter it is. In high-quality poly batting, every little fiber has 10 – 12 crimps per inch, which will be retained, no matter what. Unfortunately, in our zeal to recycle, we don't realize that those reclaimed plastic pop bottles become junk for cheap batting. The crimp cannot be recaptured, so the loft eventually compresses, and the batting looks gray. Most of the top batting companies don't use recycled fiber.

Batting arrives at the plant in 550- to 650-pound compressed bales. It is opened out and the fibers are laid either head to tail, at right angles to each other, or in a random web. The fibers can then be chemically bonded in two ways: thermal or resin. For thermal bonding, low-melt fibers are added to the mix and all is sent through an oven. The low-melt fibers act as a binder. In resin bonding, resin is sprayed and bonding occurs when the batting passes through ovens. We have embraced resin bonding in the last ten years because it has a high tensile strength, allowing us to quilt far apart, and it is resistant to the stresses of machine washings. However, the world wants less chemicals used in everything, so expect to see more thermal bonding. It has a better hand, a higher loft, and it's easier for the needle to pass through, which is important to high-speed commercial quilting. It does, however, beard more than resin-bonded batting and may pull apart in machine washing.

A third method of bonding is needle-punching, which compresses the batt and forces the fibers to intertwine. Imagine 10,000 needles, each like a tiny saw, punching through the fibers almost like a sewing machine and causing them to interlock. Since the outside fibers may be looser, bearding is more of a problem with needlepunched batts.

Two companies have unique bonding processes. Mountain Mist polyester battings are resin-bonded by a method called Glazene. They are not spray-bonded, leaving them soft and drapeable. Morning Glory is the only manufacturer with a garnetted batt, a method of orienting fibers so they interlock.

Polyester batting is also sold unbonded. Morning Glory's Great Glory is one brand and they tell me its largest concentration of use is in Utah among the Mormons and in Pennsylvania, Ohio, and Kansas, suggesting a handquilting use. When manufactured correctly, unbonded polyester does not shift or migrate.

Some quilting teachers call for a certain ounce weight of batting for projects. This can be almost meaningless, because companies do not use the same measurement system and battings manufactured to the same ounce weight are squished to varying thicknesses. For machine quilting, especially, we care more about loft than ounce weight. If you are doing extensive quilting, choose a low-loft batting. Even then, prepare for some shrinkage in overall size.

Quilts: Some of the low-loft brands are Fairfield's *Low-Loft* (bonded), *Traditional*, and *Ultra-Loft* (both needlepunched); Hobbs's *Poly-Down* and *Poly-Down DK* (a needlepunched charcoal gray batt to use with dark fabrics); Morning Glory's *Glory Bee I* (bonded); and Mountain Mist's *Quilt Lite* (bonded).

In the regular-loft category comes Fairfield's *Extra-Loft*, Buffalo Batt's *Super Fluff!*, Mountain Mist's *Glazene*, Morning Glory's *Quilter's Choice*, and Pellon's *Quilter's Fleece*. If you are doing extensive machine quilting on regular-loft batting, prepare for shrinkage of the quilt. Anita Hallock's queen-size quilt shrank from 95" x 105" to 84" x 96".

High-loft battings are usually tied. An innovative way to machine-tack a comforter has been devised by Cambridge Marking Systems. Lay an interfacing-like material marked with various designs over the top fabric and mark. Baste the quilt sandwich; then tack with a zigzag set at 0 stitch length. Fairfield's *Hi-Loft*, Hobbs's *Cloud Loft*, Morning Glory's *Glory Bee II*, Mountain Mist's *Fatt Batt*, or Buffalo Batt's *Europa* are good candidates for high-loft battings.

The RainShed has *Polarguard* for sleeping bags and comforters. This makes a *warm* covering! It has extremely long-filament polyester fibers which will not easily pull apart, allowing quilting at larger intervals.

Dacron is a brand name of polyester and is made to more rigorous standards than other poly battings. *Glory Bee III* and *Great Glory* by Morning Glory Products of 100% Dacron are especially soft and lofty, but of course are more expensive, too.

If you are making quilts for smokers, consider using Putnam's *Special Edition* batting. This is about 1/2" thick and thermal-bonded. If a lit cigarette touches the quilt, the hole won't catch fire, unlike some polyester battings, which will flame up and burn. (Most battings, however, meet stringent government standards.) On the other hand, batting is rarely used alone. The cloth surrounding it will flame instantly, so the distinction may not matter.

Garments: Hobbs's *Thermore* is a thin batt made expressly for clothing, with an additional coating of resin to discourage bearding. You could piece directly to it without a backing. It is comfortable to wear and because it is so thin, you don't feel like a walking suit of armor. It was originally developed for the Italian ski team.

Nancy Moore prefers a 1/2" loft, not needlepunched, like Fairfield's *Extra-Loft* for her unique dense quilting look. Thinner batting is too stiff and doesn't puff up enough. But you have to plan for shrinkage of the yardage. She suggests, for example, that you cut the lining 2" longer than the garment.

Warm Products also makes *Warm Winter*, which is Holofil for jackets. A thinner product is Pellon's *Thermolam Plus*, needlepunched and extremely warm.

A new product is *Timtex* by Timber Lane Press (sold by Log Cabin Dry Goods). This is a stiff yet flexible interfacing-like material which Timber Lane is using in baseball cap brims and sewing kits. It holds a definite shape but can be sewn through and is machine-washable and -dryable. Tina Bloxham says it's also perfect for placemats and costumes.

The RainShed has a *stretch needlepunch* that you can use with stretch panels in outwear.

Crafts: Use Judi Maddigan's method to assess the quality of loose fiberfill. Pull a clump of fiber apart over dark paper or material. If tiny particles drift onto the paper, you're holding a bargain brand not worth the time and energy. High-quality fiberfill comes from long-staple fibers and will not break when pulled apart. A particularly high quality fiberfill that will spoil you for anything else is made by *Jen-Cel-Lite*.

Since polyester batting melts when hot, it is not a good choice for batting in potholders.

A group of volunteers from the Maryland Bishop Method sewing group has been making quilts and toys for low-income mothers enrolled in a "Healthy Mothers, Healthy Babies" class. As an incentive to finish the classes, each parent receives handmade bibs, toys, and quilts. The filler is Morning Glory's *Down-Lite*, which is especially soft, says Maureen Thomas.

Home dec: Fusible Fleece by Pellon is attracting more and more converts. You don't have to back it with anything and it holds up well in wall hangings, placemats, and pillow fronts. Dritz also makes *Press-on Fleece*.

Morning Glory Products makes a seasonal fiberfill called *Snowsoff*, which sparkles like snow. It's perfect for holiday decorating.

In your zeal to decorate during the holidays, be careful of batts used in tree skirts. Only Putnam makes a flame-retardant tree-skirt batt, called *Special Edition*.

Warm Window is made by Warm Products. It is an insulated window-shade system that reduces heat loss through windows up to 83%. Just sew a decorated cover fabric to the fabric and make easy Roman, balloon, or hobbled shades.

Silk

Because of its cost, silk batting is primarily used in quilted jackets. It comes in rounded cone shapes called "leaves." It takes six to eight leaves to make a long-sleeved jacket. About 30 – 35 leaves make a pound of batting. You will need to sandwich silk batting between two layers of China silk before you add the top fabric and backing. This is to prevent bearding. YLI sends good instructions with their *silk batting*.

Wool

While not many people are using wool batting, it is beautiful to feel. Some brands, like Bemidji's *Pure Wool Quilt Batting*, come with or without a cheese-cloth covering. You need add only a cover if you use the tied version. The Taos Mountain *Traditional* is a low-loft batting, 94" wide and needlepunched to minimize bearding.

Harriet Hargrave has designed a wool batting for Hobbs called Heirloom Premium Wool. It is thin, lightly resin-bonded, machine-washable, and can be quilted 3" apart. The next in a signature line of battings from Harriet Hargrave and Hobbs will be silk.

The following charts are grouped by loft, then fiber (blends, cotton, polyester, silk, wool). I next list size, because I'd rather not piece batting. The batting companies, of course, would rather you choose first by brand. Finally, the listings within those two categories are alphabetical.

These are standard batting sizes, with minute variations among companies:

Crib: 36" x 45"
Twin: 72" x 90"
Full: 81" x 96"
Queen: 90" x 108"
King: 120" square

Sue Hausmann, TV hostess of The Art of Sewing With Sue Hausmann. *Photo courtesy of Sue Hausmann.*

Loft	Content	Sizes	Name	Mfg	Quilting Interval	Finish	Prewash?	Shrinkage
Low (can split layers)	80% cotton/20% polyester	36" x 45"; 81" x 96"	Cotton Classic	Fairfield Processing Corp	2" - 3"	Resin bonded	No (yes for hand quilting)	
Low	100% cotton	40" square; 45" x 60"; 90" x 108"	Old Fashion Cotton Batting	Morning Glory Products	10" - 12"	Needlepunched through scrim (unbleached)	Yes; in pillow case	
Low	80% cotton/20% polyester	90" x 108"	Heirloom Cotton Batting	Hobbs Bonded Fibers	3"	Needlepunched and bonded	Yes (don't agitate)	5%
Low (designed especially for machine quilting)	90% cotton/10% polyester	34" x 72"; 90"-wide yardage	Cotton Choice	Mountain Mist (Stearns Technical Textiles Co.)	8"	Needlepunched	No	
Low	65% polyolefin/35% polyester	60"-wide yardage	Thinsulate	3M; c/o The RainShed Outdoor Fabrics	10" – 12"	Scrim on one side	No	
Low (and stiff)	70% polyester; 30% rayon	22" wide; 4-1/2" wide; 3/8 yd. package	Timtex	Timber Lane Press	Any	Acrylic binder	No	
Low	100% cotton	124" wide yardage	Warm & Natural	Warm Products	10"	Needlepunched through scrim	Yes (don't agitate; dry cool or warm; air-dry)	1%
Low	100% cotton	90" x 108"; 120" square; 90"-wide	Clearly Cotton	Morning Glory Products	4" - 6"	Needlepunched (bleached and unbleached)		
Low	100% cotton	45" x 60"; 90" x 108"	Blue Ribbon	Mountain Mist (Stearns Technical Textiles Co.)	1-1/2" to 2"	Resin-bonded Glazene	No	
Low	100% cotton	81" x 96"; 81" x 108"	100% Bleached Cotton Batting	Mountain Mist (Stearns Technical Textiles Co.)	1/4" – 1/2"	Water-soluble resin-bonded	No	
Low	100% cotton	Usually 54"- or 60"- wide	100% cotton interlock knit	Yardage			Yes	Up to 3"/yard
Low	100% cotton	Varies	100% cotton flannel	Yardage or sheets				

Low Loft–Polyester

Loft	Content	Sizes	Name	Mfg	Quilting Interval	Finish	Prewash?	Shrinkage
Low	100% polyester	48" wide	Simplicity Poly-insulate II	Air-Lite Synthetics Mfg. Inc.		Thermal-bonded	No	
Low	100% polyester	45"-wide	Press-On Fleece	Dritz	Any	Needlepunched	No	
Low	100% polyester	45"-wide	Craft-T-Fleece	Dritz	Any	Needlepunched	No	
Low	100% polyester	36" x 45"; 45" x 60"; 72" x 90"; 81" x 96"; 90" x 108"; 120" square; 45"/81"/90"-wide	Ultra-Loft	Fairfield Processing Corp	4" – 6"	Needlepunched	No	
Low	100% polyester	45" x 60"; 72" x 90"; 81" x 96"; 90" x 108"; 120"square; 45"/81"/90"- wide	Traditional	Fairfield Processing Corp	4" – 6"	Needlepunched	No	
Low	100% polyester	45" x 60"; 81" x 96"; 90" x 108"; 120" square	Low-Loft	Fairfield Processing Corp	4" – 6"	Resin-bonded	No	
Low	100% polyester	27" x 45"; 54" x 45"; 90" x 108"; 45" roll	Thermore	Hobbs Bonded Fibers	Any	Resin-bonded	No	
Low	100% polyester	45" x 60"; 72" x 90"; 81" x 96"; 90" x 108"; 120" square	Cloud Lite	Hobbs Bonded Fibers	3" – 4"	Resin-bonded	No	
Low	100% polyester	36" x 45" wide; 36" x 22"; 45"-wide vardage	Fusible Fleece	HTC	Any		No	
Low	100% polyester	45"-wide vardage	Thermal Fleece	HTC	Any		No	
Low	100% polyester	45"-wide vardage	Glory Bee I	Morning Glory Products		Resin-bonded	No	
Low	100% polyester	45" x 60"; 81" x 96"; 90" x 108"	Quilt Lite	Mountain Mist (Stearns Technical Textiles Co.)	3"	Resin-bonded Glazene	No	
Low (can stack layers)	100% polyester	Roll batting	Comfortloft	Mountain Mist (Stearns Technical Textiles Co.)	5"		No	
Low	100% polyester		Thermolam Plus	Pellon			No	
Low	100% polyester		Fusible Fleece	Pellon			No	
Low	100% polyester	36" x 45"	Soft Shapes	Putnam	Any	Needlepunched craft fleece	No	
Low	100% polyester		Warm Winter	Warm Products			No	
Low	100% polyester		Warm Window	Warm Products			No	

Loft	Content	Sizes	Name	Mfg	Quilting Interval	Finish	Prewash?	Shrinkage
Low	100% silk		Silk	YLI Corp	Sandwich layers between China silk			
Low	100% wool		Pure Wool Quilt Batting	Bemidji Woolen Mills				
Low	100% wool	Varies	100% wool (wall hangings)	Blankets	Any	None	No	
Low	100% wool	90" x 108"	Heirloom Wool	Hobbs	3"	Resin-bonded (lightly)	No	
Regular	77.5% polyester / 22.5% polyolefin	60"-wide	Thinsulate Lite Loft	3M; c/o The RainShed Outdoor Fabrics	Any		No	
Regular	100% polyester	45" x 60"; 72" x 90"; 90" x 108"; 81" x 96"; 120" square; 45"-wide; 81"-wide; 90"-wide	Extra-Loft	Fairfield Processing Corp	4"	Resin-bonded	No	
Regular	100% polyester	45" x 60"; 81" x 96"; 90" x 108"; 120" x 120" (dark 90" x 108")	Poly-Down (Poly-Down DK)	Hobbs Bonded Fibers	3" - 4"	Resin-bonded	No	
Regular	100% polyester	45" x 60"; 81" x 96"; 90" x 108"; 120" square	Glory Bee II	Morning Glory Products		Resin-bonded		
Regular	100% Dacron		Glory Bee III	Morning Glory Products		Garnetted		
Regular	100% polyester		Quilter's Choice	Morning Glory Products		Garnetted		
Regular	100% polyester	36" x 45"; 45" x 60"; 72" x 90"; 81" x 96"; 90" x 108"; 120" square	Glazene	Mountain Mist (Stearns Technical Textiles Co.)	3"	Resin -bonded Glazene	No	
Regular	100% polyester		Quilter's Fleece	Pellon				
Regular	100% polyester	45" x 60"; 81" x 96"; 90" x 108"; 45" round tree skirt	Special Edition	Putnam Co	2" - 4"	Thermal-bonded	No	
Regular	100% wool	94"-wide yardage	Traditional	Taos Mountain Wool Works	3" - 10"	Needlepunched	Steam before using	Minimal

High Loft

Loft	Content	Sizes	Name	Mfg	Quilting Interval	Finish	Prewash?	Shrink-age
High	100% polyester	91" x 108"	Europa	Buffalo Batt & Felt Corp				
High	100% polyester	45" x 60"; 72" x 91"; 81" x 96"; 91" x 108"; 50"-wide	Super Fluff!	Buffalo Batt & Felt Corp	4"	Resin-bonded	No	
High	100% polyester	50"-wide	Thermo Batt	Buffalo Batt & Felt Corp		Thermal-bonded		
High	100% polyester	60"-wide	Polarguard HV	c/o The RainShed Outdoor Fabrics	10" – 12"		No	
High	100% polyester	45" x 60"; 90" x 108"	Hi-Loft	Fairfield Processing Corp	6" (for tying)	Resin-bonded	No	
High	100% polyester	45" x 60"; 81" x 96"; 90" x 108"; 120" square	Cloud Loft	Hobbs Bonded Fibers	3" – 4"	Resin-bonded	No	
High	100% Dacron	81" x 96"; 90" x 108"; 120" square	Great Glory	Morning Glory Products		Garnetted		
High	100% polyester	45" x 60"; 72" x 90"; 81" x 96"; 90" x 108"	Fatt Batt	Mountain Mist (Stearns Technical Textiles Co.)	4"	Resin-bonded Glazene	No	

Gina Butler, Oklahoma City, OK, dense-quilted vest inspired by Nancy Moore's book. Designs from cut paper and free-hand drawing, drawn with a Stabilo chalk pencil. Poly/cotton fabric, polyester batting. Photo by Robbie Fanning

	Mattress size	Coverlet including Standard 22" Drop and 15" Tuck	Estimated Backing Yardage for Coverlet		Approximate Continuous Binding Needed*	
			36" wide	45" wide	inches	yards
Twin	39" x 75"	83" x 112"	9-1/3	5	400	11-1/8
Full (double)	54" x 75"	98" x 112"	9-1/3	9-3/4	430	12
Queen	60" x 80"	104" x 117"	9-3/4	9-3/4	452	12-1/2
King	76" x 80"	120" x 117"	13	9-3/4	474	13-1/4
California King	72" x 84"	116" x 121"	13-1/2	10-1/4	484	13-1/2

* See charts in Edge Treatment for how many yards of fabric will yield X yards of continuous binding.

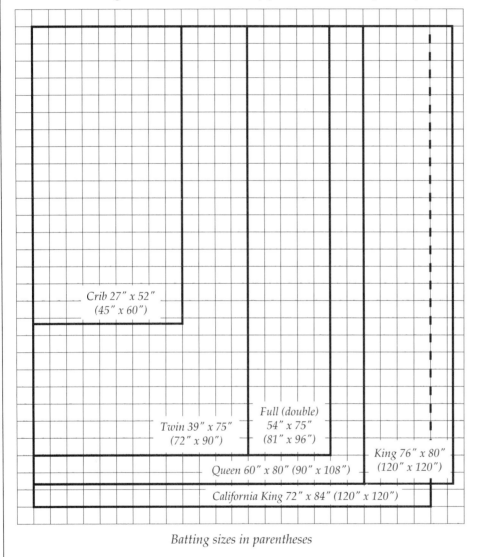

Crib 27" x 52" (45" x 60")

Twin 39" x 75" (72" x 90")

Full (double) 54" x 75" (81" x 96")

King 76" x 80" (120" x 120")

Queen 60" x 80" (90" x 108")

California King 72" x 84" (120" x 120")

Batting sizes in parentheses

Bias, Joining. See *Binding, Joining; Joining 45° Ends;* and *Joining 90° Ends.*

Binding, Bias. Fabric cut in strips at 45° to the crosswise or lengthwise grain. Preferred when rounding corners. Can be cut single-fold or double-fold. See also *Binding, Joining; Bias Binding, Making;* and *Edge Finishes.*

Binding, Making Bias. Fold the upper left corner down to meet the lower edge, forming a square. Mark the diagonal line this fold makes (which is true bias). Cut along the diagonal line and move the triangle formed to the right crosswise edge of the fabric. Sew a 1/4" seam.

Machine Quilting

On the rightside of the fabric, mark diagonal lines across the parallelogram you just made as wide as your binding requires. Be careful: the bias width is "a", not "b", as shown. The bias width "a" is perpendicular to the diagonal lines; "b" is larger than the width you need.

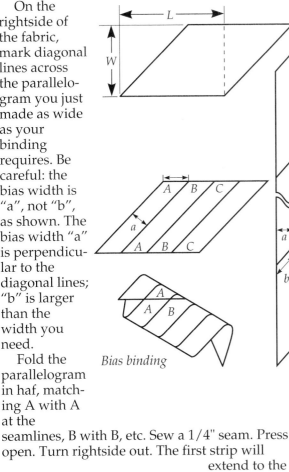

Bias binding

Fold the parallelogram in haf, matching A with A at the seamlines, B with B, etc. Sew a 1/4" seam. Press open. Turn rightside out. The first strip will extend to the left of the seam. Cut along the marked lines for a continuous bias srip.

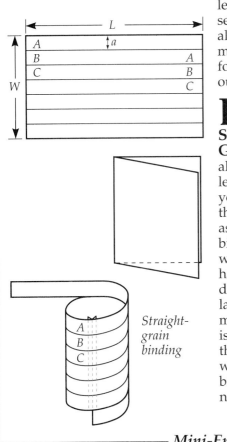

Straight-grain binding

Binding, Making Straight-Grain.

Mark along the length of your fabric on the rightside as wide as binding. You will probably have to discard the last section marked, if it is less wide than the width of binding you need.

Fold the fabric in half and match A to A, B to B, and so forth. The first width of binding will extend above the folded fabric. Sew 1/4" seam. Press open. Turn rightside out.

Cut along the marked lines and your binding will be continuous.

Binding, Double-fold. Can be used on straight-grain or bias binding. Decide whether to join ends before turning (see page 238), to lap ends (see page 236), to miter corners during first stitching (see page 237), or to stitch a double miter (see page 234).

Cut the bias strip *six times* as wide as what you want to show on the front and *add* the loft to allow for quilt thickness. Be sure to test before you cut a lot of yardage.

Fold the strip in half lengthwise, wrongsides together, and press lightly. On the underside of the quilt, stitch the binding to backing, raw edges together. Fold the binding up over the quilt edge and pin a little beyond the seam on the topside. Edgestitch.

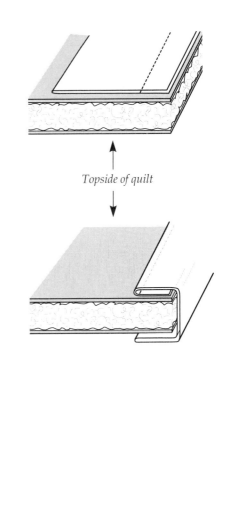

Topside of quilt

Binding, Joining. I learned this handy way to join bias strips from Ann Person in *The Stretch & Sew Book of Sewing on Knits.* Cut binding 7" – 10" longer than your calculations. Start binding on the underside of the quilt halfway down one side. Don't start bindings at a quilt corner. Cut 3" off one end for a joining template. Press in half the long way. Set aside.

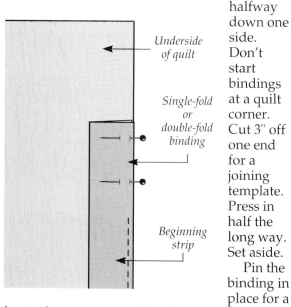

Underside of quilt

Single-fold or double-fold binding

Beginning strip

Pin the binding in place for a few inches, raw edge of binding matching raw edge of quilt and rightsides together. When beginning, leave 2" of binding unstitched, to be joined to other end. When you are 3" from where you started, stop stitching and break threads. Don't trim end of binding yet.

Lay joining template over beginning strip, leaving 1" of beginning strip to left of joining template. Place a pin as a marker in the quilt aligned with the halfway press mark on the joining template. Trim beginning strip even with the upper side of the joining template.

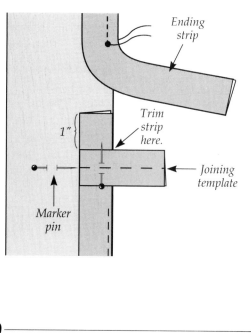

Ending strip

Trim strip here.

1"

Joining template

Marker pin

Remove joining template. Fold back beginning strip. Lay ending strip along edge of quilt. Lay joining template over ending strip, aligning fold with marker pin in quilt. Trim ending strip even with lower side of joining template.

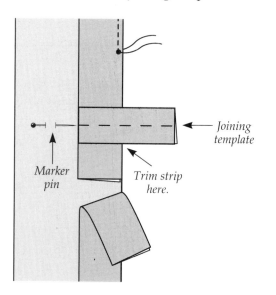

Joining template

Marker pin

Trim strip here.

Place ends of two strips rightsides together at a 90° angle and pin. Draw from corner of top strip to corner of underlying strip. Baste along line with pin or thread. Check to be sure join is exact before final stitching. Stitch. Press seam open, then trim seam. Clever, huh?

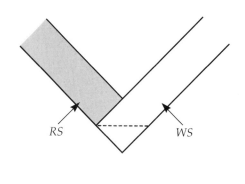

RS   *WS*

Binding, Single-fold.

Binding, **Single-fold.** Can be used on straight-grain or bias binding. Decide whether to join ends before turning (see page 238), to lap ends (see page 236), to miter corners during first stitching (see page 237), or to stitch a double miter (see page 234).

Cut the bias strip *four times* as wide as what you want to show on the front and *add the loft* to allow for quilt thickness. Be sure to test before you cut a lot of yardage.

Rightside of binding against rightside of backing, seam all around the quilt in a minimum 1/2" seam (a smaller seam is tricky—if you are inaccurate in seaming, the quilt may pull away from the binding).

Fold in the raw edge to the raw edge of the quilt; then fold the fold up to and a little beyond the seamline on the topside. Pin in place and edgestitch. *Optional:* Use a walking foot to keep the fabric from shifting and invisible thread in the bobbin if you fear your stitching line will wobble back and forth over the binding seam line on the back. Or use a binding foot.

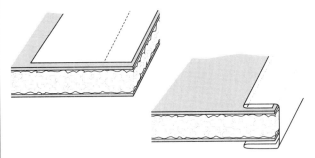

Binding, Straight-Grain.

Binding, **Straight-Grain.** Binding strips cut on the crosswise or lengthwise grain (rather than cut on the bias). Preferred by the same sort of people who press seam open and speed-piece without guilt. See *Joining 90° Ends.* Do not use continuous straight-grain binding if corners are rounded (binding will cup). Crosswise straight-grain binding will stretch slightly. Lengthwise grain is more stable.

Binding, Yardage Needed.

Binding, **Yardage Needed.** Ask yourself four questions:

1. What method of binding, single or double fold?
2. Straight-grain or bias binding?
3. How wide a finished edge on the front?
4. How wide is the fabric you're buying/using?

To find out how many yards of fabric to buy to get the number of inches (yards) of continuous binding you need, consult the appropriate table on the following page:

Continuous Straight-grain Binding, Single Fold.
Continuous Straight-grain Binding, Double Fold.
Continuous Bias Binding, Single Fold (for widths of 36", 45", 54", 60").
Continuous Bias Binding, Double Fold (for widths of 36", 45", 54", 60").

(*Note:* All calculations based on useable fabric width—e.g., after trimming 36"-wide fabric, useable width is approximately 34".)

How to use the tables

Example 1. For a king-size coverlet, the Standard Bed Size Chart says we need 474" of continuous binding. We choose to make a double-fold straight-grain binding 1/2" wide. Our chosen fabric is 45" wide. We look at the chart for 45"-wide fabric.

For a finished 1/2" edge, one yard of fabric will yield 465" of bias strips cut 3-1/4" wide. We need 9" more. Each strip is 60" long across the fabric, so we need one more strip.

1 strip x 3.25" each strip = 3-1/4" = 1/8 yd.

We need one yard + 1/8 yd. = 1-1/8 yd. to cover the edge of the king-size coverlet in continuous binding.

Example 2. In Europe you bought one yard of gorgeous 36"-wide fabric. You want to use it for binding on a double-bed coverlet. What is the best width and method of binding to use without running out of binding fabric?

The Standard Bed Size Chart says you need 430" binding. Looking at each table under 36"-wide fabric, you see that you have enough fabric to make a 1/2" straight-grain single-fold binding, but not enough for any wider edge or for bias or double-fold edges.

Continuous Straight-Grain Binding, Single-fold

Finished Front Width	Cut Strip this Wide	36" Fabric Width		45" Fabric Width		54" Fabric Width		60" Fabric Width	
		# of Strips / yard	Total length / yard	# of Strips / yard	Total length / yard	# of Strips / yard	Total length / yard	# of Strips / yard	Total length / yard
0.25"	1.25"	28	952"	28	1176"	28	1456"	28	1624"
0.50"	2.25"	16	544"	16	672"	16	832"	16	928"
0.75"	3.25"	11	374"	11	462"	11	572"	11	638"
1.00"	4.25"	8	272"	8	336"	8	416"	8	464"
1.50"	6.25"	5	170"	5	210"	5	260"	5	290"
2.00"	8.25"	4	136"	4	168"	4	208"	4	232"

Continuous Straight-Grain Binding, Double-fold

Finished Front Width	Cut Strip this Wide	36" Fabric Width		45" Fabric Width		54" Fabric Width		60" Fabric Width	
		# of Strips / yard	Total length / yard	# of Strips / yard	Total length / yard	# of Strips / yard	Total length / yard	# of Strips / yard	Total length / yard
0.25"	1.75"	20	680"	20	840"	20	1040"	20	1160"
0.50"	3.25"	11	374"	11	462"	11	572"	11	638"
0.75"	4.75"	7	238"	7	294"	7	364"	7	406"
1.00"	6.25"	5	170"	5	210"	5	260"	5	290"
1.50"	9.25"	3	102"	3	126"	3	156"	3	174"
2.00"	12.25"	2	68"	2	84"	2	104"	2	116"

Continuous Bias Binding, Single-fold

Finished Front Width	Cut Strip this Wide	36" Fabric Width			45" Fabric Width			54" Fabric Width			60" Fabric Width		
		# of Strips / yard	Length of Bias Strip	Total length / yard	# of Strips / yard	Length of Bias Strip	Total length / yard	# of Strips / yard	Length of Bias Strip	Total length / yard	# of Strips / yard	Length of Bias Strip	Total length / yard
0.25"	1.25"	20	47"	940"	20	58"	1160"	20	72"	1440"	20	81"	1620"
0.50"	2.25"	11	47"	517"	11	58"	638"	11	72"	792"	11	81"	891"
0.75"	3.25"	7	47"	329"	7	58"	406"	7	72"	504"	7	81"	567"
1.00"	4.25"	5	47"	235"	5	58"	290"	5	72"	360"	5	81"	405"
1.50"	6.25"	4	47"	188"	4	58"	232"	4	72"	288"	4	81"	324"
2.00"	8.25"	3	47"	141"	3	58"	174"	3	72"	216"	3	81"	243"

Continuous Bias Binding, Double-fold

Finished Front Width	Cut Strip this Wide	36" Fabric Width			45" Fabric Width			54" Fabric Width			60" Fabric Width		
		# of Strips / yard	Length of Bias Strip	Total length / yard	# of Strips / yard	Length of Bias Strip	Total length / yard	# of Strips / yard	Length of Bias Strip	Total length / yard	# of Strips / yard	Length of Bias Strip	Total length / yard
0.25"	1.75"	14	47"	658"	14	58"	812"	14	72"	1008"	14	81"	1134"
0.50"	3.25"	7	47"	329"	7	58"	406"	7	72"	504"	7	81"	567"
0.75"	4.75"	5	47"	235"	5	58"	290"	5	72"	360	5	81"	405"
1.00"	6.25"	4	47"	188"	4	58"	232"	4	72"	288"	4	81"	324"
1.50"	9.25"	2	47"	94"	2	58"	116"	2	72"	144"	2	81"	162"
2.00"	12.25"	2	47""	94"	2	58"	116"	2	72"	144"	2	81"	162"

Block Sizes and Borders.

	Twin, 39" x 75"			Full, 54" x 75"		
Finished Block	Number of Blocks	Border Around Each Block	Gives a Pillow tuck of *	Number of Blocks	Border Around Each Block	Gives a Pillow tuck of *
6"	6 x 12	1/4"	3"	9 x 12	0	3"
8"	4 x 9	1/2"	5"	6 x 9	1/4"	6"
10"	3 x 7	3/4"	3"	5 x 7	0	5"
12"	3 x 6	1/4"	0	4 x 6	0	6"
14"	not recommended			3 x 5	1/2"	5"

	Queen, 60" x 80"			King, 76" x 80"		
Finished Block	Number of Blocks	Border Around Each Block	Gives a Pillow tuck of *	Number of Blocks	Border Around Each Block	Gives a Pillow tuck of *
6"	10 x 13	0	2"	12 x 13	0	0
8"	7 x 10	0	0	9 x 10	0	0
10"	6 x 8	0	0	7 x 8	1/4"	0
12"	5 x 6	1/4"	16"	6 x 6	1/4"	16"
14"	4 x 5	0	10"	5 x 5	1/4"	20"

* Add on one or two blocks to length for a deeper pillow tuck.

Note: This chart does not include side or end drop measurements, only mattress top measurement.

Blocks. See *Quilt-As-You-Go Blocks, Joining.*

Borders. See *Block Sizes and Borders.*

Continuous Bias Binding. See *Binding, Making Bias.*

Continuous Straight-Grain Binding. See *Binding, Making Straight-Grain.*

Double-Fold Binding. See *Binding, Double-fold.*

Double-mitered Edge. See *Edge Finishes, Double-mitered.*

Edge Finishes, Blindhem. We called this A Machine Curiosity in the first edition. Finish the double-fold binding edge as described in *Edge Finishes, Mitered.* Join ends as described in *Binding, Joining.* Turn binding to topside of quilt and miter corners. Pin edge in place with heads of pins facing the quilt center.

Fold binding to underside so only a tiny bit shows at the edge of the fold. Place quilt edge on water-soluble stabilizer if your machine doesn't like to stitch on nothing. Set up the machine for blindhem stitch. Loosen top tension.

Stitch along the edge of the quilt. The straight stitches stitch on air; the zigzag barely catches the fold of the quilt—adjust width of bite. Stitch one side at a time and tie off threads.

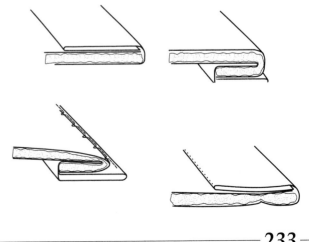

Edge Finishes, Continuous.

This is the simplest of all bindings. Sew one long piece of bias-cut material around all the quilted edges, without mitering. To do so, round off the corners of your work, using the edge of a teacup, plate, pocket former, or French curve to make a smooth line. Zigzag or straight stitch the edge of your quilt

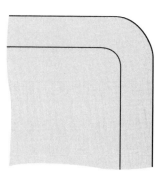

before applying the binding; it makes it easier to fold the binding over the edge. *Optional:* Use your steam iron to shape the binding before turning. See *Bias, Joining,* for how to join ends. See also *Binding, Single-fold* and *Binding, Double-fold.* To calculate yardage needs, see page 232.

Edge Finishes, Double-mitered.

This edge is completely machine-sewn. It is mitered on both the front and back. Use double-fold straight-grain binding and add 4" to the length of each strip. See page 232 for how wide to cut strips. Lay the first binding strip rightsides together against the *underside* of the quilt, raw edges matching. Let the binding overhang at the top about 2". Start and end stitching exactly a seam allowance from each end of quilt. Lock stitches with auto-lock or back stitches.

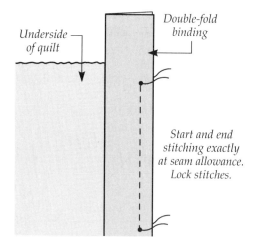

Underside of quilt

Double-fold binding

Start and end stitching exactly at seam allowance. Lock stitches.

This method was first shown to me in 1980 by Bev Soderlund, then of Kenwood, CA. In 1993, Linda Goodmon Emery showed me her Corner Mark-It tool, which does the same thing (but is calibrated only for 1/4″ seam allowances). Then Joan Bechtel of Midland, TX, sent her home-made miter tools, also calculated only for 1/4″ seam allowances. My method uses any seam allowance.

Remove quilt from machine and fold seam allowance toward quilt. Pin to hold. Use a ruler to draw a line on the binding at right angles to the stitched seam.

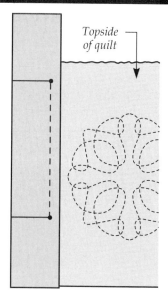

Topside of quilt

Fold the outside edge to the seam allowance and finger-press to mark center point. Open flat. Measure distance from seam allowance to press-marked point. Measure same distance on fold line toward end of strip and make dot.

Connect dot with seam allowance and with line at outside edge.

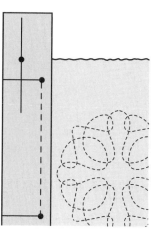

Place second binding strip directly behind marked binding strip, matching short ends and outside folded edge. Pay attention to matching the folded edges exactly. Pin strips together.

If your machine eats delicate points, put water-soluble stabilizer under the binding. With a short stitch length (1.5mm or 18 – 20 stitches per inch), sew along the marked line, taking two tiny stitches across the point. Lock stitches at both ends of stitching. Trim seam allowance to 1/8". Don't turn yet.

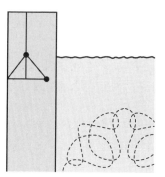

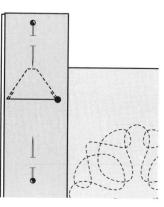

Turn quilt clockwise. Push completed corner to the left and pin second binding strip in place, matching raw edges with the quilt. Begin stitching at the end of the miter seam and stop a seam allowance from the next edge. Repeat methods.

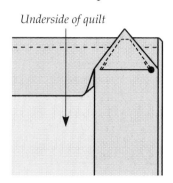

Underside of quilt

Stitch second binding strip.

After completing all four corners, finger-press miter seams open. Turn miter rightsides out, using a point turner to push out the corners. Pin the binding in place on the topside and edgestitch, blindhem, zigzag,

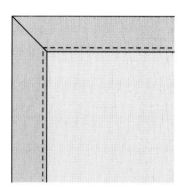

or use a decorative stitch to hold the binding in place.

Edge Finishes, Easy Miter. Use this finish to bring the backing of a quilted object over the edge to the top. It also works at the edge of napkins. Make a miter guide by cutting gridded template plastic across a line of 1" squares. Save both parts. I call the larger piece with the 135° angle the miter guide and the smaller triangle with the 45° angle the little miter guide. (An easier method is to buy a miter guide like Holiday Designs' Miterite.)

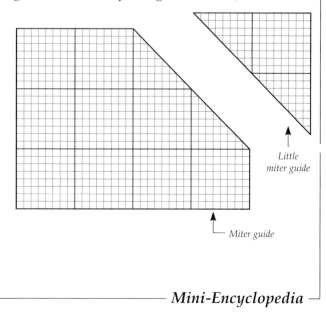

Little miter guide

Miter guide

Extend the edge of the quilted object to the edges of the backing. Make sure the intersections form 90° angles. Turn up seam

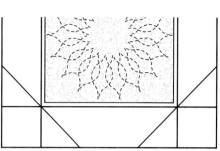

allowances and press. Use the miter guide to mark a 45° angle at each corner, bisecting the right angle formed by the seam allowances.

Fold the quilt, underside together, on the diagonal. Stitch on the angled line you drew, making certain the outside edges meet exactly. Trim 1/8" away, finger press, and turn to the topside. Repeat for each corner.

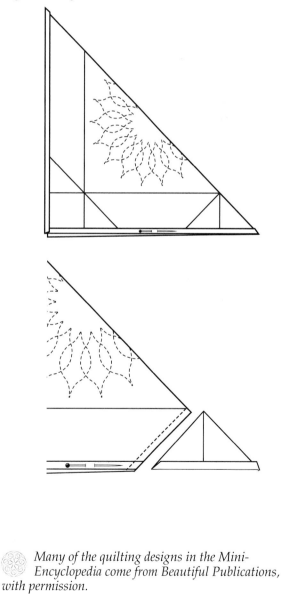

Many of the quilting designs in the Mini-Encyclopedia come from Beautiful Publications, with permission.

Edge Finishes, Inserted. Any number of decorative treatments can be inserted at the edge—large rickrack, ruffles, piping, triangles, prairie points, etc. Fold back the top and batting. Sew the pre-shrunk trim to the backing only, rightsides together. The part of the trim that extends to the left of the seamline toward the center of the quilt will stick out of the finished quilt edge. Trim the batting close to the stitching line. Fold the backing over the batting on the stitched line. Press gently. Fold the quilt top and pin it in place. Edgestitch.

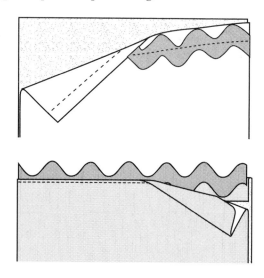

Another way to insert an edge is to lay the decorative insertion (rightsides together) against the quilt top. Lay a ribbon or piece of bias binding on top, rightside to the insertion's wrongside. Stitch. Grade seam to remove excess bulk. Then fold bias to underside and handstitch in place.

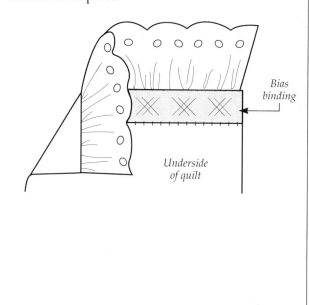

Bias binding

Underside of quilt

Edge Finishes, Lapped. Bind two opposite edges of the quilt, using single-fold or double-fold binding. Then bind the other two edges, including the binding you just finished. Be sure to turn under the top and bottom edges 1/4". Handstitch the ends closed, using a ladder stitch. This edging can be made from either the bias or the straight-grain of the fabric.

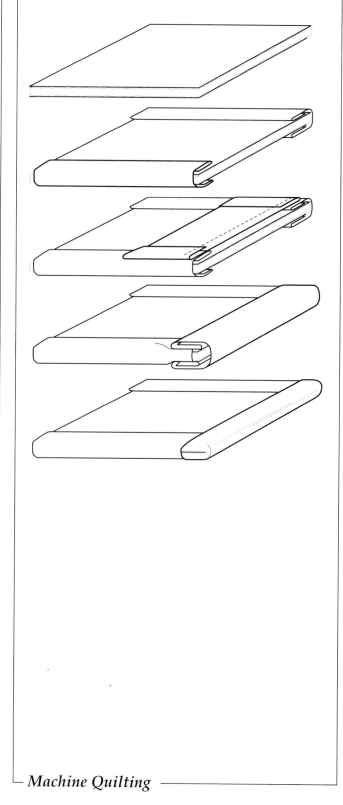

Edge Finishes, Mitered. Use this all-machine method for applying continuous binding to an edge. The finished binding size equals the seam allowance. See page 232 for how much binding to cut.

Raw edges together, pin binding to back of quilt along one edge. Leave 3" unstitched at beginning. Before stitching, put pin in binding at lower edge of corner. Use a marking pen to make a dot at the intersection of the two seam allowances at the corner. If your presser foot is not open enough to see the dot easily, put a pin

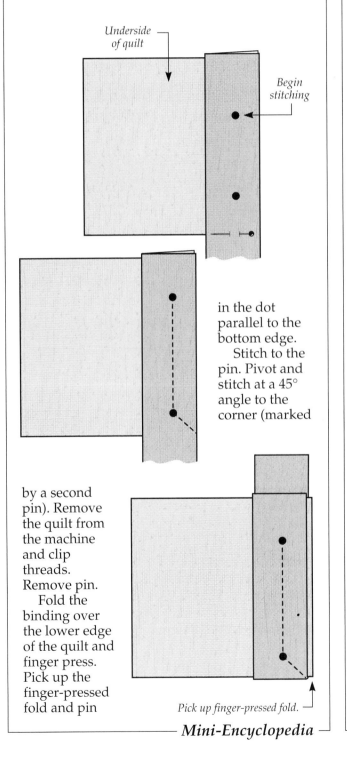

Underside of quilt

Begin stitching

in the dot parallel to the bottom edge.
Stitch to the pin. Pivot and stitch at a 45° angle to the corner (marked

by a second pin). Remove the quilt from the machine and clip threads. Remove pin.
Fold the binding over the lower edge of the quilt and finger press. Pick up the finger-pressed fold and pin

Pick up finger-pressed fold.

the two outside edges together. Pivot the fold to match the first edge you stitched. The raw edges of the binding should now match the raw edges of the second side of the quilt. Underneath is a 45° fold. Pin binding in place.

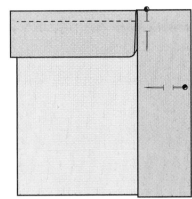

To sew the second edge, start in a bit from the edge and backstitch to the edge. Stitch a seam allowance away from the second side.

Repeat for remaining three corners.

Fold binding over edge, using fingers to miter both corners. Edgestitch binding to top

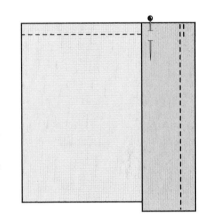

of quilt. *Optional:* Machine- or handstitch mitered corners in place (not necessary unless seam allowance is wide).

Support fabric artists— collect machine-quilted art.

Fabric Care Chart.

Fiber	Machine Washing	Machine Drying	Ironing	Dye Class	Beware
Cotton/poly	warm	low	warm	union	
100% cotton	hot water	regular	hot	fiber reactive direct	shrinks a lot
100% polyester	warm water	low	low-moderate	disperse acid	
Nylon	warm	low	cool (melts under high heat)	acid disperse	picks up colors from other fabrics in wash
Rayon	hand-wash	drip-dry	low-moderate on wrong side	fiber reactive direct	
Linen	hot	regular	hot	direct	
Silk	hand-wash or dry-clean	hand-wash or dry-clean	medium on wrong side; no steam	fiber-reactive acid	water spots
Wool	hand-wash in cool water or dry-clean	hand-wash in cool water or dry-clean	medium with press cloth	acid	shrinks drastically if exposed to heat (hot water or hot dryer air)

Fabric/Thread/Needle Chart for Quilting.

Fabrics	Threads	Needles American/European
Very sheer (lace, net, chiffon, voile, pantyhose)	Extra-fine	10/70
Lightweight/ transparent (organza, tricot, taffeta, organdy)	Extra-fine cotton, rayon, polyester	10/70
Lightweight cottons (gingham, calico, etc.), doubleknits, silk	Ordinary cotton, Size A silk twist	12/80
Medium-weight cottons (poplin, kettlecloth, wool, jersey, flannel, prequilted fabrics, velour, felt, fake fur, ski-weight nylon	Ordinary cotton, cotton-covered polyester, silk twist, nylon monofilament	14/90
Heavy woven (denim, corduroy, sailcloth, duck)	Heavy-duty	16/100
Leather, imitation suede, vinyl, heavy upholstery fabrics	Heavy-duty	18/100

Flat Sheet Yardage. *See Yardage, Flat Sheet.*

Inserted Edge. See *Edge Finishes, Inserted.*

Joining 45° Ends. If ends are already cut at 45° angle, match seam allowances, not cut ends. Stitch. Then press seam open gently. See also *Binding, Joining.*

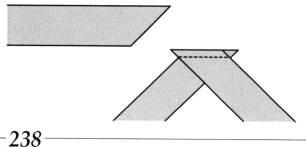

Joining 90° Ends. Overlap ends at right angles. Draw line from outside edge to outside edge, connecting corners. Stitch along line. Trim seam and press open gently. See also *Binding, Joining.*

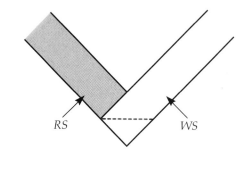

Ladder Stitch.

Lapped Edges. See *Edge Finishes, Lapped.*

Miter, Easy Lining. See *Edge Finishes, Mitered.*

Mitered Edge. See *Edge Finishes, Mitered.*

Needles. Good needles are the foundation of good sewing, yet we take the history, manufacture, and function of sewing-machine needles for granted. It seems obvious now, but it took almost 100 years after the first attempts to build a sewing machine to invent a crucial part: the eye-pointed needle (by Walter Hunt about 1833). Moving the eye from its position for hand sewing down to the point led to today's lockstitch sewing machine.

Today needles are made by only seven companies worldwide, most based in Germany. The best known are Schmetz and Singer. Making a quality needle is an intricate operation involving 45 major production steps, with 100 machines involved. The needles are cut from coiled steel wire in the various diameters of the shank. Then the scarf and eye are stamped out. Some manufacturers use a chemical process to deburr the eye, but a quality manufacturer such as Schmetz mills the eye and polishes it with a cotton thread dipped in abrasive paste.

Needle Parts

Understanding the parts of a needle and their functions will improve your sewing.

The *shank* is flat on the back rather than completely round, so it can be held firmly in the machine. When the shank is shaved flatter by the manufacturer, it brings the needle closer to the bobbin hook, so that stitches aren't dropped.

The *groove* on the topside above the eye allows the thread to nestle in the needle as the point pierces the fabric. Without a groove, the hole poked would need to be larger to accommodate thread/needle as it passes through the fabric.

The *eye* is highly polished and large enough to surround the thread without squeezing it. Burrs in the eye would wear away the thread, which passes through the eye 40 – 60 times in the process of forming a stitch. If the eye were not large enough for the thread, the fibers would be cut and would break. Polyester and monofilament threads do not saw at the eye, but it's too soon to know about the long-range effect of metallics.

The *scarf*, scooped out above the eye on the underside, allows the bobbin hook to pass close to the needle and pick up the loop of thread formed as the needle rises. Twenty years ago, European needles had deeper scarfs than Singer needles. That's why you got a skipped stitch if you put a Singer needle in your European machine.

The *point* makes a hole for the thread. It is with the type of point and with needle size that you can make a difference in your stitch quality.

Point Types

Singer uses a color code for points. Red Band is for woven; Yellow Band, for knits. Occasionally, Green Band

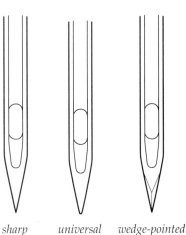

sharp   *universal*   *wedge-pointed*

needles turn up. These are made for special promotions. Use Yellow Band needles for decorative stitching. They have a deeper scarf and form a bigger loop underneath (no skipped stitches).

Schmetz, which makes needles for Bernina and Elna, as well as under its own name, uses this code for points:

H: A slightly rounded point, called a universal point, that allows you to sew almost all fabrics, woven or knit. The point usually slips between the fibers. H stands for "Hohlkehle," the German word for scarf. It is engineered with a long scarf for zigzag, so that at no position during the formation of a stitch would the needle hit or deflect off the bobbin hook. The scarf made this an engineering breakthrough. Before, you could not sew on knits without backing them with paper. Otherwise, the needle would catch on the fabric, forcing it down into the needle hole and destroying the chance of the hook picking up the thread: skipped stitches galore.

H-SUK: A full ballpoint tip, which slips between the fibers instead of piercing them. Used for loose knits and extremely stretchy fabrics with spandex or elastic girdle-like material. SUK refers to "synthetic." Knit fabrics have memory. They will return to their original position and close around the thread. Interestingly, even though we are routinely told to use this point on knits, Gale Grigg Hazen finds that holes sometimes develop in the seams after washing. She prefers to use a universal or H-S Stretch point (after testing, of course).

H-S: Same tip as the H-SUK with a flatter shank, to bring the needle closer to the hook, and a special construction at the eye. It was developed for flimsy knits, like Qiana, silk jersey, Lycra, and similar materials, to prevent the fabric from being dragged into the bobbin case. Using a wide presser foot and/or single-hole needle plate helps prevent this. These come blue-tipped in only two sizes and are called Stretch needles. The blue coating keeps the needle cool. Gale Hazen likes an 11/75 H-S for Ultrasuede, which has a knit backing.

H-J: A sharper point, to pierce the fibers on tightly woven fabric. Until recently, we've used these needles for denim-weight materials in appropriate needle sizes (J stands for "jeans"), but now they are also available in fine sizes: 10/70) and 12/80. If you want an absolutely straight stitch for topstitching or piecing quilts or for sewing microfibers, use the fine H-J needles, rather than the traditional H point. (Because the H point slips between the fibers,

you may get a slight wobble to a straight stitch.) But beware: goofs may remain as holes.

H-LL: A sharp cutting point, used only for real leather. Its wedge point slits the skin. Expert Gail Brown, however, tests before using this harsh point. For softer leathers, she prefers a universal point.

Four new needles appeared in 1993, three from Schmetz and the fourth from Lammertz/Sullivans.

H-E: Designed with a larger eye to accommodate heavier embroidery threads like metallics, with a scarf which reduces the risk of skipped stitches and a slightly rounded point to avoid damage to thread and material. Available in 11/75 and 14/90.

H-M: Microfibers are fine, tightly woven polyesters that resist penetration by traditional needles. The new H-M points are slim and free of burrs or sharp edges. Available in 9/60, 10/70, 12/80, and 14/90; colored violet at the shank end.

H-Q: Developed for piecing and quilting, this is similar to the H-J jeans needle but with a tapered point. Comes in 11/75 and 14/90; colored green at the shank end.

The **Metafil** from Lammertz/Sullivans is a needle specially designed for metallic and rayon threads. It has a specialized eye and scarf that eliminates stripping and splitting of these threads. Available in 12/80.

Needle Sizes

Needle sizes refer to the diameter of the needle blade (the European size is in hundredths of a millimeter). As a needle increases in size, its eye becomes bigger. Equivalent sizes in American/European are: 8/60, 9/65, 10/70, 11/75, 12/80, 14/90, 16/100, 18/110, 20/125.

Try to use the smallest size needle you can, depending on the thread you've chosen. Match the thickness of your thread to your fabric; then the size of your needle to the thread; then the point of the needle to the task. For example, in constructing a 100% interlock knit shirt with a collar, you might use fine polyester thread and a 12/80 needle with a universal point to construct the garment, but for topstitching the collar, which has been fused so it no longer has the qualities of a knit, you might change to a 12/80 H-J point, to get a straight stitch.

Needle sizes for sergers are generally limited to 12/80 and 14/90, with a universal point. Since you aren't forming a lockstitch in the fabric, needle point and size are not quite as particular.

I can never remember what size needle I left in the machine, especially since I sew on so many. When I remember, I leave Post-it Notes on the machine. If I remove a needle temporarily, I thread it through a Post-it Note with annotation. For two of my machines, I made sewing-machine covers with a dial pointing to the last needle size used (not point, though). Supposedly, the lid in a case of Schmetz needles is a built-in magnifier, but my eyes are not good enough. Instead, I keep a linen tester next to the machine, which magnifies the print on the shank. Hold the eye to the left and read the number printed on the round shank. Gale Hazen bought herself a 30-power lighted magnifier from a science specialty store. Not only does she use this on needles, but she examines fiber structure, puckering, and lots more with it.

Schmetz Needle Sizes (European Sizes)	
Universal (H)	60, 65, 70, 75, 80, 90, 100, 110, 120
Jeans (H-J)	70, 80, 90, 100, 110
Stretch (H-S)	75, 90
Ballpoint(H-SUK)	70, 80, 90, 100
Leather (LL)	70, 80, 90, 100, 110
Twin	2.0/75, 3.0/75, 1.6/80, 2.0/80, 2.5/80, 4.0/80, 3.0/90, 4.0/90, 4.0/100, 6.0/100
Stretch Twin	2.5/75, 4.0/75
Wing	100, 120
Twin Wing	100
Triple	2.5/80, 3.0/80
Topstitch	80, 90, 100
Self-Threading	80, 90
Spring Needle	Universal—70, 80, 90; Stretch—75, 90; Denim—100; Machine Embroidery—75, 90
Machine Embroidery	75, 90

Specialty Needles

One blade: The *topstitching needle* (130N) has an elongated eye to accommodate thicker threads. This makes it a weaker needle. Don't try to use it on heavy fabrics. I like to use it with specialty threads when filling in a shape with thread in machine embroidery. It easily pierces many layers of thread, even though it's only slightly ballpoint.

The *wing needle* punches a large hole in closely woven fabric and produces a hemstitch effect. Expert Carol Ahles, however, prefers a large-size universal point (110 H or 120 H). It's

cheaper, too. She says the wing often damages or distorts lace or tatting.

The *basting needle* (130/705 R-H) has two eyes, one above the other (sometimes it's called the "magic needle"). Thread only the upper eye and use the blindstitch. The stitch forms only on the jag of the blindstitch, skipping all other stitches and forming a long basting stitch.

The *spring needle* has a wire cage around it that acts like a presser foot only at the moment the needle enters the fabric, after which the cage rises. This makes free-machine embroidery easier. It comes in sizes from 70 to 90 in four point types (H, H-S, H-J, H-E).

The *slotted or self-threading needle* is open on one side for easy threading. This weakens the needle, so extra care must be taken when sewing: don't pull the material and don't sew fast.

Two blades: *Twin needles* come in universal, jeans, machine-embroidery, and stretch points (see chart). The widest setting is 6.0, but you may not be able to use this, depending on the opening of your needle plate. Always test twin needles by handwalking the wheel through a complete revolution. If your machine comes up in left-needle position when you turn it on, such as the New Home, don't leave the twin needles in overnight. You may forget to center the needles and break them with the first stitch. Some computer machines have twin-needle settings that automatically prevent too-wide stitches.

To make a twin-needle stitch lie flat, loosen or bypass the bobbin tension. This should also prevent skipped stitches. Also, if you are topstitching with twin needles (2.5/75 Stretch recommended) on the crossgrain of knits, as on a hem, fuse the hem up first to stabilize it, so that it won't be rippled. I like to use woolly nylon in the bobbin, as it is stretchy but strong so the stitches won't pop when stretched. Be careful: It's difficult to make anything wider than 2.5 lie flat.

When upper tension is tightened, twin needles produce pintucks. On lightweight fabric like batiste, you should stay with the 1.6/70. A 2.0 would be a nicer width but the smallest size is 80, which can cause puckering. If that occurs, you may have to loosen top tension or cord the pintuck.

On a 6.0 twin needle, the right needle is slightly shorter to avoid the bobbin hook.

The Elna 7000 must use the black-bar twin needle, not the red-bar. The difference is related to the angle of the needle clamp. If a 7000 owner uses a red-bar needle, she may get skipped stitches; however, a simple modification by a dealer can be made in two minutes, allowing the use of the red bar. Mechanical Elnas use the maroon-bar twin needles.

You can buy a wing needle/straight needle combination, called a *double wing.*

Three blades: These triple needles are used for decorative topstitching. Some people use them to make two pintucks at once. You can use them with decorative stitches as long as you don't set the stitch width too wide for your needle plate.

If you do not see these needles out at your dealer's, ask. Often the specialty needles are kept in a drawer. Your dealer can order you any needle. He or she may not know about some of the newer needles, such as the fine HJ points. You can also order these through mail-order.

Serger Needles

Serger needles are not yet standardized like sewing-machine needles. You must use the needles specified for your machine. Some use standard household needles; others use industrial needles. There doesn't seem to be a difference in stitch quality between the two.

If you have more than one serger, keep track of the needles. I once was baffled when my Baby Lock would not form a stitch. After much tearing out of hair, I discovered I'd put a White Superlock needle in it by mistake.

The following sergers use Schmetz needles: Bernina, Elna (can also use ELx, which has a groove in the back and front for a tighter stitch), Pfaff, Viking, White.

The following sergers use Organ household needles: New Home, Juki (Schmetz OK on light to midweight fabrics).

Babylocks use DCX1 or DCX1F (newer models). The 4/2-thread uses BLX 1.

Singer 14U uses #2054 in sizes 10, 12, 14, 16; 14U64 uses standard Singer sewing-machine needles.

Threading the Needle

Machine manufacturers are aware that at about age 40, the eyes go—and the majority of us home sewers are 40+. That's why the newer machines come with built-in needle threaders or with shanks behind the eye painted white. If you find yourself swearing while you try to thread the needle, try any of these tricks: 1) Put a piece of white paper behind the needle. It's easier to see the eye. 2) Cut the thread at an angle, then slide it down the groove until it pops into the eye. 3) Wet the needle, not the thread. Supposedly capillary action pulls the thread through. 4) Take out the needle, thread

it, and reinsert the needle. 5) Buy a long skinny wire needle threader from Clotilde. It's particularly good for monofilament thread and for your serger. 6) Have many children with good eyes, spacing them so that you'll have live-in needle threaders for years to come.

Sew Carefully

You can prevent broken needles in two ways. 1) Insert the needle with the flat side to the back all the way up inside the holder. 2) Improve your handling of fabric while at the machine. Don't let the fabric fall off the extension plate of the machine. It may pull the needle and cause it to break against the needle plate. Similarly, don't tug at the fabric while you're sewing. When pivoting, leave the needle down in its lowest position, raise the presser foot, turn the fabric, lower the presser foot, and handwalk the first stitch. Never change needle position or stitch selection while the needle is in the fabric, including pushing the reverse button. When you remove material from the machine, pull it out to the side or back, never to the front, which could bend the needle. And if you sew a lot and fast, consider wearing safety glasses. I've heard some gruesome stories about eye damage from flying needles.

Care of Needles

Ensure success in sewing and serging by using the needle system specified for your machine. The machine is timed to strike the bobbin loop at a certain distance from the needle. If you have a new machine, throw out old needles. For example, if you use a Singer needle in a Viking sewing machine or HuskyLock serger, you could ruin the machine.

The finishes used on many woven, knit, and synthetic fabrics and interfacings tend to dull the tip of the needle, which is why you should change to a new needle for each major sewing and serging project. One way to test on newer sewing machines whether you need a new needle is to sew a straight stitch on a small 3" – 4" long strip of fabric, with no help from your hands. If the strip feeds to the left or right instead of straight, the needle is bending. Throw it away. Every dealer I know has a story about the person who is proud of using the same needle for twenty years. Don't get cheap with needles. Buy the best in a range of sizes and points, then change them frequently.

Gert Boldt of Schmetz tells me the worldwide average number of sewing-machine needles used per year by the home sewer is six. As avid machine quilters, let's up the average.

Piping. For width, cut bias strips the cord circumference plus 1". For filler, use cotton cording (preshrink if quilted object will be washed), acrylic yarn, rayon rattail, pearl cotton, or nothing. Fold bias over cording and

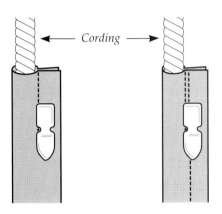

Cording

pin at the beginning. If you don't have a piping foot, use a zipper foot to stitch next to the piping. If you can decenter your needle, make the piping with the needle closest to the foot. Then decenter it slightly closer to the piping when applying to quilt edge. First stitching will not show. If you have a piping foot, you can make piping and apply it in one step. To join piping ends, see *Piping, Joining*. See also *Edge Finishes, Inserted*.

When going around corners, stop at the corner with the needle in the fabric. Raise the presser foot. Clip the piping seam allowance only to the needle, parallel with the bottom edge. The piping will spread and you will be able to pivot and stitch the next edge.

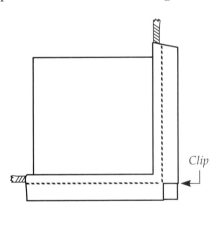

Clip

Piping, Joining. For narrow piping with thin or no filling, taper off seam allowance where it won't show. Gently pound the join with a rubber mallet to flatten filler.

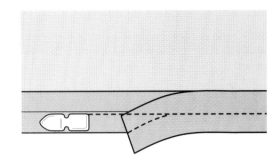

For heavier piping, rip stitches on each end for about 3". Cut cording to butt. Then use method for joining shown under *Binding, Joining*.

I don't recommend overlapping ends. It looks sloppy.

Problem-Solving Clinic. See next page.

Ruth B. McDowell, detail of **Scramble,** *88-1/2" x 77-1/2", 1992. Free-machine alphabet in background with outline of pieced figure drawn free-hand Photo courtesy of the artist.*

THREAD PROBLEMS

Problem Caused by	Solution
Upper thread breaks	
the machine is not threaded properly	re-thread
needle inserted wrong way round or at wrong height	insert properly
upper tension too tight	loosen
thread caught below spool on spindle or nick of spool	use tapestry needle; turn spool upside down
thread too dry and brittle	buy better thread; leave outside overnight
thread is cheap and poorly made	buy better thread
thread too thick for needle or material	change thread or needle—see chart, Ch. 1
needle bent or blunt	change needle
presser foot not lowered	lower presser foot
burrs on edges of needle plate hole	file with emery cloth
material too thick or dense (e.g., leather)	use heavier needle
take-up lever not in highest position when removing fabric from machine	set take-up lever in highest position
Top thread loops show on back	
bobbin tension too tight and/or upper tension too loose	re-adjust
threads used in top and bobbin of uneven weight or tensile strength	use same thread for both or hide loops by using small print on back
Lower thread breaks	
lower tension too tight	loosen
thread is unevenly wound on bobbin or brought up incorrectly	read your instruction manual
burrs on edges of needle plate hole	file with emery cloth
Lower thread loops show on top	
upper tension too tight and/or bobbin tension too loose	re-adjust
threads used on top and bobbin of uneven weight or tensile strength	use same or heavier thread (and larger needle) on top
Threads jam at start of sewing	
top thread not held securely behind presser foot for first few stitches, pulling it into bobbin snarl	hold thread
cat or baby walked on unattended machine's foot pedal	watch out; get a canary
presser foot not down at start of sewing	lower presser foot
Stitches are skipped or uneven	
bobbin innards are linty and clogged	clean and oil
broken threads in bobbin case	clean and oil
needles being used are not made expressly for machine	use correct needles
wrong type needle for material being used	use ballpoint, sharp, or leather needle (Ch. 1)
machine incorrectly threaded or needle inserted wrong	check threading and needle
fabric(s) were not touching the needle plate at moment the stitch was formed	press down on fabric near needle with fingers

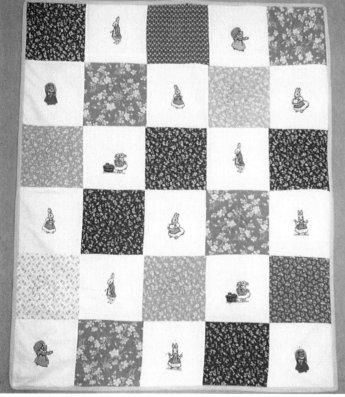

Upper left: *Moyra McNeill, West Wickham, Kent, England, detail of larger panel of shells. Silk and felt, solidly machined with occasional slashing to reveal felt. Photo courtesy of the artist.*

Upper right: *Kandy Schneider, McHenry, IL, detail, Pacific Sunset, 38" x 48". Mock handquilting, embellished by Kandy's Kan Scan designs for the New Home 8000 and its Scan 'n Sew. Photo courtesy of the artist.*

Left: *Irene Stratton, Oxford, England, Peter Rabbit quilt with alternate blocks stitched by built-in designs on the New Home Memory Craft 8000. Photo by Dr. Anne Clark.*

Quilt-As-You-Go Blocks, Joining.

Choose from eight methods of joining finished quilt-as-you-go blocks. I prefer to use 1/2" seams for durability.

1. Handle each block as if it were one layer, not three. Undersides together, sew a 1/2" seam. Trim the batting to the seamline and the top allowances to 1/4". Gently press open the seam and lay 1" wide bias binding, lace, ribbon, or strips of fabric over the seam. Edgestitch the strips by machine. If you have quilted close to the seamlines, you must use this method or #6.

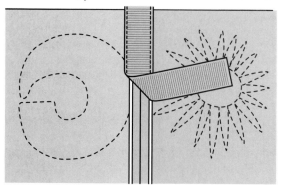

2. Pin the top and batting of both blocks out of the way.
Rightsides together, join the backs in a 1/2" seam. Press open the seam, using a press cloth to protect the iron. Trim the batting to the seamline. Lay the two blocks on a table, rightsides up. Fold under 1/2" on one top and lap it over the second. Pin-baste. Then zigzag, edgestitch, or use a decorative stitch to secure the seam. You can't use this method if you've stitched too close to the seam allowance. Leave two times the seam allowance free all around the unfinished block (e.g., don't stitch closer than 1" with a 1/2" seam allowance).

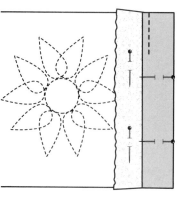

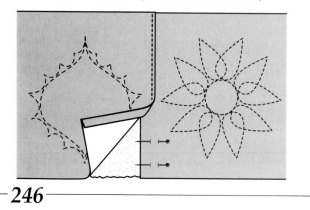

3. Pin the tops out of the way. Join the backing and batting in a 1/2" seam—press open lightly, using a press cloth to protect the iron. Trim the batting to the seamline. Unpin one top and pin it down. Turn the two blocks over and pin again from the back. Remove pins from the topside. Stitch in the ditch (right down the seamline). Turn over and unpin the remaining top. Fold it under a few threads less than 1/2". Edgestitch with a straight stitch, narrow zigzag, or blindhem stitch.

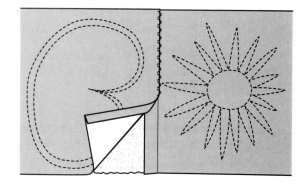

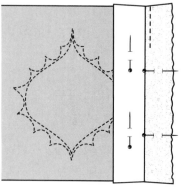

4. Pin one top out of the way. Wrong sides together, join the two blocks. Trim the batting to the seamline. Trim the fabrics to 1/4". Press all three layers lightly toward the pinned-back top. Unpin the remaining top and press it under 1/2". Lap over the fabrics and topstitch near the edge.

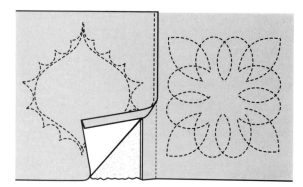

5. Work the one-step quilting in manageable modules with a low-loft batting. Lay the modules onto another backing and butt them up against each other. Cover the join with strips of fabric, ribbon, or binding edgestitched in place.

If the blocks are not bigger than 6" square, you can add another layer of batting, which is quilted by the topstitching lines. The perfectionist starts and stops these lines 1/2" away from the top and bottom, on the seam allowance of the cross-seam.

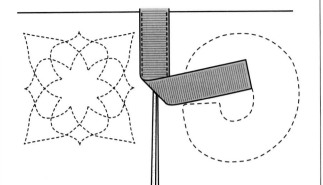

6. Join one-step quilting by sandwiching both top and backing with strips of fabric laid rightsides together against the blocks. Sew a 1/2" seam through all layers.

Open out the two strips and press. Match the right side of the second block's backing to the right side of the backing strip. Sew a 1/2" seam through all layers. Press seam lightly.

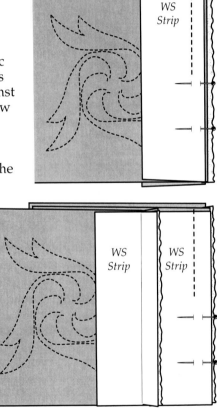

Lay the blocks on a hard surface, rightside up. (If the added strip is wider than two times your seam allowance (1" here), cut batting to fit from seam to seam.) Fold under 1/2" on top strip. Pin it in place over the batting. Topstitch with a straight stitch or narrow zigzag. *Optional:* Topstitch the other side of the strip. If batting was added, nothing has yet secured the batting

between the strips and it will shrink in over the years of washing unless you do secure it, so machine quilt at least 1/4" from each side.

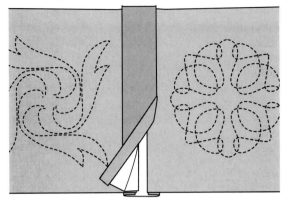

7. This is McRee Hickman's method. Cut the backing and batting about 4-1/2" larger than the top. After quilting, put the backings rightsides together and sew a 1-1/2" seam allowance. Trim batting, press seam open, turn under raw edges, and edgestitch them. To order McRee's booklet, see the Bibliography and Directory.

Use extra-wide backing and large seam allowances to make mock sashing.

8. Include ribbon or tape on the sides or corners of finished modules. Then tie the modules together. See the Great Batting/Wheel Cover test on page 174.

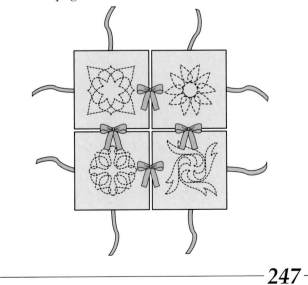

Above: *Pat Autenrieth,
Hyattsville, MD, Leafheart, 70-1/
2" x 97", 1991.
Photo courtesy of the artist.*

Left: *Jan Brashear, Atlanta, GA,
Birds of a Feather #1, 46" x 45",
1994. Machine embroidery with
Madeira rayon, some silk threads,
worked on a Pfaff 7550.
Photo courtesy of the artist.*

Ruffles. Cut fabric at least two times the length of the perimeter. Anything less looks skimpy. The easiest way to prepare the ruffles is with a ruffler attachment for your machine, which gathers and attaches in one operation. Alternately, try monofilament in the top, a tight top tension, and a long stitch. Test to see if that gathers the fabric enough. If not, zigzag over crochet cotton or dental floss and pull cord to gather. See *Edge Finishes, Inserted*.

Scissors. In one form or another, scissors have been in continuous use for over 2,000 years. We use them so often that we take them for granted. Yet scissors are a fairly complicated piece of machinery. They are actually mini-levers, with the pin acting as the fulcrum. As your hands exert force on one end, the sharpened blades on the other end move together and part the material sidewards. The top blade is called the finger blade and the blade below the fabric is called the thumb blade.

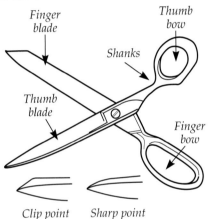

Finger blade *Thumb bow* *Shanks* *Thumb blade* *Finger bow*

Clip point *Sharp point*

Shears are different from scissors. They have different-size bows (handles) and/or are 6" or greater in length. Scissors have identical bows. Thus, you could own 5" shears, but no 7" scissors—they automatically become shears beyond 6". For simplicity, we're calling them all scissors here.

Two Types

There are two types of scissors. In one, blades connect with a spring, like ice tongs or thread snips. This kind appeared as early as the third century BC. In the other kind, two blades are connected by a pin or screw. These were popular by the Middle Ages. The latest innovation of the second type has been the pinking shears, invented in the 20th century. Before their appearance, dressmakers had to pound the edge of seams with a serrated mallet onto a lead block. (Incidentally, the first tooth on pinking shears never cuts.)

Scissors can be made in two ways. The lightweight kinds are stamped out of flat stainless steel, processed, and have plastic handles added. More expensive kinds are hot-drop forged. That means round steel bars that look something like a dowel are heated and placed in half of a scissors die on an anvil. Then the hammer drops with the other half of the die. The excess steel flows outside the die and is called flashing. It is removed and pivot holes are put in both blades. The scissors go through something like 73 process steps on their way to the finishing line. One important part is matching up the correct blades. If you look inside the blades of your scissors, you may find a matching number or letter on each. If the blades are not matched, one blade may grind down faster than the other.

The finish on scissors can be either nickel-plated, nickel-plated and painted, or chrome over nickel, the latter being the best (and of course, the most expensive). Painting, for example, can hide scale marks in the handles.

The variety in scissors comes from differences in length, shape and edge of the blades, bow shapes, and uses. It is educational to look at various professions and crafts for the scissors used—hemostat scissors from the medical world, scissors with a tiny rounded piece of metal on the thumb blade point from the lacemaking world, slant scissors from the hand-embroidery world. In fact, scissors make much-appreciated gifts to sewers and others, from the classic stork scissors to duck-billed appliqué scissors, raised-handle machine-embroidery scissors, wavy-lined pinking shears, and more.

How to Buy

In buying scissors, don't be bamboozled by name alone. For example, don't make the mistake of asking for Solingen scissors. Clotilde tells me that this is a town in Germany where many cottage industries make the various parts of scissors. Solingen, therefore, is not one particular brand and some scissors coming from there are good; some, less good.

Weight is not necessarily important, either, unless you have weak hands or arthritis. A well-made pair of lightweight shears will cut fabric almost as well as a forged pair. More important is to choose the right tool for the job. Watch the garment industry to see what they use. Those who are paid by the piece use efficient tools—bent trimmers when standing to cut, straight trimmers at the machine.

If you know someone who has lost strength in her grip, give her a set of spring-band scissors, recommended by Deb Wagner. You grasp the large spring; a light squeeze cuts the fabric; then the handles and blades spring open. They are available from Access to Recreation, Inc.

The edge of the blades will matter in the long run and there are five kinds: traditional, double knife, true knife, knife/serration, and scissors. The angles of the edges usually total 70°, but top and bottom blades are ground to different bevels. Knife-edged shears do cut through fabric like butter—in the beginning—but it's harder to keep them sharp for a long time. Thus, you may want to include additional kinds of edges in your scissors collection. A newer variation of the knife-edged shear matches a knife-edged finger blade with a micro-serrated thumb blade, which prevents slippery fabrics like sand-washed silk from shifting.

The most important part of owning scissors is caring properly for them. This is where we're all guilty. How many times have you wiped your scissors clean of lint, oiled the pivot point, and wiped the scissors again? The answer is likely to be "Never." Lint and dirt can build up at the pivot point, just as they do in the bobbin case area of your sewing machine. Your scissors will last much longer if you clean them often and replace them in their pouch.

Scissor Myths

In fact, many of the myths about scissor sharpness have more to do with lack of cleanliness than dull edges. For example, it's often repeated that cutting paper dulls scissors. Not true. Paper has a film on it that transfers to the blade. If you wipe the film off, the scissors will still be sharp.

Never force a pair of scissors to cut. If they won't cut the fabric easily, they are either too lightweight for the fabric or the blades are dull.

Can you sharpen them yourself? You can reshape the edge. Yet there is a big difference between edging scissors—bringing up an edge that's folded over from use—and grinding them to reshape the edge. When you take a pair to a store and leave them for "sharpening," someone will take a few minutes and use an abrasive to "edge" them. Periodically, consider looking in the Yellow Pages for a grinder. He or she will actually take the scissors apart to sharpen them. Every snip of your newly sharpened scissors will repay you for your time and effort.

You can send Ginghers back to the company for sharpening and reconditioning. It costs about $4 in 1994 and takes about two weeks.

Another alternative is to use the ScissorPro, a home sharpening machine. We tested it in our office, first sharpening a cruddy pair of kitchen scissors I use for cutting herbs; then with some

trepidation, Pam Swierczynski's Gingher shears, with which she had nicked a pin. The tiny electrical sharpening machine uses a two-step process. You insert the blade under a clip, which has a combination of magnets and springs to hold the blade while you draw it through several times. Then you repeat the process with a finer diamond sharpening wheel. For knife-edged scissors like Ginghers, you attach an additional guide which ensures the severe angle is maintained. We were very pleased with the results and think $49.95 is a fair price for this handy tool.

If you take care of your scissors, mainly by cleaning them constantly, they will last a long time. Mundial, Inc., one of the world's largest manufacturers of scissors, once tested a pair of shears by cutting continuously. They lasted 5,000 cuts through 27 miles of fabric—longer than the Boston Marathon.

Single-Fold Binding. See *Binding, Single-fold.*

Spring Needle. See *Needles,* page 241.

Square Knot.

Square knot

Straight-Grain Binding. See *Binding, Making Straight-Grain.*

Threads. If there is anything we machine-quilting enthusiasts take for granted, it's threads. We know what we like, but we usually have no idea of the subtle differences between types of thread. How are the various threads manufactured? What are their strengths and weaknesses? What do the numbers on the spools mean?

We couldn't easily use thread in the sewing machine until 1866, when George Clark developed a six-cord, soft-finished cotton thread that was even and not too wiry. This thread, which revolutionized the sewing industry, was called "Our New Thread" or ONT, the trademark for the Clark Thread Company product.

Two types of yarns are used to make thread: filament and staple. *Filament yarns*, which come from silk and man-made fibers like rayon and polyester, are extremely long, thin, smooth, and lustrous; *staple yarns*, like cotton and linen, are shorter, thicker, fibrous, and without luster.

To produce sewing thread, slivers of the yarns are fed into rollers and drawn out in strands. These strands are spun counter-clockwise as they emerge, to increase the strength of the yarn. This is called an S-twist. When two strands are then twisted together into, say, a two-ply machine-embroidery thread, they are twisted in a clockwise direction so they won't come untwisted. This is called a Z-twist. Sewing machines require Z-twisted sewing threads.

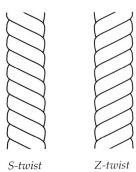

S-twist   *Z-twist*

The reasons you choose a thread for constructing a garment are not the same as for decorating it. For example, 100% cotton thread has a low stretchability. If you were to sew a seam in a knit garment with cotton thread, the stitches might pop. On the other hand, extra-fine machine-embroidery cotton is soft and tends to untwist a bit on the surface, giving its satin stitch a better coverage without piling up thread in the stitches.

The usual advice for selecting thread for construction is to match your thread type to your garment fiber. If you were to use a polyester thread on 100% cotton, in the long run the fabric might tear before the stronger thread would break, a non-fixable situation.

But in decorating fabric, anything goes—and that's where the fun of exploring threads starts. Carol Ahles, co-author of *Know Your Elna*, says, "One of the most useful charts I have in my notebook is a piece of doubled fabric with line after line of satin stitches on it. Each row is stitched using a different type of thread. I recommend that you make one, too. More important than telling you which thread to use, your chart will graphically convince you that what is called machine-embroidery cotton is usually more lustrous and covers an area more quickly and more beautifully than regular sewing thread. It's easy to compare differences among threads."

Cotton
Pros: In high-quality threads, is composed of long staples that are soft and flexible, with a lower amount of thread drag in the machine than synthetics. Resists untwisting. Comes in a wide variety of colors and several weights. Washable.

Cons: Weak, breaks easily. Absorbs moisture and perspiration, rotting quickly (beware underarm seams!). Has a matte finish unless mercerized. Does not stretch, so is unsuitable for sewing knit garments. Cheaper threads (e.g., inexpensive basting thread), composed of short staples, can throw off a lot of lint into your machine.

Details: The higher the number, the finer the thread. Two most common sizes for machine embroidery are size 50 and 60 (DMC has recently dropped size 30). Madeira has a very fine size 80 (Tanne, pronounced *tan-ay*), used for French handsewing. If the thread spool carries a second number after a slash (e.g., 60/2), it refers to the number of thread plies. Thus, a 60/2 is finer than a 60/3.

Cotton thread for hand quilting with a glacé finish should not be used in the machine, as it will shed its wax coating into your machine's tension dials. The exception is Metrosene's machine-quilting thread, which is a high-quality 100% cotton thread designed for machine use. Back in the mid-80s, Swiss-Metrosene received complaints about this quilting thread from hand quilters. After much research, they discovered that left-handed quilters quilt differently from right-handed quilters. Swiss-Metrosene changed the twist on the thread and everybody was happy.

Brand names: Coats & Clark, DMC, Madeira, Mettler, The Thread Shed, Zwicky

Polyester
Pros: Strong, lustrous, widely available.

Cons: More thread drag through machine than cotton, requiring lower top tension (also be sure machine is well-oiled). Leaves more fluff in bobbin case area and around tension disks. Stretches. Tends to untwist, making it harder to thread the needle. Can cut natural fibers like cotton, causing fabric to tear before seam would break.

Details: Be sure to wind your bobbins slowly, to minimize stretching. If you wind them fast, the thread will relax once it's in the seam, which will cause puckering. In order to meet the speediness needs of sergers, new manufacturing processes have been invented which have also benefitted sewing-machine thread. The newest method is air-texturing, which eliminates the old spinning techniques. This produces a strong, almost perfectly round thread with high tensile strength and hardly any defects or "nebs" (these get caught in your machine's tension guides and needle eye, causing the thread to break). Because the thread is round, it reflects light like silk.

Cotton-wrapped polyester is an attempt to combat the weaknesses of both threads. The regular size can be too coarse for construction or decorative work, but Coats & Clark's extra-fine Dual Duty Plus is an excellent thread for garment construction. Yvonne Perez-Collins, author of *Soft Gardens: Make Flowers on Your Sewing Machine*, uses two strands of cotton/poly through the needle with pearl cotton in the bobbin for sashiko, stitching underside up. The cotton/poly should be the same color as the fabric. These two strands are pulled to the surface and cover the pearl cotton at each lock stitch, giving the appearance of a hand running stitch.

Madeira's Bobbinfil is a fine 100% polyester thread that's often used in the bobbin for machine embroidery because you can get a lot of it onto the bobbin, yet it's strong enough not to be pulled to the surface by the top thread. Be sure to wind the bobbin slowly.

Metrolene is a thin serger thread, the equivalent of size 80. It is recently available again because so many consumers asked for it (we have power when we act).

A new polyester thread is Scanfil by Sullivans. It has a polyester core with a long-staple polyester wrap and no left or right twist, which minimizes seam puckering. This has been available only to manufacturers until now.

Brands: Coats & Clark Dual Duty Plus, Gutermann, Madeira's Super Sheen, Maxi Lock, Metrosene Plus, Mölnlycke, Signature, Sullivans

Rayon
Pros: Shiny, takes dye well so comes in wide variety of colors, washable. Beautiful in any decorative work in the serger or sewing machine, such as rolled edge, flatlocking, decorative stitches, and satin stitch.

Cons: Weak and breakable. When wet, loses strength and disintegrates. Slips off thread spool and wraps around spindle, causing breakage. Sometimes cranky in the machine, requiring fiddling with tension dials. High thread drag.

Details: Called "the poor man's silk," rayon is a wood by-product but it's still considered manmade. In the highest quality brands like Sulky, it is extruded, not spun, before it is twisted into two plies in a Z-twist. It requires testing on your

machine to find the right combination of top tension and needle size to prevent fraying and breaking. If that happens, try a larger needle.

Not all rayons are twisted identically; some are looser than others and may require a *tighter* tension to keep them from rolling or untwisting. You must test first.

To prevent the slippery thread from wrapping around the thread spindle and breaking, try any of these solutions: Put a thread net on the spool. Use a horizontal spindle. Use a thread stand behind the machine. Sew slowly and consistently, so the thread doesn't jerk.

Don't use rayon in seam construction if the item will be washed. Use it to embellish.

Sulky, made in Germany, is the best-known and most widely available rayon. It comes in two sizes, 40 and 30 (larger). Natesh is finer, closer to a size 50. Aardvark Adventures, which imports Natesh from India, has put together Designer Sets, 10 spools for $18.95 of colors coordinated by well-known artists.

Brands: Coats & Clark, Madeira's MEZ Alcazar (carried by Pfaff dealers), Natesh, Pearl Crown Rayon, Signature, Sulky, Union, YLI

Silk
Pros: Flexible, shiny, strong.

Cons: Hard to find, some brands not washable, expensive.

Details: Remember when you could buy silk in two sizes on wooden spools in any fabric store? Those days are long gone. Fortunately, we still have two good sources of silk for decoration and construction.

Maggie Backman of Things Japanese has a filament silk that works beautifully in the sewing machine and serger (see page 35). It is machine-washable and has a 25% natural elasticity.

Frank Bates of Gutermann reminds us that the often-repeated advice to baste with silk thread can be disastrous if the silk is colored. When you steam the basted item, the dye in the silk discharges into the fabric. Use only white or natural-colored silk to baste.

Don't forget that you can wind 1/8" silk ribbon onto your bobbin, work underside up, and do gorgeous decorative work with even the most simple stitches, like a zigzag.

Brands: Gutermann, Janome/New Home, Tiré, YLI (also distributes Belding Corticelli)

Nylon
Pros: Strong, inexpensive, washable.

Cons: Hard to thread and control in machine, stretchy, may damage machines. Rots in sunlight.

Details: The best-known nylon thread is monofilament, which comes in several weights and two colors (clear and smoke). For quilting, use only the finest: .004.

Some people have trouble threading the needle. Not only is the thread fine and wiry, resisting the aid of needle threaders, but you can't see it to begin with. I suggest you thread the machine down to the last thread guide and pull out some extra thread. Then take the needle out of the machine, thread it by eye or with a needle threader, and reinsert it into the machine.

If you have trouble with whiplash, where the thread spool jerks around, causing either loops on the underside or bobbin loops on the topside, try any of these solutions: Put a metal washer on top of the spool to weight it. Use metal bobbins instead of plastic, for more weight (ask your dealer for them). On some machines, such as the Pfaff, the bobbin alert does not work with metal bobbins. Put a thread net on the spool. Use a horizontal spindle. Use a thread stand behind the machine. Sew slowly and consistently, so the thread doesn't jerk.

Don't worry about your iron melting monofilament. It becomes soft at 360°F and doesn't melt until 485°F. You'll scorch your fabric before you'll melt the thread.

Two concerns about monofilament are: does it damage machines and is it dangerous for babies and animals? Scott Blackman of YLI tells me that they have a metal winding machine for monofilament that has been used every day since 1969, sometimes 24 hours a day. It is just now showing a small groove where the monofilament rubs the metal. He does not think home sewers are pushing their machines to that extent; therefore, we don't need to worry. The head technician at Pfaff, on the other hand, is seeing some damage to tension disks. Whether this comes from heavy usage, like a drapery shop, he does not know.

Someone wrote to *Quilter's Newsletter* about her dog eating some monofilament and needing surgery. The dog later died. Pat Merrell of Sew-Art International says that her daughter raised three children practically in their warehouse, surrounded by thread ends, with no problems.

Pat also said that the whiplash problem happens with a new spool or when the thread is almost gone. She suggested turning the spool upside down, so it's unreeling differently.

If you use monofilament in the bobbin, be sure to wind slowly. Otherwise, it can heat up and cause a plastic bobbin to explode or worse, stick in the bobbin case. You may want to wind bobbins only half-full.

Other kinds of nylon are woolly nylon, used primarily for sergers, and lingerie thread, a fine nylon with which machine embroiderers like to fill bobbins. Gayle Domorsky winds woolly nylon into her bobbin and stitches underside up with a satin or decorative stitch. She likes the extra texture of the thread.

Brands: Madeira, Sew Bob lingerie thread; Sew-Art, Clotilde, or YLI Wonder Thread, YLI Woolly Nylon

Metallics

Pros: Give instant pizzazz to anything.

Cons: Weak, breaks, gives off harsh fluff in tension disks.

Details: In the past, it was difficult to sew with metallics through the needle, so we often wound them on the bobbin and sewed underside up. Today, however, metallics have gotten softer and thinner, so we can use them topside. Most metallics require not only a larger needle eye, but a larger scarf. Therefore, start with a 14(90) needle and if you're having trouble with breakage, make it a stretch needle (H-S point), which has a larger scarf. You can also try a topstitching needle, which has an enlarged eye. Ann Boyce, the queen of glitz, recommends using a clear fluid called Sewer's Aid and painting it directly on the spool. This acts as a lubricant to facilitate sewing. Ann says, "This product may be used on the bobbin thread, needle, and even on the bottom of the presser foot. Although it feels greasy to the touch, it does not leave a stain on fabrics or threads." A similar product is Sew Slick.

Fred Drexler of Sulky says that all of a sudden, metallic threads are selling like crazy, especially among quilters. One artist sewed 18,000 yards of metallics into one garment for the Fairfield Fashion Show. Sulky has now put nine of their 24 colors on king-size cones and added 12 more colors.

Brands: Coats, DMC, Dritz, Gutermann, Kanagawa, Kreinick, Madeira's Super Twist, Signature, Talon, Tire, YLI's Candlelight, Sulky

Novelty Threads

Sew-Art International has a washable wool/acrylic blend called *Renaissance.* Used with a topstitching needle and sewing weight thread in the bobbin, it fluffs up like a thin crewel yarn and looks wonderful used with decorative stitches. Yvonne Perez-Collins likes to use it in the bobbin for sashiko (see explanation under

Yardage Charts

cotton-wrapped polyester). Madeira's *Burmilana* is similar.

Janome/New Home sells a package of *acrylic thread* in brilliant colors, used with their built-in large designs. The thread shines like rayon.

Susan Rock, who designs for Madeira, advises us to investigate their *neon polyester* threads. "On the spool, the colors look juvenile," she says, "but I think people are missing how sophisticated these threads look when worked on black fabric." She sent a sample and it was downright stunning.

Madeira also has a brand-new thread they don't know how to publicize. It's called *Chameleon* and it's light-sensitive. It looks white indoors, but when you go outside, it changes to a color.

Ann Kennedy's *Threadfuse* is a strand of thread twisted with a strand of glue. Loaded into the bobbin or bottom looper, the thread can be used it for fusing hems, appliqués, serger chain, etc. Threadfuse is distributed by YLI, who also distributes a water-soluble basting thread called *Wash-A-Way*.

Yardage, Approximate Whole Cloth.

These are figured for 45"-wide fabric (usable width 42") and standard batting sizes.

Crib: 1-3/4 yds. for each side
Twin: 5 yds. for each side
Double: 5-1/2 yds. for each side
Queen: 6 yds. for each side
King: 10-1/8 yds. for each side

Yardage, Flat Sheet.

	Finished Size: inches	Yards of fabric	
		36" wide	45" wide
Twin	66 x 96	5	4-3/8
Full (double)	81 x 96	6-1/2	5-3/4
Queen	90 x 102	7-1/2	6-5/8
King	108 x 102	9-1/8	8
Standard pillowcase		1-1/8	1
King pillowcase		1-3/8	1-1/4

> *"The best intelligence test is what we do with our leisure."*
>
> Dr. Laurence J. Peters

Yardage Conversion Chart.

If your pattern calls for material this wide...					...but you want to use material this wide instead, then for each yard your pattern calls for, use this many yards instead.
36"	45"	54"	60"		
1 yd (1.00)	1-1/4 yd (1.25)	1-1/2 yd (1.50)	1-2/3 yd (1.67)	36"	...but you want to use material this wide instead, then for each yard your pattern calls for, use this many yards instead.
7/8 (0.88)	1 (1.00)	1-1/4 (1.25)	1-1/3 (1.33)	45"	Example: The project calls for 2-1/2 yd of 45"-wide fabric. Your fabric is 36" wide. What length of 36"-wide fabric do you need?
3/4 (0.75)	7/8 (0.88)	1 (1.00)	1-1/8 (1.13)	54"	For every yard of 45"-wide, you need 1-1/4 yd of 36"-wide.
5/8 (0.63)	3/4 (0.75)	7/8 (0.88)	1 (1.00)	60"	2-1/2 times 1-1/4 yd = 3-1/8 yd. (Use your calculator: 2.5 x 1.25 = 3.125).

More on Machines

Sewing Machine Chart

Here are some of the features of current machines. Each company wants to help you quilt better, so stay in touch with a good dealer for the latest information, accessories, and techniques.

Peggy Bendel says "Because writing about sewing is my occupation, I've made it my business to learn what the new machines can do. But because the act of sewing is my hobby, I appreciate the way programmable machines encourage play. I like to have three or four machines set up, each with a different color of thread, then wheel on an office chair from one to the other."

Brand and model	Darning foot?	Walking foot?	Quilting guide?	Straight- stitch needle plate?	Needle up/down?	Auto-lock?	Drop feeds?	Decenter needle positions
Babylock Esanté	Yes	Yes	Yes	No*	Yes	Yes	With tool	14
Bernina 1630	Yes	Yes	Yes	No	Yes	Yes	Yes	11
Bernina 1530	Yes	Yes	Yes	Yes	Yes	Yes	Yes	11
Bernina 1230	Yes	Yes	Yes	Yes	Yes	No	Yes	5
Bernina 1090	Yes	Yes	Yes	Yes	Yes	No	Yes	5
Brother XL 2010-3010	No	Yes	No	Yes	No	No	Darning plate	2
Brother PS 1200	Yes	Yes	No	Yes	No	No	Darning plate	3
Brother PC-7000	Yes	Yes	Yes	No	Yes	Yes	Yes	13
Brother PS-5000	Yes	Yes	No	No	Yes	Yes	Yes	26
Elna Diva (9000), 8000	Yes	Yes	Yes	No	Yes	No	Yes	5
Elna 1600	Yes	Yes	Yes	No	No	No	Darning plate	2
Elna 1400	Yes	Yes	Yes	No	No	No	Yes	2
New Home 8000	Yes	Yes	Yes	Yes	Yes	Yes	Yes	15
New Home 4000	Yes	Yes	Yes	No	Yes	Yes	Yes	14
New Home 3123	Yes	Yes	Yes	Yes	Yes	No	Yes	Yes
New Home 3015	Yes	Yes	Yes	No	No	No	Yes	None
JC Penney 868-1363	Yes	Yes	Yes	No*	No	No	Darning plate	3
Pfaff 7550 & 1475	Yes	Yes	Yes	Yes	Yes	Yes	Yes	19
Pfaff 6250	Yes	Yes	Yes	Yes	Yes	Yes	Yes	13
Pfaff 6230	Yes	Yes	Yes	Yes	Yes	Yes	Yes	3
Pfaff 6150	Yes	Yes	Yes	Yes	No	No	Yes	3
Riccar REC6000	Yes	Yes	Yes	No*	Yes	No	Darning plate	7
Simplicity SL9240LCD	Yes	Yes	Yes	No*	No	No	Darning plate	3
Singer 9240, 9217, 9210	Yes	Yes	Yes	Yes	No	No	Darning plate	Infinite
Singer XL100	Yes	Yes	Yes	No	Yes	No	Yes	Infinite
Viking Husqvarna #1	Yes	Yes	Yes	Yes	Yes	Yes	Yes	25
Viking Husqvarna 500, 400	Yes	Yes	Yes	No	Yes	Yes	Yes	25
Viking Husqvarna 210	Yes	Yes	Yes	No	No	No	Yes	Infinite
White 9800	Yes	Yes	Yes	Yes	Yes	Yes	Yes	25
White 5823	Yes	Yes	Yes	No	No	No	Yes	Infinite
White 221	Yes	Yes	Yes	No	No	No	Darning plate	None

*(foot available)

Portables

Need a machine for classes? Tired of lugging Old Faithful? You may want to buy a lighter weight machine (and luggage wheels) just for classes. Here are some golden oldies (many no longer manufactured):

Babylock: BL2000

Bernina: 730, 801, Bernette 100

Elna: Lotus Compact SP, Lotus Compact TSP, Stella TX, 1400 Quilter's Machine, Elnita 225

New Home: Travel Mate, CombiDX (2-thread serger combined with sewing machine)

Pfaff: 1229

Singer: Featherweight

Viking: Vanessa series, Sew Easy series (weighs 14 pounds)

White: Quilter's Friend 221

Stephanie Cornet tells me "I save my computerized machines for piecing and embellishment. I like to use old (1940s) straight-stitch machines for machine quilting. I find that a good sewing machine repair person can adjust the presser foot height for a darning foot. That way the machine is always ready to quilt and I do not have to worry about overuse of my good machine. I quilted over 300 quilts on a 1940 Pfaff before it needed a new motor (which cost only $25). If you can afford it, a second machine is definitely the way to go."

For a complete discussion of bobbin systems, feed dogs, motors, and more about machines, see *The Complete Book of Machine Embroidery*.

How to Buy a Sewing Machine

My one key advice in buying a new machine is: don't hurry. A sewing machine is a major tool and must be selected with great care. All brands are not the same, no matter what a salesperson will tell you. Take the time to do each of the following and the machine you eventually buy will last a lifetime.

1. Go to the public library and look up the issue of *Consumer Reports* that rates new machines. (Ask your reference librarian for help if you need it.) In some ways, these reports are like comparing apples and oranges, but at least you will find out which models of which brands you can expect to malfunction. Look at the machine chart on page 255 for features desirable to machine quilters.

2. Talk to consumers about their preferences—other machine quilters, sewing and home-ec teachers, quilt guild members, home sewers. This can be amusing, because those who love their brand of machine are usually wildly enthusiastic about it and will make unfounded snipes at other perfectly good brands.

The Creative Machine Newsletter publishes a yearly sewing machine and serger survey, compiled from the vast experience of its readers. The Survey is available only to subscribers. See Resource list.

If possible, machine quilt on as many models as you can before buying one. Find out which machines have terrible repair records. As for my own preference, I've sewn on all machines and have four or five favorite brands, each with some unique feature. I'd like one of each but my bank account objects. I feel it is worth buying the top-of-the-line model of the brand you've chosen, even if you have to get a loan to do so or buy one used. You always rise to the level of your tools.

3. After you buy and before you leave the store, make the salesperson machine quilt (not just sew pretty stitches on one or two layers of stiffened fabric) on *your* machine—not a floor model. Contrary to popular delusion, the floor models are often the finest tuned in the store. Make sure yours, fresh from bouncing around in a factory box, is in as good a shape as the demonstrator machine.

4. Don't cut corners in buying a machine. Top-notch machines cost money. To stay in top-notch shape, they need top-notch repair people, who truly care about sewing machines. Nothing is more frustrating than buying an extremely expensive machine at a discount store for $100 less than the store charges—and taking home a machine out of tune that never sews right and is never really fixed correctly. Establishing a close relationship with a good fabric/sewing-machine dealer will bring you years of pleasure in your machine quilting.

To help you think about features you don't notice during the sales pitch, here is a list compiled from the *1993 Creative Machine Sewing-Machine and Serger Survey* of what people wish they had.

Sewing Machine Wish List

Buttonholes
better buttonholes
more buttonhole styles
uniform automatic buttonholes

Bobbin
low-bobbin warning
better bobbin winder
bypass for heavy threads
slow speed for bobbin winding

Design
more accurate seam guide
needle plate markings in inches, not metrics
ability to lower feeds
adjustable presser foot pressure
brighter light
built-in needle threader that works
differential feed on sewing machine
knee-lift
light to remind that presser foot lever is up
second light
skinnier free arm
variable speed control
DC motor

Education
advanced handbook
better instruction manual
decent dealer
fairer trade-in and upgrade policy
reliable source of information on new
    accessories and techniques
video

Feet
1/4" presser foot
beading foot
better zipper foot
built-in walking foot
higher lift to presser foot

Needle
more needle positions
needle up/down button
needle up/down by tapping foot pedal

Programming
infinite updateability
permanent memory (not lost when machine is
    turned off)
turnover memory feature both top/bottom and
    side to side
variable stitch width/length on
    preprogrammed stitches
more memory

Stitches
Utility:
    adjustable blindhem
    long basting stitch
    sideways stitch motion
    lock-off button

Decorative:
    built-in monogramming
    cursive or script alphabet
    larger letters and numbers
    more alphabet styles
    smoother satin stitch
    more decorative stitches
    single-pattern button or dial

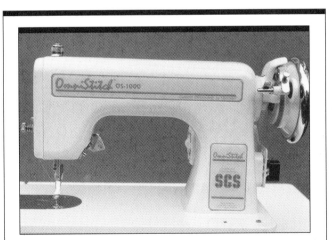

The OmniStitch has no feed dogs.

Special Quilting Machines

You can supplement your family income by machine quilting for other people. You may be surprised at your customers. Many could quilt for themselves, but prefer to design tops.

If you are starting a quilting business, you have several choices of specialty machines.

The first is the *OmniStitch*, a sewing machine that has been adapted to free-machine embroider easily. There are no feed dogs or regular presser feet. You can adjust the height of the darning foot to accommodate bulk. The OmniStitch is more often used to apply yarns and cord as surface embellishment. It has no more space between the needle and head than an ordinary home sewing machine. The OmniStitch is distributed by SCS, Inc.

Halfway between a home sewing machine and a room-size quilting machine is the *Chandler Darning Machine*. It has 30" between the needle and head and no feed dogs. The machine arrives with its own 72" x 36" table, which weighs 250 pounds. Nansi Bainard of Richland, WA, runs a quilting business using this machine. She says it took her a while to adjust to its speed—1500 stitches per minute. She put a 2x4 under the foot so she couldn't push it all the way down. Nansi bought her machine from an industrial sewing-machine dealer. Even though she has a large table surface to support the quilt bulk, she still uses two card tables, one on each side of her as she works.

The next step up is a *room-size quilting machine*. These cost from $1500 up, depending on whether you build the table frame yourself and how big the opening between the rollers is. The machines have no feed dogs or foot control. They roll along the length of the quilt while the operator guides padded handles that look like bicycle handlebars. Speed is adjusted with a thumb-operated control. At the side of the machine is an upside-down L. This is the stylus with which the operator follows a long, continuous machine-quilting design.

While some dismiss this kind of quilting as "next thing up from a mattress pad," it's no different from any machine quilting: quality and design depend on the operator, not the machine. Some operators apply machine-quilting lines that do not relate to the design; others improve the quilt-top design.

Quilting services can be used for other purposes than quilting quilts. I had Julie Nodine of Belmont, CA, who runs Julie's Quilting Service, baste my daughter's king-size quilt on her 12'-long Noltings Long-Arm Quilter. I had neither space nor time to baste the quilt and the money was well-spent. I was then able to finish the quilt before Kali's wedding. Joan Wilson of El Paso, TX, who owns a KenQuilt, quilted 3-1/2 yards of 60"-wide fabric for herself. Then she cut out a simple jacket and sewed it together that afternoon.

Many companies make room-size quilting machines. See the Resource list and watch the ads in quilting magazines.

Unfortunately, most of these companies are not education-oriented. Therefore, take your time before buying. Talk to other quilters in business. Set up a network so that you can get help when you need it—and do the same for other beginners once you are launched.

Sergers

These tiny machines have caused many people to fall in love again with sewing. If you haven't seen one, it's the machine that makes little railroad tracks of thread on the seams of ready-to-wear. The machine trims a seam, overcasts it, and seams it all at once.

Do you need a serger for quilting? By the strictest definition of quilting—attaching three layers with thread—no.

But I can't imagine sewing life before the serger. It neatens seam allowances, allows you to play with decorative threads, and makes insides of garments look professional. I like to use monofilament in the lower looper of a 2-thread serger to finish teaching samples.

Sergers sew twice as fast as sewing machines. They have differential feed to prevent layers of fabric from creeping (somewhat like walking feet). And the best part is that you don't have to stop to wind bobbins. (See information on serger needles in the Mini-Encyclopedia on page 242.)

The machines are changing rapidly. The newest sergers have LED read-outs, computer chips to control stitches, and easy threading. Stay in touch with the latest through your local dealer.

Kali and Jonathan's wedding quilt being basted on Julie Nodine's 12' long Noltings Long-Arm Quilter.

Resources

Please ask your sewing-machine or fabric dealer to order you any product she or he doesn't stock. If you do not have access to a complete store, try mail order. The addresses for these companies are in the Directory on page 261. As a courtesy, please include a pre-addressed, stamped envelope when inquiring. While we have tried to be accurate and complete, addresses change, businesses move or die, and we make regrettable omissions by mistake (advance apologies to anyone we left out). Please send updates to us at PO Box 2634-MQ, Menlo Park, CA 94026-2634.

Art Supplies
Jerry's Catalog
Me Sew Inc (light table)
Ruth's Country Creations (light table)

Batting Manufacturers
Air Lite
Airtex
Bemidji Woolen Mills
Buffalo Batt & Felt Corp
Dritz
Fairfield Processing
Hobbs Bonded Fibers
HTC
Jen-Cel-Lite Corp
Log Cabin Dry Goods
Morning Glory Products
Pellon
Putnam Co
RainShed Outdoor Fabrics
Stearns Technical Textiles Co (Mountain Mist)
Taos Mountain Wool Works
Warm Products
YLI

Bias Bars
Celtic Designs Co
Collins, WH
Heirloom Stitches

Books, Mail-Order
Dover Needlecraft Catalog
Dover Street Booksellers
Open Chain (Sewing Notebook)
Purchase For Less
Quilting Books Unlimited
Unicorn Textile Book Catalog

Charms
Stylex

Computer Bulletin Boards
America Online
Compuserve
Crafts Board
Genie
Prodigy

Cutters
Dritz Corporation (Kai)
Fiskars Manufacturing Corp
Olfa/O'Lipfa
LP Sharp (sharpens rotary blades)

Fabric Manufacturers
Artweave Traders
Benartex
Britex Fabrics
Chapel House
Concord Fabrics
Daisy Kingdom
Dan River
EZ International
Fabri-Quilt
Fabric Traditions
FASCO
Gutcheon Patchworks
Haber Fabrics
Hancock's
Hoffman California Fabrics
John Kaldor Fabricmaker
Kona Bay Fabrics
Marcus Brothers Textiles Inc
Mission Valley Textiles
P&B Textiles
RJR Fashion Fabrics
Robert Kaufman Co
Spartex Inc
Spectrix
Springs Industries
VIP

Fabrics, Hand-Dyed
Cherrywood Quilts & Fabrics
Katie's Collection
Kwilt & Kloze
Legacy In Stitches
Lunn Fabrics
Marbled Fabric & Accessories
Myhre Shibori Hand-Dyed Fabric
Shades Inc
Skydyes
Sonya Lee Barrington

Fabrics, Mail-Order
Britex Fabrics
Cotton Club
Dharma Trading Co
Fabulous Furs (Fabu-Leather)
Fields Fabrics
G Street Fabrics
Hancock's
Kirk Collection
Oppenheim's
Osage County Quilt Factory

Furniture
Hold Everything
Sirco Tables

Fusibles and Glues
Aleene's Division Of Artis, Inc
Beacons
Dritz
Eclectic Products
EZ International
HTC
Osage County Quilt Factory
Pellon
Plaid
Sew-Art
Slomons
Solar-Kist
Therm O Web

Groups
American Quilters Society
National Quilting Association
Seattle Textile Computer Users
Wearable Art Connection

Irons
Ardco Templates
Custom Sewing (Seam Stick)
June Tailor, Inc.
Rowenta
Sussman
Tower Hobbies

Machine Accessories
Kanscan
See also Presser Feet

Magazines & Newsletters
American Quilter
Art/Quilt Magazine
Canada Quilts Magazine
Creative Machine Newsletter
Creative Quilting
Down Under Quilting
Lady's Circle Patchwork Quilts
McCall's Quilting
Miniature Quilts Magazine
MiniWorks
Patchwork Patter
Quick & Easy Quilting
Quilt
Quilt Craft
Quilt World
Quilter's Newsletter Magazine
Quiltessence
Quilting International
Quilting Today Magazine
Quiltmaker
Scattered Patchers
Sew News
Stitch 'n Sew Quilts
Threads Magazine
Traditional Quilter
Traditional Quiltworks
Wearable Wonders

Mail Order, General
Clotilde
Connecting Threads
Crazy Ladies & Friends
Ghee's
Keepsake Quilting
Nancy's Notions
National Thread & Supply Corp
Newark Dressmaker Supply
Quilting Bee
Quilts & Other Comforts
SCS
Sew-Art International
Sew/Fit Company
Sewing Emporium
Speed Stitch
Treadleart

Magnifiers
PS Uniques (Extra Hands)

Manuals, Sewing Machine
Paris Connection

Markers
Custom Processing (Ultimate
   Marking Pencil)
Smocks & Kisses
Stencil Company

Marking Systems
Cambridge Marking Systems

Mats
Dritz
Douglas Products
Kai
Olfa-O'Lipfa
Omnigrid
Sew/Fit Company
Voster Marketing (Spaceboard)

Needles
Schmetz
Sullivans

Notions
Birch Street Clothing (Prym Vario
   snap kit)
Clotilde
Clover
Creative Hearts (Sew Perfect)
Crowning Touch, Inc. (Fasturn)
Dritz
EZ International
Little Foot
Nancy's Notions
Paula Jean Creations (Kwik Klip)
Quilted Ribbon (Corner Marker)
Stan Rising (Innovations Needle
   Release)
See also Mail Order, General

Paper, Acid-Free
Light Impressions

Patterns
Artful Illusions
Birch Street Clothing
Just My Imagination
Nansi's Fancies
Osage County Quilt Factory
Sally Lampi (Sally's Jacket)
Stretch & Sew

Phone Headset
Hello Direct

Presser Feet
Creative Feet
Little Foot Ltd
Paris Connection
See also Mail Order, General

Professional Machines
American Professional Quilting
Chandler Machine Co
Design-A-Quilt
Gammill Quilting Machine Co
Granny's Patchwork & Mfg
Kenquilt Mfg Co
Noltings
Northwest Industrial
Nustyle Quilting Frame Co
SCS (Omnistitch)

Quilt Hangers
Dianne Larson Quiltworks
Hang Ups

Quilting Patterns
Beautiful Productions
Quilts and Other Comforts
EZ International

Quilting Services
Julie's Quilting Services
Nansi's Fancies
Quilt Works
Dorie Whipple

Recorded Books
Books On Tape

Rulers
C-Thru Ruler Co
Cutting Edge Quilt Designs
Dritz
Flynn Frame Co (Cutting Edge)
Holiday Designs
Omnigrid
Quilter's Rule Int'l, Inc
That Patchwork Place

Sashiko Supplies
Kasuri Dyeworks

Scissors
Access to Recreation
Back Street Designs
Edgecraft
Fiskars
Gingher, Inc.
Mundial

Sewing Machine Companies
Allyn International
Brother International
Elna of America
Juki American
New Home Sewing Machine Co
Pfaff American Sales Corp
Sears Laboratories
Singer Company
Tacony Corp
Viking White Sewing Machine
   Co

Software
Electric Quilt Company
MetaTheory
PC-Quilt
QuiltSOFT
SPPS (Quilt Top Designer)

Stabilizers
Aardvark
HTC
Madeira
Magic Needle
Palmer/Pletsch
Pellon
Sew-Art
Sew-Art International
Stretch & Sew Fabrics
Sulky
Sullivans

Stamps
Pelle's

Stencils
Creative Woodburning
Harriet's Treadle Arts
Kasuri Dyeworks
Stencil Company
StenSource

Threaders
Clotilde (wire)
Palmer/Pletsch (Perfect Sew)

Threads
A&E
Aardvark
Coats & Clark
Craft Gallery Ltd
DMC Corporation
Elna of America
Gutermann Of America
Horn Of America, Inc
Kreinik Mfg Co Inc
Madeira Thread
National Thread & Supply
New Home
Rosecrest Farms
Sew-Art International
Sulky
Things Japanese

Thread Discount Sales
Thread Shed
Sullivans
Viking/White
Web Of Thread
YLI

Tracing Materials
Sewing Place, The (Mönster Paper)
Stretch & Sew (Do-Sew)
Titus & Son, FD

Transfer Systems
Saral Paper Co
Stretch & Sew Fabrics (Artist Delight System)
Tolin' Station

Travel
A-1 Travel

June Inouye, Mt. View, CA, detail of Sunkist. *June used techniques from* Barbara Johannah's Crystal Piecing *on ColorBar fabric to make half-square triangles. She continued the design of the sunflowers onto the plain area, using Sulky metallics and rayons, Warm & Natural batting. Photo by Robbie Fanning.*

Directory

A&E, 400 E Central Ave, Mt Holly, NC, 28120, 704 827 4311

A-1 Industry, 908 N Glenstone, Springfield, MO, 65802, 417 831 0033

A-1 Travel, 2701 Sunset Point Rd, Clearwater, FL, 34619, 800 677 9412

Aardvark, PO Box 2449, Livermore, CA, 94550, 510 443 2687

Access to Recreation, 2509 E Thousand Oaks Blvd, Thousand Oaks, CA, 91362

Adams, Shirley, 922 Cheltenham Way, Plainfield, IN, 46168, 317 745 1501

Air Lite Synthetics Mfg Inc, 342 Irwin St, Pontiac, MI, 48341-2982, 313 335 8131

Airtex, 150 Industrial Park Rd, Cokato, MN, 55321, 612 286 2428

Aleene's Division of Artis, Inc, 85 Industrial Way, Buellton, CA, 93427, 800 825 3363

Allyn International, 1075 Santa Fe Dr, Denver, CO, 80204, 303 825 5200

America Online, 8619 Westwood Center Dr, Vienna, VA, 22182-2285, 800 827 6364

American Professional Quilting Systems, Inc, Hwy 30-East, Carroll, IA, 51401, 712 792 5870

American Quilter's Society, PO Box 3290, Paducah, KY, 42002-3290, 502 989 7903

American Quilter, PO Box 3290, Paducah, KY, 42002-3290, 502 898 7903

Ardco Templates, 252 Cedar Rd, Poquoson, VA, 23662

Art/Quilt Magazine, 9543 Meadowbriar, Houston, TX, 77063-3812

Artful Illusions, PO Box 278, Ector, TX, 75439

Artweave Traders, 7520-R Fullerton Rd, Springfield, VA, 22153, 800 932 8317

ASN Publishing, 1455 Linda Vista Dr, San Marcos, CA, 92069

Back Street Designs, 100 E Washington St, Athens, AL, 35611, 800 228 2319

Bantam Doubleday Dell, 666 Fifth Ave, New York, NY, 10103, 212 765 6500

Barrington, Sonya Lee, 837 47th Ave, San Francisco, CA, 94121, 415 221 6510

Beacon Chemical Co, 125 Macquesten Pkwy S, Mt Vernon, NY, 10550, 914 699 3400

Beautiful Productions, 13340 Harrison St, Thornton, CO, 80214-1403, 303 452 3337

Bemidji Woolen Mills, PO Box 277, Bemidji, MN, 56601, 218 751 5166

Benartex, 1460 Broadway, New York, NY, 10036, 210 840 3250

Bernina, 300 Thayer Ct, Aurora, IL, 60504-6182, 708 978 2500

Betterway Books, 1507 Dana Ave, Cincinnati, OH, 45207, 800 289 0963

Birch Street Clothing, PO Box 6901, San Mateo, CA, 94403, 415 578 9729

Bonesteel, Georgia, 150 White St, Hendersonville, NC 28739

Books on Tape, PO Box 7900, Newport Beach, CA, 92658, 800 626 3333

Boyd Publishing, PO Box 6753, Wheeling, WV, 26003, 800 437 4442

Brenan Daniel Publications, PO Box 27757, Tempe, AZ, 85285-7757, 602 838 0347

Britex Fabrics, 146 Geary St, San Francisco, CA, 94108

Broadway Press, 12 W Thomas St, Shelter Island, NY, 11964, 516 749 3266

Brother International, 200 Cottontail Lane, Somerset, NJ, 08875, 908 356 8880

Buffalo Batt & Felt Corp, 3307 Walden Ave, Depew, NY, 14043, 716 683 4100

C&T Publishing, 5021 Blum Rd #1, Martinez, CA, 94553, 510 370 9600

Cambridge Marking Systems, PO Box 21428, Salt Lake City, UT, 84121-0428, 801 485 5218

Canada Quilts Magazine, PO Box 39, Station A, Hamilton, Ont, Canada, L8N 3A2, 416 549 1055

Cardinal Creations, 304 Brentwood Lane, Muncie, IN, 47304

Carikean Publishing, Box 11771, Chicago, IL, 60611-0771, 312 533 7704

Celestial Arts, Box 7123, Berkeley, CA, 94707, 510 845 8414

Celtic Designs Co, PO Box 2643, Sunnyvale, CA, 94087-0643

Chandler Machine Co, Ayer, MA, 01432, 508 772 3393

Chapel House, PO Box 295, West Cornwall, CT, 06796, 203 672 6830

Cherrywood Quilts & Fabrics, 361 Cherrywood Dr N, Baxter, MN, 56401, 218 829 0967

Chitra, 2 Public Ave, Montrose, PA, 18801, 717 278 1984

Clotilde, 2 Sew Smart Way, Stevens Point, WI, 54481-8031, 305 491 2889

Clover, 1007 E Dominguez St Ste L, Carson, CA, 90746, 213 516 7846

Coats & Clark, 30 Patewood Dr, Ste 351, Greenville, SC, 29615, 803 234 0331

Collins, WH, 21 Leslie Ct, Whippany, NJ, 07981, 201 887 4900

CompuServe, PO Box 20212, Columbus, OH, 43220, 800 368 3343

Concept Videos, 7910 Woodmont Ave, Ste 1214, Bethesda, MD, 20814

Concord Fabrics, 1359 Broadway, New York, NY, 10018, 800 223 5678

Connecting Threads, 5750 NE Hassalo, Portland, OR, 97213, 800 754 6454

Cotton Club, PO Box 2263, Boise, ID 83701

Craft Gallery Ltd, Box 145, Swampscott, MA, 01907, 617 744 6980

Crafts Board, 3617 McFarland Blvd N, Northport, AL, 35476, 205 333 8045

Crazy Ladies & Friends, 1606 Santa Monica Blvd, Santa Monica, CA, 90404

Creative Feet, 302 W Willis St Ste 105, Prescott, AZ, 86301, 602 778 0998

Creative Hearts, 12317 149th St E, Puyallup, WA, 98374, 206 845 1235

Creative Machine Newsletter, PO Box 2634, Menlo Park, CA 94026-2634, 415 366 4440

Creative Quilting, 950 Third Ave, 16th floor, New York, NY, 10022, 212 888 1855

Crown Publishing Group, 201 E 50 St, New York, NY, 10022, 212 572 6117

Crowning Touch, Inc, 2410 Glory C Rd, Medford, OR, 97501, 503 772 8430

C-Thru Ruler Co, PO Box 356, Bloomfield, CT, 06002, 203 243 0303

Custom Processing, Queensbury, NY, 12804

Custom Sewing by Barrick, 5643 W Townley Ave, Glendale, AZ, 85302, 602 934 8459

Cutting Edge Quilt Designs, PO Box 75, Edmonds, WA, 98020, 206 546 2064

Cy De Cosse Inc, 5900 Green Oak Dr, Minnetonka, MN, 55343, 612 936 4700

Daisy Kingdom, 134 NW 8th Ave, Portland, OR, 97209

Dan River, 111 W 40th St, New York, NY, 10018, 212 554 5555

Dav-a-lyn Enterprise, PO Box 88682, Seattle, WA, 98188

David & Charles, Box 257, North Pomfret, VT, 05053, 802 457 1911

Design-A-Quilt, 11936 Lebanon Rd, Mt Juliet, TN, 37122, 615 758 9969

Dharma Trading Co, PO Box 150916, San Rafael, CA, 94915, 800 542 5227

Dianne Larson Quiltworks, 3583 Richie Rd, Verona, WI, 53593, 608 829 3583

Dick, Karen L, Box 207, Main St, Beallsville, PA, 15313, 412 769 3242

DMC Corporation, 10 Port Kearny, South Kearny, NJ, 07032, 201 589 0606

Doheny Publications, PO Box 75, Edmonds, WA, 98020, 206 546 2064

Douglas Products, PO Box 2606, Rohnert Park, CA, 94928, 707 585 2786

Dover Needlecraft Catalog, 31 E 2nd St, Mineola, NY, 11501, 301 822 9329

Dover Street Booksellers, Ltd, PO Box 1563, Easton, MD, 21601, 410 822 9329

Down Under Quilting, PO Box 529, Beenleigh, Queensland, Australia 4207

Dritz Corporation, PO Box 5028, Spartanburg, SC, 29304, 803 576 5050

E&P Sewing, 135 N Main, Gunnison, CO, 81230, 800 736 4281

Eclectic Products, Inc, Carson, CA, 90479

Edgecraft, PO Box 3000, Avondale, PA, 19311-0915, 215 268 0500

Electric Quilt Company, 1039 Melrose St, Bowling Green, OH, 43402, 419 352 1134

Elegant Design, PO Box 323, Huntsville, UT, 84317

Elna Inc, 7642 Washington Ave S, Eden Prairie, MN, 55344, 612 941 5519

Eric's Press, Box 5222, Salem, OR, 97304, 503 364 6285

EZ International, 95 Mayhill St, Saddle Book, NJ, 07662, 201 712 1234

Fabri-Quilt, 901 E 14th Ave, North Kansas City, MO, 64116, 816 421 2000

Fabric Traditions, 1350 Broadway #2106, New York, NY, 10018, 212 279 5710

Fabulous Furs, 700 Madison Ave, Covington, KY, 41011, 800 848 4650

Fairchild Publishing, 7 W 34th St, New York, NY, 10001

Fairfield Processing, PO Box 1157, Danbury, CT, 06810, 203 744 2090

FASCO, 6250 Stanley Ave S, Seattle, WA, 98108, 206 762 7886

Fields Fabrics, 1695 44th St SE, Grand Rapids, MI, 49508, 800 678 5872

First Star, 2201 N Camino Principal, Ste 7B, Tucson, AZ, 85715, 602 885 7278

Fiskars Manufacturing Corp, PO Box 8027, Wausau, WI, 54402-8027, 715 842 2091

Flynn Frame Company, 1000 Shiloh Overpass Rd, Billings, MT, 59106, 406 656 8986

G Street Fabrics, 11854 Rockville Pike, Rockville, MD, 20852, 301 231 8998

Gammill Quilting Machine Co, 1452 W Gibson St, West Plains, MO, 65775, 800 659 8224

GEnie, PO Box 6403, Rockville, MD, 20849-6403, 800 638 9636

Ghee's, 106 East Kings Hwy Ste 205, Shreveport, LA, 71104

Gingher, Inc, PO Box 8865, Greensboro, NC, 27419, 919 292 6237

Granny's Patchwork & Mfg, 105 E Dallas, Mt Vernon, MO, 65712, 417 466 7080

Gutcheon Patchworks, 917 Pacific Ave, Ste 305, Tacoma, WA, 98402, 206 383 3047

Gutermann of America, PO Box 7387, Charlotte, NC, 28217, 704 525 7068

Haber Fabrics, 1720 E Highway 356, Irving, TX, 75010

Hancock's, 3841 Hinkleville Rd, Paducah, KY, 42001, 800 845 8723

Hang Ups, PO Box 1011, Ashland, OR, 97520

HarperCollins Publishers, 10 E 53 St, New York, NY, 10022, 212 207 7000

Harriet's Treadle Arts, 6390 W 44th Ave, Wheatridge, CO, 80033, 303 424 2742

Harry N Abrams Inc, 100 Fifth Ave, New York, NY, 10011, 212 206 7715

Heirloom Stitches, 626 Shadowood Lane, Warren, OH 44484, 216 856 7384

Hello Direct, 5884 Eden Park Pl, San Jose, CA, 95138-1859, 800 444 3556

Hickman, McRee , Box 84, Tioga, TX, 76271-0084, 817 437 2437

Hobbs Bonded Fibers, PO Box 3000, Mexia, TX, 817 562 5998

Hoffman California Fabrics, 25792 Obrero Rd, Mission Viego, CA, 92691, 800 547 0100

Hold Everything, PO Box 7807, San Francisco, CA, 94120-7807, 800 421 2264

Holiday Designs, Rte 1 Box 302P, Mineola, TX, 75773, 903 569 0462

Horn of America, Inc, Box 608, Sutton, WV, 26601, 304 765 7254

HTC, 24 Empire Blvd, Moonachie, NJ, 07074, 201 641 4500

Inglis Publications, PO Box 400, Chelsea, MI 48118

Islander School of Fashion Arts, PO Box 66, Grants Pass, OR, 97526, 503 479 3906

Jen-Cel-Lite Corp, 954 E Union St, Seattle, WA, 98122

Jerry's Catalog, PO Box 1105, New Hyde Park, NY, 11040, 800 827 8478

John Kaldor Fabricmaker, 500 7th Ave, New York, NY, 10018, 212 221 8270

Judith Dahlin Designs, PO Box 130831, St Paul, MN, 55113

Juki America, 3555 Lomita Blvd, Ste H, Torrance, CA, 90505, 310 325 5811

Julie's Quilting Services, 1081 Alameda #61, Belmont, CA, 94002, 415 598 0970

June Tailor, Inc, PO Box 208, Richfield, WI, 53076, 414 644 5288

Just My Imagination, 6719 Braden Circle, Kerrville, TX, 78028, 210 257 2408

Kali House, PO Box 2634, Menlo Park, CA, 94026-2634, 415 366 4440

KanScan, 1419 Edgewood Lane, McHenry, IL, 60050, 815 344 0694

Kasuri Dyeworks, 1959 Shattuck Ave, Berkeley, CA, 94704, 510 841 4509

Katie's Collection, 230 Rancho Alegre, Santa Fe, NM, 87505, 505 471 2899

Kaye Wood Publishing, 4949 Rau Rd, West Branch, MI, 48661, 517 345 3028

Keepsake Quilting, PO Box 1618, Rt 25, Centre Harbor, NH, 03226, 603 253 8731

Kenquilt Mfg Co, 113 Pattie St, Wichita, KS, 67211, 316 262 3438

Kirk Collection, 1513 Military Ave, Omaha, NE, 68111, 800 398 2542

Kona Bay Fabrics, 1928 Kalani St, Honolulu, HI, 96819, 800 531 7913

Kreinik Mfg Co Inc, 9199 Reisterstown Rd, Ste 209B, Owings Mills, MD, 21117, 410 581 5088

Kwilt & Kloze, PO Box 4602, Flint, MI, 48504

Lady's Circle Patchwork Quilts, 152 Madison Ave, #905, New York, NY, 10016

Lamb Art Press, Inc, PO Box 38, Parsons, IN, 38363

Legacy in Stitches, 720 N Green, Kennewick, WA, 99336, 509 783 7804

Leone Publications, 198 Castro St, Mt View, CA, 94041, 415 969 1714

Light Impressions, PO Box 940, Rochester, NY, 14603-0940, 800 828 6216

Little Foot Ltd, 605 Bledsoe NW, Albuquerque, NM, 87107, 505 345 7647

Live Guides, 10306 64th Pl W, Everett, WA, 98204, 206 743 6885

Log Cabin Dry Goods, E 3445 French Gulch Rd, Coeur d'Alene, ID, 208 664 5908

Lone Tree Press, 4790 N Road G, Vale, OR, 97918

Lunn Fabrics, 357 Santa Fe Dr, Denver, CO, 80223, 303 623 2710

Madeira Thread, 600 E 9th St, Michigan City, IN, 46360, 219 873 1000

Magic Needle, RR 2 Box 172, Limerick, ME, 04048

Marbled Fabric & Accessories, 325 4th St, Petaluma, CA, 94952, 707 762 7514

Marcus Brothers Textiles Inc, 1460 Broadway, New York, NY, 10018, 212 354 8700

McCall's Quilting, 405 Riverhills Business Park, Birmingham, AL, 35242, 205 995 8860

McGraw-Hill Inc, 1221 Ave of the Americas, New York, NY, 10020, 212 512 2000

Me Sew Inc, 24307 Magic Mountain Pkwy, Ste 195, Valencia, CA, 91355, 800 846 3739

MetaTheory, 2701 Ridge Rd #301, Berkeley, CA, 94709, 510 540 0822

Miniature Quilts Magazine, PO Box 1762, Riverton, NJ, 08077

MiniWorks, Rt 1, Box 44B, Brevard, NC, 28712

Mission Valley Textiles, PO Box 311807, New Braunfels, TX, 78131-1807, 800 628 2513

MIT Press, 55 Hayward St, Cambridge, MA, 02142, 617 253 5646

Morning Glory Products, PO Box 979, Taylor, TX, 76574-0979, 800 234 9105

Mundial, 50 Kerry Pl, Norwood, MA, 01062, 617 762 8310

Myhre Shibori Hand-dyed Fabric, 1135 N 32 St, Billings, MT, 59101, 406 252 5431

Nancy's Notions, PO Box 683, Beaver Dam, WI, 53916, 800 833 0690

Nansi's Fancies, 1111 Birch, Richland, WA, 99352, 509 943 4755

National Quilting Association, PO Box 394, Ellicott City, MD, 21041

National Thread & Supply, 695 Red Oak Rd, Stockbridge, GA, 30281, 800 847 1001

Newark Dressmaker Supply, Box 20730, Lehigh Valley, PA, 18002-0730

New Home, 100 Hollister Rd, Teterboro, NJ, 07608, 201 440 8080

Noltings, Rt 3 Box 147 Hwy 52 East, Stover, MO, 65078, 314 377 2713

Northwest Industrial, 2129 NE Broadway, Portland, OR, 503 282 2254

Nustyle Quilting Frame Co, Box 61-194, Stover, MO, 65078, 800 648 2240

Olfa/O'Lipfa, 3822 Waldo Pl, Columbus, OH, 43220, 614 442 1177

Omnigrid, 1560 Port Dr, Burlington, WA, 98233, 206 757 4743

Open Chain Publishing, PO Box 2634, Menlo Park, CA, 94026-2634, 415 366 4440

Openheim's, 120 E Main, North Manchester, IN, 46962-0052

Osage County Quilt Factory, 400 Walnut, Overbrook, KS, 66524, 913 665 7500

P&B Textiles, 1580 Gilbreth Rd, Burlingame, CA, 92668, 415 692 0422

Palmer/Pletsch, PO Box 12046, Portland, OR, 97212, 503 294 0696

Paris Connection, 4314 Irene Dr, Erie, PA, 16510, 814 899 7496

Patchwork Patter, PO Box 394, Ellicott City, MD, 21041

Paul Jean Creations, 1601 Fulton Ave, Sacramento, CA, 95825, 916 488 3480

PC-Quilt, 7061 Lynch Rd, Sebastopol, CA, 95472

Pelle's, PO Box 242, Davenport, CA, 95017, 408 425 4743

Pellon, 20 Industrial Ave, Chelmsford, MA, 01824, 508 454 0461

Pfaff American Sales Corp, 610 Winters Ave, Paramus, NJ, 07653, 201 262 7211

PH Press, 630 Cloutier Dr, Winnipeg, MN, Canada, R3V 1L2

Plaid Enterprises, PO Box 7600, Norcross, GA, 30091-7600, 404 923 8200

Possibilities, 8970 E Hampden Ave, Denver, CO, 80231

Powell Publications, PO Box 513, Edmonds, WA, 98020

Power Sewing, 185 5th Ave, San Francisco, CA, 94118, 800 845 7474

Prentice Hall Press, 15 Columbus Cir, New York, NY, 10023, 212 373 8000

Prodigy, 445 Hamilton Ave, White Plains, NY, 10601, 800 822 6922

PS Uniques, 3330 S Columbine Cir, Englewood, CO, 80110, 303 761 7433

Purchase For Less, 231 W Floresta, Menlo Park, CA, 94028

Putnam Co, PO Box 310, Walworth, WI, 53184, 414 275 2104

Quick & Easy Quilting, 306 E Parr Rd, Berne, IN, 46711-9509, 219 589 8741

Quilt Craft, 152 Madison Ave, #906, New York, NY, 10016

Quilt Digest Press, PO Box 1331, Gualala, CA, 95445

Quilt Works, 1920 E Palomino Rd, Tempe, AZ, 85284-2555, 602 345 2706

Quilt World, 306 E Parr Rd, Berne, IN, 46711-9509, 219 589 8741

Quilt, 1115 Broadway, 8th Floor, New York, NY, 10010, 212 807 7100

Quilted Ribbon, PO Box 811, Derby, KS, 67037, 316 788 4123

Quilter's Rule Int'l, Inc, 2322 NE 29th Ave, Ocala, FL, 34470

Quilter's Newsletter Magazine, 6700 W 44th Ave, Wheatridge, CO, 80033-4700, 303 420 4272

Quiltessence, RR2, Box 121, Thief River Falls, MN, 56701

Quilting Bee, 198 Castro St, Mt View, CA, 94041, 415 969 1714

Quilting Books Unlimited, 1911 W Wilson St, Batavia, IL, 60510-1680

Quilting International, 243 Newton-Sparta Rd, Newton, NJ, 07860, 201 383 8080

Quilting Today Magazine, PO Box 1762, Riverton, NJ, 08077

Quiltmaker, 6700 W 44th Ave, Wheatridge, CO, 80033-4700, 303 420 4272

Quilts & Other Comforts, PO Box 394, Wheatridge, CO, 80034, 303 420 4272

QuiltSOFT, PO Box 19946, San Diego, CA, 92159-0946, 619 583 2970

RainShed Outdoor Fabrics, 707 NW 11th, Corvallis, OR, 97330, 503 753 8900

RJR Fashion Fabrics, 1261 S Boyle, Los Angeles, CA, 90023, 213 780 1565

Robert Kaufman Co, 135 W 132nd St, Los Angeles, CA, 90061, 310 538 3482

Rodale Press Inc, 33 E Minto St, Emmaus, PA, 18098, 215 967 5171

Rodgers, Pat, 46 Clinton St, Sea Cliff, NY, 11579

Rosecrest Farm, 5256 W 10400 S, Payson, UT, 801 465 4184

Rowenta, 281 Albany St, Cambridge, MA, 02139, 617 661 1600

Ruth's Country Creations, PO Box 1739, Paradise, CA, 95967, 800 568 8991

Sally Lampi, 2261 Beckham Way, Hayward, CA, 94541, 510 886 1943

Saral Paper Co, 322 W 57th Ste 30, New York, NY, 100019, 212 247 0460

Scattered Patchers, HCR #1 Box 67, Toivola, MI, 49965

Schmetz, 10613 Lexington Dr, Knoxville, TN, 37932, 800 221 9897

SCS, 9631 NE Colfax, Portland, OR, 97220, 503 252 1452

Sears Laboratories, National HQ/Sears Tower, Chicago, IL, 60684, 708 286 2173

Seattle Textile Computer Users, PO Box 17506, Seattle, WA, 98107

Seth Publications, PO Box 2606, Rohnert Park, CA, 94928, 707 585 2786

Sew News, PO Box 1790, Peoria, IL, 61656, 309 682 6626

Sew-Art International, PO Box 550, Bountiful, UT, 84011, 800 231 2787

Sew/Fit Company, PO Box 397, Bedford Park, IL, 60499, 800 547 4739

Sewing Emporium, 1087 Third Ave, Chula Vista, CA, 92010, 619 420 3490

Sewing Place, The, PO Box 111446, Campbell, CA, 95011, 800 587 3937

Shades Inc, 585 Cobb Pkwy S, The Nunn Complex, Studio O, Marietta, GA, 30062, 800 783 3933

Sharp, LP, HC 3, Box 48A, Emily, MN, 56447

Silver Star Publishing, RR 4, Box 413, Tunkhannock, PA, 18657, 717 836 5592

Singer Company, 200 Metroplex Dr, Edison, NJ, 08818, 908 287 0707

Sirco Tables, Box 2463, Missoula, MT, 59806, 800 621 3792

Skydyes, 83 Richmond Lane, West Hartford, CT, 06117, 203 232 1429

Slomons, 2550 Pellissier Pl, Whittier, CA 90601, 213 686 0678

Smocks & Kisses, PO Box 334, La Jolla, CA, 92038-0334, 619 457 0045

Solar-Kist Corp, PO Box 273, LaGrange, IL 60525, 708 352 2973

SoSew Press, 210 Estates Dr, Ste 401, Roseville, CA, 95678-2300

Spartex Inc, PO Box 1149, Roebuck, SC, 29376, 803 585 7186

Spectrix, 20-21 Wagaraw Rd, Fairlawn, NJ, 07410, 210 423 5525

Speed Stitch, PO Box 3472, Port Charlotte, FL, 33949, 813 629 3199

SPPS, PO Box 9200-135, Fountain Valley, CA, 92728

Sprayway, Inc, Addison, IL 60101

Springs Industries, 104 W 40th St, New York, NY, 10018, 212 556 6548

Stan Rising Co, 5332 Twin City Hwy N, Port Arthur, TX, 77642-6023, 800 654 4476

Stearns Technical Textiles Co (Mountain Mist), 100 Williams St, Cincinnati, OH, 45215-4683, 513 948 5252

Stencil Company, PO Box 1218, Williamsville, NY, 14221, 716 656 9430

StenSource International, 19411 Village Dr, Sonora, CA, 95370, 209 536 1148

Sterling Publishing Co, Inc, 387 Park Ave S, 5th Fl, New York, NY, 10016-8810, 212 532 7160

Stitch 'n String, PO Box 140876, Nashville, TN, 37214

Stitch 'n Sew Quilts, 306 E Parr Rd, Berne, IN, 46711, 219 589 8741

Stretch & Sew Fabrics, 19725 40th Ave, Lynnwood, WA, 98036, 206 774 9678

Stretch & Sew, PO Box 185, Eugene, OR, 97440, 800 547 7717

Stylex Worldwide, 12A Oak St Terr, Shrewsbury, MA, 01545, 508 842 9058

Sulky, PO Box 3472, Port Charlotte, FL, 33949, 813 629 3199

Sullivans, 224 William St, Bensenville, IL, 60106, 708 238 8033

Summa Design, Box 24404, Dayton, OH, 45424, 800 869 0625

Sussman-Automatic Corp, 43-20 34th St, Long Island City, NY, 11101

Tacony Corp, 1760 Gilsinn Lane, Fenton, MO, 63026, 314 349 3000

Taos Mountain Wool Works, PO Box 327, Arroyo Hondo, NM, 87513, 505 776 2925

Taunton Press, 63 South Main St, Newtown, CT, 06470-5506, 800 926 8776

Thames & Hudson Inc, 500 Fifth Ave, New York, NY, 10110, 212 354 3763

That Patchwork Place, PO Box 118, Bothell, WA, 98041, 206 483 3313

Therm O Web, 770 Glenn Ave, Wheeling, IL, 60090, 708 520 5200

Things Japanese, 9805 NE 116th St, Kirkland, WA, 98034, 206 821 2287

Thread Discount Sales, 10222 Paramount Blvd, Downey, CA, 90241, 310 928 4029

Thread Shed, PO Box 898, Horse Shoe, NC, 28742, 704 692 5128

Threads Magazine, 63 S Main St, Newtown, CT, 06470-2344, 203 426 8171

Ticknor & Fields, 215 Park Ave S, New York, NY, 10003, 212 420 5800

Titus & Son, FD, 9410 Topanga Canyon Rd, Ste 202, Chatsworth, CA, 91311, 800 767 6339

Tolin' Station, PO Box 8206, Greensboro, NC, 27419, 910 855 8932

Tower Hobbies, PO Box 778, Champaign, IL, 61820, 217 298 3630

Traditional Quilter, 243 Newton-Sparta Rd, Newton, NJ, 07860

Traditional Quiltworks, PO Box 1737, Riverton, NJ, 08077

Treadleart, 25834 Narbonne Ave , Lomita, CA, 90717, 310 534 5122

Unicorn Textile Book Catalog, 1338 Ross St, Petaluma, CA 94954-6502, 800 289 9276

Viking White Sewing Machine Co, 11760 Berea Rd, Cleveland, OH, 44111, 216 252 2032

VIP, 1412 Broadway, New York, NY, 10018, 212 730 4600

Voster Marketing, 190 Mt Pleasant Rd, Newtown, CT, 06470, 203 370 7190

Walnut Hollow, Rt 1, Dodgeville, WI, 53533

Warm Products, 16120 Woodinville-Redmond Rd #5, Woodinville, WA, 98072, 206 488 4464

Wearable Art Connection of Southern California, 23344 Park Hacienda, Calabasas, CA, 91302-1715

Wearable Wonders, 306 E Parr Rd, Berne, IN, 46711, 219 589 8741

Web of Thread, 3240 Lone Oak Rd, Ste 124, Paducah, KY, 42003, 800 955 8185

Whipple, Dorie, 7705 Isabel, Cotati, CA, 94931

YLI, PO Box 109, Provo, UT, 84603, 801 377 3900

Linda Denner, Garden City, NY, Fred and Ginger. Cotton, silk, satin, and Ultrasuede, with background machine-quilted with silver threads. Photo courtesy of the artist.

Bibliography

This is a small taste of the books available. Don't wait to buy a good book—unfortunately, it will not stay in print forever. If you can't find one of these books, ask your favorite storeowner to order the book for you. Otherwise, order from one of the companies listed under Books, Mail-Order, or General Mail Order on the Resource list. Most quilt books are in the 746.4 – .6 section of the public library. Your library can order almost any book on inter-library loan.

Please also consult the Chilton books listed in the front of the book, especially the Contemporary Quilting series.

Most publishers' addresses are in the Directory .

Machine Quilting

Clawson, Eileen, *Simply Elegant Machine Quilts*, Elegant Design, 1984.

Cody, Pat, *Continuous Line Quilting Designs Especially for Machine Quilting*, Chilton Book Co, 1984.

Devlin, Nancy, *Guide To Machine Quilting*, Starshine Stitchery Press, 1976.

Haight, Ernest B., *Practical Machine-Quilting For The Homemaker*, self-published, 1974.

Hargrave, Harriet, *Heirloom Machine Quilting*, C&T Publishing, 1990.

Haywood, Dixie, *The Contemporary Crazy Quilt Projectbook*, Crown Publishers, 1977.

Johnson-Srebro, Nancy, *Featherweight 221/The Perfect Portable*, Silver Star Publishing, 1992.

Malone, Maggie, *Quilting Techniques & Patterns for Machine Stitching*, Sterling Publishing Co, 1985.

Malone, Maggie, *Quilting*, Sterling Publishing Co, 1985.

Nilsoon, Shirley, *Stitching Free*, C&T Publishing, 1993.

Marsh, Pat, *Easy Machine Quilting*, Cardinal Creations, 1990.

Quilt Projects by Machine, Singer/Cy DeCosse Inc, 1992.

Quilting by Machine, Singer/Cy DeCosse Inc, 1990.

Quilting Concepts in Sulky, Sulky of America, 1993.

Roberts, Sharee Dawn, *Creative Machine Arts*, American Quilter's Society, 1992.

Skjerseth, Douglas Neil, *Stitchology*, Seth Publications, 1979.

Smith, Lois Tornquist, *Fun & Fancy Machine Quiltmaking*, American Quilter's Society, 1989.

Thompson, Shirley, *Designs for Continuous Line Quilting*, Powell Publications, 1993.

Tyrrell, Judi, *Beginner's Guide to Machine Quilting*, ASN, 1990.

One-Step Quilting

Greene, Marilyn, *Sew Simple Quilts*, Dav-a-lyn Enterprise, 1988.

Hickman, Elva McRee Hickman, *Quiltmaking— Fast and Easy*, self-published, 1990.

Michell, Marti, *Weekend Log Cabin Quilts for People Who Don't Have Time to Quilt*, ASN, 1991.

Millett, Sandra, *Quilt-As-You-Go*, Second Edition, Chilton Book Co, 1994.

Murphy, Anita, *Reversible Quilts*, ASN, 1991.

Wood, Kaye, *Turn Me Over...I'm Reversible*, Extra Special Products, 1984.

Sashiko

Allen, Alice, *Sashiko Made Simple*, Bernina Books Limited, 1992.

Rostocki, Janet K., *Sashiko for Machine Sewing*, Summa Design, 1988.

Takano, Saikoh, *Sashiko and Beyond*, Chilton Book Co, 1993.

Innovative Piecing

Anderson, Mary Lou, *Precision Machine Piecing*, Stitch 'n String, 1987.

Brackman, Barbara, *Encyclopedia of Pieced Quilt Patterns*, American Quilter's Society, 1993.

Daniel, Nancy Brennan, *Delectable Mountains*, Brenan Daniel Publications, 1990.

Doheny, Marilyn, *Woven Ribbons*, Doheny Publications, 1991.

Flynn, John, John Flynn's Braided Borders, Flynn Quilt Frame Company, 1990.

Johnson, Carolyn R., *Taking Off With Flying Geese*, Boyd Press, 1990.

Kime, Janet, *Log Cabins/New Techniques for Traditional Quilts*, Cutting Edge Quilt Designs, Inc., 1992.

Kramer, Monta Lee, *New Path*, Lamb Art Press, Inc., 1989.

McCloskey, Marsha, *Lessons in Machine Piecing*, That Patchwork Place, 1990.

Phillips, Cheryl, *Quilts Without Corners*, E&P Sewing.

Schaefer, Becky, *Working in Miniature*, C&T Publishing, 1987.

Schaffeld, Barbara, and Bev Vickery, *Log Cabin in the Round Designs*, Lone Tree Press, 1992.

Speckmann, Doreen, *Pattern Play/Creating Your Own Quilts*, C&T Publishing, 1994.

Stothers, Marilyn, *Curved Strip-Piecing/A New Technique*, PH Press, 1988.

Thomas, Donna Lynn, *A Perfect Match/A Guide to Precise Machine Piecing*, That Patchwork Place, 1993.

Young, Blanche, and Helen Young Frost, *Nine Patch Wonders*, First Star, 1991.

General Quilting

Chainey, Barbara, *The Essential Quilter*, David & Charles, 1993.

Danita Rafalovich and Kathryn Alison Pellman, *Backart on the Flip Side*, Leone Publications, 1991.

Dietrich, Mimi, et al, *The Quilters' Companion*, That Patchwork Place, 1994.

Doak, Carol, *Quiltmaker's Guide: Basics and Beyond*, American Quilter's Society, 1992.

Great Quilting Techniques, Threads Magazine, Taunton Press, 1994.

McClun, Diana, and Laura Nownes, *Quilts! Quilts!! Quilts!!!*, Quilt Digest Press, 1988.

McClun, Diana, and Laura Nownes, *Quilts, Quilts, and More Quilts!*, C&T Publishing, 1993.

Orlofsky, Patsy and Myron, *Quilts in America*, McGraw-Hill, 1974.

Piecemakers, *Picking up the Pieces*, EZ International, 1992.

Quilt Shop Series (many books, all worth owning), That Patchwork Place, various dates.

Rolfe, Margaret, *Australian Patchwork*, Lloyd O'Neil Pty Ltd, 1985.

Ryker, June, *Log Cabin Rondelay*, Possibilities, 1990.

Schneider, Sally, *Painless Borders*, That Patchwork Place, 1992.

Schneider, Sally, *Scrap Happy/Quick-Pieced Scrap Quilts*, That Patchwork Place, 1990.

Seward, Linda, *The Complete Book of Patchwork, Quilting, and Appliqué*, Prentice-Hall, 1987.

Townswick, Jane, *Quiltmaking Tips and Techniques*, Rodale Press, 1994.

Voudrie, Sylvia Trygg, *Tiny Traditions*, Chitra Publications, 1992.

Walker, Michele, *The Passionate Quilter*, Ebury Press, 1990.

White, Tonee, *Appliquilt*, That Patchwork Place, 1994.

Wiechec, Philomena, *Celtic Quilt Designs*, Celtic Design Co., 1980.

Wood, Kaye, *Quilting for the 90's*, Kaye Wood Publishing, 1992.

Clothing

Adams, Shirley, *The Sewing Connection 8*, Shirley Adams Publications, 1993.

Avery, Virginia, *Wonderful Wearables*, American Quilter's Society, 1991.

Davis, Marian L., *Visual Designs in Dress*, Prentice-Hall, 1980.

Doriss, Barbara Bell, *The Original Log Cabin Jacket & Vest Book*, Yours Truly, 1983.

Ericson, Lois, *The Great Put On*, Eric's Press, 1992.

Gadia-Smitley, Roselyn, *Wearable Quilts*, Sterling Publishing Co , 1993.

Larkey, Jan, *Flatter Your Figure*, Prentice-Hall, 1991.

Leone, Diana, *Investments*, Leone Publications, 1982.

McGehee, Linda, *Texture With Textiles*, Ghee's, 1991.

Mackelburg, Kay M., *The "Me" Vest*, SoSew Press, 1993.

Marano, Hara Estroff, *Style Is Not a Size/Looking and Feeling Great in the Body You Have*, Bantam Books, 1991.

Mashuta, Mary, *Wearable Art for Real People*, C&T Publishing, 1989.

Murrah, Judy, *Jacket Jazz*, That Pathwork Place, 1993.

Oblander, Ruth, and Joan Anderson, *The Sew/Fit Manual*, Sew/Fit Co, 1993.

Rasband, Judith, *Fabulous Fit*, Fairfield Publishing, 1994.

Rostocki, Janet, *Jazz Shirts*, Summa Designs, 1990.

Tilke, Max, *Costume Patterns And Designs*, Frederick A. Praeger, 1957.

Zieman, Nancy, and Robbie Fanning, *The Busy Woman's Fitting Book*, Open Chain Publishing, 1989.

Interiors

Babylon, Donna, *Quilter's Guide to Home Decorating for the Nursery*, ASN, 1991.

Jacobson, Anthony and Jeanne, *Quilting Around Your Home*, Chilton Book Co, 1993.

Martin, Nancy J., *Make Room for Quilts*, That Patchwork Place, 1994.

Videos

Betzina, Sandra, and Gale Grigg Hazen, *Power Sewing's Fitting Solutions #3*, Power Sewing, 1993.

Beyer, Jinny, *Color Confidence!*, Concept Videos, 1991.

Dahlin, Judith, *Machine Quilting Techniques*, Judith Dahlin Designs, 1993.

Hausmann, Sue, *The Art of Sewing*, many tapes, Viking White Sewing Machine Co, many dates.

Hazen, Gale Grigg, *Sewing Machine Savvy*, Islander School of Fashion Arts, 1993.

Rogers, Pat, *Free Motion Embroidery and Beading by Machine*, Pat Rogers, 1993.

Ruddy, Kathy, and Sherri Clark, *OmniStitching*, Live Guides, 1991.

Webster, Sandra Betzina, *Power Sewing's Handwoven and Quilted Garments*, Power Sewing, 1993.

Creativity

Bender, Sue, *Plain and Simple*, HarperCollins Publishers, 1989.

Fanning, Tony and Robbie, *Get It All Done and Still Be Human/A Personal Time-Management Workshop*, Kali House, 1990.

SARK, *A Creative Companion/How to Free Your Creative Spirit*, Celestial Arts, 1991.

Steward, Jan, and Corita Kent, *Learning by Heart*, Bantam Books, 1992.

Design

Cory, Pepper, Quilting Designs from the Amish, C&T Publishing, 1985.

Goldsworthy, Andy, *A Collaboration with Nature*, Harry N. Abrams, Inc., 1990.

Humbert, Claude, *Islamic Ornamental Design*, Hastings House, 1980.

Laury, Jean Ray, *Imagery on Fabric*, C&T Publishing, 1992.

Laury, Jean Ray, *No Dragons on My Quilt*, American Quilter's Society, 1990.

McDowell, Ruth B., *Pattern on Pattern*, Quilt Digest Press, 1991.

Peter S. Stevens, *Handbook of Regular Patterns*, MIT Press, 1980.

Phillips, Peter, and Gillian Bunce, *Repeat Patterns*, Thames & Hudson, 1993.

Tubau, Ivan, *How to Attract Attention with Your Art*, Sterling Publishing Co, 1970.

Color

Beyer, Jinny, *Color Confidence for Quilters*, Quilt Digest Press, 1992.

Horton, Roberta, *An Amish Adventure*, C&T Publishing, 1983.

McKelvey, Susan Richardson, *Color for Quilters*, Yours Truly, 1984.

McKelvey, Susan Richardson, *Light & Shadows*, C&T Publishing, 1989.

Penders, Mary Coyne, *Color and Cloth*, Quilt Digest Press, 1989.

Westray, Kathleen, *A Color Sampler*, Ticknor & Fields, 1993.

Wolfrom, Joen, *The Magical Effects of Color*, C&T Publishing, 1992.

Sourcebooks

Association of Theatrical Artists and Craftspeople, *The New York Theatrical Sourcebook*, Broadway Press, 1993.

Boyd, Margaret A., *The Crafts Supply Sourcebook*, Betterway Books, 1992.

Burgess, Maryanne, *Designer Source Listing*, Carikean Publishing, 1993.

Dick, Karen L., Editor, *The Whole Costumer's Catalogue*, 11th edition, 1994.

Hari Walner, Thornton, CO, Dolly, 14" x 16". Quilted with one of Hari's machine-quilting designs from her company, Beautiful Productions. Photo by Blake Karsh.

Machine Quilting

Index

*Hari Walner's partner, Gordon Snow,
built a clever electric track on a quilt
with a tiny sewing machine on it, to
demonstrate the concept of her
continuous-line quilting designs. In
June 1994 the little machine had
traveled 362 miles. At the model-
railroad ratio of 1:160, it has traveled
58,000 "real" miles. Photos courtesy
of Hari Walner.*

Are you interested in a quarterly
newsletter about creative uses of
the sewing machine and serger?
Write to:

The Creative Machine
PO Box 2634-MQ
Menlo Park, CA 94026-2634